Unconventional Wisdom

Gender, Theology and Spirituality

Series Editor
Lisa Isherwood, University of Winchester
Marcella Althaus-Reid, University of Edinburgh

Gender, Theology and Spirituality explores the notion that theology and spirituality are gendered activities. It offers the opportunity for analysis of that situation as well as provides space for alternative readings. In addition it questions the notion of gender itself and in so doing pushes the theological boundaries to more materialist and radical readings. The series opens the theological and spiritual floodgates through an honest engagement with embodied knowing and critical praxis.

Gender, Theology and Spirituality brings together international scholars from a range of theological areas who offer cutting edge insights and open up exciting and challenging possibilities and futures in theology.

Published:
Resurrecting Erotic Transgression
Subjecting Ambiguity in Theology
Anita Monro

Patriarchs, Prophets and Other Villains
Edited by Lisa Isherwood

Forthcoming in the series:

Women and Reiki
Energetic/Holistic Healing in Practice
Judith Macpherson

For What Sin was She Slain? A Muslim Feminist Theology
Zayn R. Kassam

Our Cultic Foremothers
Sacred Sexuality and Sexual Hospitality in the Biblical
and Related Exegetic Texts
Thalia Gur Klein

Through Eros to Agape
The Radical Embodiment of Faith
Timothy R. Koch

Baby, You are my Religion: Theory, Praxis and Possible Theology of
Mid-20ᵗʰ Century Urban Butch Femme Community
Marie Cartier

Radical Otherness
A Socio/theological Investigation
Dave Harris and Lisa Isherwood

Unconventional Wisdom

June Boyce-Tillman

LONDON   OAKVILLE

Published by Equinox Publishing Ltd.
UK: Unit 6, The Village, 101 Amies St., London SW11 2JW
USA: DBBC, 28 Main Street, Oakville, CT 06779

www.equinoxpub.com

First published 2007

British Library Cataloguing-in-Publication Data
A catalogue record for this book is available from the British Library.

ISBN-13 978 1 84553 099 0   (hardback)
         978 1 84553 100 3   (paperback)

Library of Congress Cataloging-in-Publication Data

Tillman, June
Unconventional wisdom / June Boyce-Tillman
   p. cm. — (Gender, theology and spirituality)
Includes bibliographical references and index.
ISBN 978-1-84553-099-0 (hb) — ISBN 978-1-84553-100-3 (pb)
1. Feminist theology. 2. Christianity and culture. 3. Knowledge, Theory of (Religion)
I. Title. BT83.55.T55 2007
230.082 — dc22
                    2007000746

Typeset by S.J.I. Services, New Delhi
Printed and bound in Great Britain by Lightning Source (UK) Ltd, Milton Keynes

CONTENTS

ACKNOWLEDGEMENTS

It is difficult to name everyone who has been part of that journey. There is the University of Winchester (King Alfred's College) that provided me with both time and money to pursue foreign travel and creative exploration. In that community I would like to thank especially Dr Inga Bryden, Professor Joy Carter, Professor Anthony Dean, Dr Malcolm Floyd, Professor Paul Light, Dr Graham Harvey, Professor Joyce Goodman, Jane Erricker, Alma Jones, Prof. Elizabeth Stuart, Prof. Lisa Isherwood, and the late Professor Mike Llewellyn and all my research students past and present.

Spiritually I owe a great debt to The Revd Canon Gonville ffrench Beytagh, the Revd Canon Ian Ainsworth Smith, the Revd Canon Andrew Todd, Penelope Eckersley, Monica Furlong, Dr Nicola Slee and more recently, the Revd David Page and the Revd Canon Prebendary Bill Scott and Dr Adriana Marian, my homeopath. It was Mary Grey whose feminist theology first inspired me to look further in this area. Much of this was written during my time as Proctor Fellow at The Episcopal Divinity School, Cambridge, Massachusetts, where I would like to thank particularly Professor Carter Heyward, Professor Kwok Pui Lan, Jane Ring Frank and Bishop Stephen Charleston with my friends Kate Sullivan, Brigitte Loewe and Betsy Ewalt. I am grateful to the composers Michael Finnissy and Sir John Tavener who have provided considerable support, encouragement and advice.

The most formative musical/theological influences were Sydney Carter, Bernard Braley and the Galliard Press, Carol and Keith Wakefield and Nick Williams at Stainer and Bell. There were also the festivals organized by Brian Frost at which I first met Ianthe Pratt who has been a constant source of support, helping me to publish the first collections of my work through the Association for Inclusive Language. Dr Ian Sharp of the Hymn Society has provided regular support and advice.

Some of the material in this book was developed as part of my ordination training in the diocese of Southwark where I work in St Paul's Furzedown.

I would also like to thank Norma Beavers, my copy editor for her patience and understanding in this process and my sons Matthew and Richard for their faith in me.

Contexts that have been particularly supportive are:
- Womenchurch Reading and my very good friend Carol Boulter.
- The Sisters of the church at Ham Common, especially Sisters Aileen and Jennifer and the Mother Superior, Anita.
- Holy Rood House especially Elizabeth and Stanley Baxter.
- Catholic Women's Network (now Women/Word/Spirit), especially Veronica Seddon, Gillian Limb, Lala Winkley and Lillalou Hughes.
- Catholic Women's ordination especially my very good friend, Myra Poole SND and Susan Roll, who organizes liturgies in US and Canada.
- The Sisters of the Glorious Ascension at Prasada, Provence, Sisters Jean and Cecile and my good friend, Pam Gladding.
- St James' Piccadilly especially the Revd Charles Hedley.
- Greenspirit and my good friends who have provided me with so much hospitality, Chris and Isabel Clarke.
- The Church of St Paul's, Furzedown, South London, especially John and Janet Driver, the priests, Peter Jones, the Reader and his wife Jean and John Mitchell the organist and the associated Interfaith group.
- Lucy Neal OBE for the inspiring work on Mary Neal.
- Alex Hoare for the inspiration of her Women Space project.
- Mary Jo and Patrice SSHM at the Noddfa retreat Centre.
- Professor Grenville Hancox at Christchurch University Canterbury.

In New Zealand, my good friend Stuart Manins, has also provided me with helpful feedback on the models.

Introduction

THE PATTERN OF THE BOOK

Blessed Trinity

Son of man they call you,
A divine title of ancient origin,
But what if you had been born of girl?
Daughter of woman,
How's that?
It doesn't seem to have the same ring,
The same historical authenticity.
It just isn't as grand.

Why not?
Maybe because there is no representation in higher circles.
At least in England before the reformation
There was a token woman
In the divine hierarchy.
But even she got deposed
Because her followers got out of hand.

Men's worst fears were realized.
Better be safe than sorry –
You know where you are with the Trinity.
Or was it the Triumvirate?

I'm not sure I fancy them as a jury at the Last Judgement.
Most British juries have to be balanced now.
Strange that the group responsible for the ultimate verdict
Should be so
Unbalanced. (Tillman 1988: 16)

I have always had a problem with belonging and it has taken me a
lifetime to work out why. Although a bright and able child,

1. All hymns reprinted with kind permission of Stainer and Bell,
http://www.stainer.co.uk.

fascinated by the Anglican Church with which I was associated from my cradle – I always seemed somehow to be outside it – never outside of God – just the Church.

This book is about that search – through the academy, through practical theology, through music – to locate the source of the problem. In many ways it is an anthology of that search – drawing on many different disciplines – both critiquing them and rejecting and accepting them.

My Theological Background

I was brought up in the context of rural Anglicanism – not too high and not too low! At Oxford University, I explored a number of different theological positions ranging from a fairly conservative evangelicalism to a quite liberal Anglo-Catholicism. While working in London in Notting Hill post the race riots in the 1960s, I worshipped with the Methodists for seven years – quite 'High' Methodists who tried a great deal of liturgical experiment and innovation. I enjoy Quaker worship although I have remained always a communicant member of the Anglican Church with which I have often had a 'love-hate' relationship. At the time of writing I am an Anglican deacon and some of the text in this book was developed as part of that journey. My main spiritual nurturing has been through a variety of 'alternative' liturgy groups like Women Word Spirit (formerly Catholic Women's Network), an informal group that met in Wimbledon, Women Church reading, an informal group of middle-aged women called Wild Women and liturgies for conferences on women's ordination and feminist theology and so on – all embracing a strong feminist theology (although not all of them were composed exclusively of women). However, I write hymns and liturgical music, which are finding a place in more 'mainstream' Christianity (Boyce-Tillman 2006a). At the same time there has been a great exploration of other faith traditions particularly Jewish, Hindu, Sikh, Islam and a variety of the burgeoning pagan traditions and an enduring commitment to Interfaith dialogue.

The discovery of the Wisdom traditions has been very important for me. Julian of Norwich was an important guide in the journey. She came at a time in my life when I was sort of at a crossroads. Largely through the ministrations of the Beatles, Transcendental

Meditation came to the UK with the Maharishi and I, like hundreds of others from many backgrounds, learned it. Despite being brought up in the Church I had encountered nothing like the peace of the twenty-minute practice and there was no one to talk about it to in Christianity which seemed to regard it as devilish. Then I found Gonville ffrench-Beytagh, ex-Dean of Johannesburg, with whom I discovered the Christian contemplative tradition, the way of unknowing and of darkness. That for me was the beginning of the Wisdom journey, which was tightly tied up with the feminine in God. I think, as with so much of my life, at first I did it my way. For me it was to do with finding the other half of one of the binary divides that characterize the Christian tradition –

- The darkness that balances the light.
- The unknowing that balances the aggressive pursuit of knowledge which has led theology in its patriarchal form to reduce God to a series of creedal statements.
- The intuitive God who cannot be held by the reasoning mind alone.
- The feminine images to balance the male images.
- The accepting God to balance the judgmental God that had peopled my childhood fears, who I think I would describe at that time as a blessed all-embracing darkness where I could take refuge from the worst of the excesses of the so-called Enlightenment that took its stranglehold on Europe in the late eighteenth century.

My Musical Background

For most of my life I have been a musician – mostly in some form of education, often in liturgical music, now often in the context of healing. Here too I have felt that I have not quite belonged in any particular genre or style and have had a somewhat nomadic life. Musically the patterns of knowing that had been presented by my education were very limited and many of them conceived theologically. As a child I was not allowed to sing in the church choir which was only boys. How I longed to be part of that tradition especially in the Anglican cathedrals! Only in my teens did I find a 'good' church choir that included women at St Mary's Southampton. This was a time of spiritual awakening for me. There were theological study groups (although members of the choir were not supposed to join them as they did not associate with the congregation!). I was trained as a musician at Oxford University in the 1960s where sexist jokes were the common currency of the lecture hall and, in general, unquestioned by men or women. Because for most of pre-Enlightenment Europe most 'high art' music was written for the Church, the 'objective' underpin of much musicology can be laid at the door of the notion of God as constructed by mainstream theologians during that period.

My further musical exploration represented an embracing of a musical freedom that I could not find in a classical training that ended in a music degree at Oxford University which consisted of history and analysis and written composition in the style of composers from 1550–1900. My grandfather had been the village dance band pianist in a New Forest village and played by ear; but he wanted his granddaughter to enter the world of classical music (epitomized by his 78rpm recording of Jose Iturbi playing Chopin's *Fantaisie Impromptu*). I was too young when he died to realize what I had missed by not learning his skills. Already, I realized there is a sort of sanctity surrounding certain composers – with busts of them taking a prominent place on my music teacher's piano, not unlike the status of saints. In fact, as a child, I was glad of the containment of the classical tradition. I knew where I was by learning how to read the notes and enjoyed the poise and elegance of Mozart and Haydn who were my favourites at that time. I was terrified of improvisation in any form. The printed notes offered the security that I needed. I had not yet encountered the improvisatory Pentecostal traditions. It was through exploring sound with children in school that I found that freedom and this was followed by playing folk guitar and (much later) buying a djembe. Twenty-five years after leaving Oxford I dared to improvise in public and felt that I could claim that musical freedom.

My route into Oxford consisted largely of a set of challenges called examinations and as a child I remember my musical and academic life as a series of hurdles. No sooner was one surmounted, the next one loomed on the horizon. The notion of using music for relaxation was not a possibility and indeed was discouraged by teachers of musical analysis who despised what they called 'wall paper' music and set listening up as something to engage the whole mind and certainly never to be indulged in while doing something else. It took the discovery of therapeutic massage to introduce me to the use of music to nurture and heal, as an accompaniment to other activities. Indeed, my main experience of nurture was via the natural world with which I always had a deep sense of connection; this was at least partly due to my being an only child with few human playmates.

Although I composed a few original pieces at Oxford (not as part of the academic course) I wrote few classical pieces for the next twenty years. Oxford had taught me that composers were usually male, German or Italian-speaking and dead. The theology I met resembled them – all male, mainly priests and bishops. The hymns were similarly alienating.

It was during a prolonged illness that I started to compose again and became aware that this process was actually part of my own healing process, that in combining and recombining the ideas musically I was actually changing parts of myself. At this point composing was essentially an individual activity done at the piano or on paper, as I had been taught it to be. I was a pianist, an essentially individual instrument. I enjoyed accompanying but the examination system dictated that I was always examined as an individual. My parents could only afford for me to learn the cello in a class, so advanced orchestral playing was not available. Choral singing was the only communal music-making experience open to me. Playing folk guitar for large gatherings in the 1960s offered me an experience of communal music making that had largely been denied.

My first move into other musical traditions was the protest song movement in Notting Hill in the 1960s and I can remember the sense of rebellion in going back to Oxford to sing at my college and using a song entitled *O That Greedy Landlord* which I accompanied on the guitar in my essentially classical programme. I discovered folk music in the context of worship and a strand of music challenging the church and its failure to address social action. These were the days of the Christian Aid competitions entitled *Songs from the Square* – ordinary people writing songs sent in on tape – a democratizing musical tradition that my upbringing had not included. The scene was set for the embracing of musical diversity as a way of exploring different parts of my own psyche. It has led me through various New Age groups, into ethnic traditions and an exploration of the tenets of music therapy. At first I was concerned about the diversity and discrepancies between what was the dominant tradition for me – classical music – and the other ones. Now I rejoice in the diversity and realize that each represents a different aspect of my persona and can be respected in the same way as I teach respect for difference in the course in World Musics and in my interfaith dialogue. This is as true internally as it is externally in terms of society.

Through these other traditions, especially the drumming, I discovered a much greater awareness of the role of my body in music making at about the same time as I discovered body theology. Although I necessarily spent much time on technical exercises in learning the piano and was aware of how the state of my physical health affected my singing, the tradition I was being initiated into did not show a great concern for the role of the body and concentrated largely on the role of the mind which was seen to be the ruler of the body. I sang in Church (but not in the choir) for as long as I can remember and was a deeply religious child. When later I did sing in a choir that included girls, I found that most of the members of the church choir had little sense of the religious meaning of music (less so often than the congregation). It took explorations into Hinduism and New Age to discover a group of people who genuinely believed in the transcendent power of music and indeed, sometimes linked this with the embodied art of dancing.

What Does This Book Hope to Do?

This book hopes to rework the Wisdom tradition in the context of the twenty-first century and in the light of ways of knowing that are marginalized in contemporary society (Foucault and Gordon 1980). It is in itself a challenge to the dominant orthodoxy because it crosses disciplinary boundaries. But, for most of us, the boundaries of academe are artificial and do not reflect the way that our lives are lived. As you can see from my own background, I am constantly crossing disciplines – theology, musicology, performance, education, psychology, to name only the chief of them. So this book draws on a variety of disciplines, bringing them together in new ways. The ideas have been tried out in many circles during the process of writing it, and in most contexts, this interdisciplinarity has been received with excitement and enthusiasm. So it represents in itself a flow between diversity and unity as the various disciplines come together and then separate and then re-synthesize.

Each chapter begins with a hymn that I have written which encapsulates some of the ideas in the chapter. Stories are also often included. The first chapter – *Subjugated Ways of Knowing* – examines through this lens the value systems that have become subjugated in Western culture. Chapter Two examines Wisdom theology through a feminist lens. The remaining chapters examine the ways in which the dominant and subjugated ways of knowing interact in society and how various groups of people find a way of negotiating their way through them to achieve a healthy balance. Chapter Three: *Creating Identity* looks at how people negotiate the dilemma of belonging and individualism to create an identity and also how the splitting of diversity and unity have led to chaos and darkness being demonized and pathologized even though they are part of everyone's life experience.

Chapter Four: *An Integrated Manifestation* looks at how various groups of people are represented in society – who is private, who is public. It also looks at the need for the valuing of process in an aggressively product based economy. Chapter Five: *The Rhythm of Growth* examines the increasing speed of our society and the devaluation of nurturing activities. It looks at reasons for the collapse of many people because the right balance is not struck. In Chapter Six: *Understanding Wisdom* we examine the place of the visionary experience in the balancing of the rational and the intuitive; it also looks at the dilemma of holding body and soul together in our fragmentary/fragmented society. Chapter Seven: *Dancing in Wisdom's Ways* examines the need for flow between the different parts of our lives and the way in which that might influence the prevailing value systems.

Summary

The route to this book has been a journey that has included academic scholarship, personal friendship and liturgical and musical involvement. It is only a beginning in examining what a counter narrative to the dominant culture might look like in terms of theology. The limitations of size and cost has meant that certain choices have been made but I hope that it will illuminate the position of subjugated knowers in particular, as well as giving examples of how people have negotiated their own integrity within contemporary society; many of these people have been companions on my journey and I am very grateful to them. It is a book of hope, of transformation, of understanding, all part of the Wisdom tradition. I have indicated some of the signposts that might direct such a journey and I look forward to continuing on it with old and new companions – both supportive and infuriating, both dead and living, from the human and the natural world. The past is always with us and is always shaping the present. I hope that this book gives some pointers as to how it can be seen as a source of energy and power – in fact, the Understanding of Unconventional Wisdom.

Chapter One

SUBJUGATED WAYS OF KNOWING

1. God of justice, wind the circle,
   Making all the cosmos one,
   Show us in millennial visions,
   How on earth Your Will is done;
   Help us see the mercy flowing
   From the wounding of Christ's side;
   Heal us with compassion spreading
   As a purifying tide.

2. God of dreams and intuition
   Inspiration from the night,
   Temper reason's rigid systems
   With the leap of faith's insight.
   God of passion, fill our knowing
   With Divine authority,
   And a sense of mystery leading
   To a right humility.

3. God of faith's heroic journey
   May Your Truth direct our way;
   Guide our footsteps, give us courage
   In the challenge of each day.
   God of Wisdom's spinning spiral,
   Soothe us with your gentle charms,
   Weave our lives into the pattern
   Of Christ's all-embracing arms.

4. God of order, God of chaos,
   In love's creativity
   Move the mountains of tradition
   Stifling earth's fertility

Break the barriers, guide the learning,
Bind the wounds and heal the pain,
Bring to birth our human yearning,
Integrate the world again.
(Boyce-Tillman 2006a: 32–33)

Ways of Knowing

Deep in the desert there lives an old woman. She is secret and private. She is a crower and a cackler; she is fat. She lives in a dark, hidden cave. And her task is the gathering of bones, which is why they sometimes call her La Trapera – the one who gathers. She creeps around the desert collecting whatever bones she can find – deer, birds and snakes and other animals that are likely to die out; but she specializes in the bones of wolves, which is why sometimes she is called La Loba – the wolf woman. And she brings the bones back to her deep, dark cave and lays them out on the rocky floor. And when she has a complete beautiful skeleton she starts to find the right sound for the bones. And she sits by the fire exploring all the lost sounds of the world. And when she has found it she starts to sing. And gradually the bones come together. And she sings and she breathes. And gradually the bones grow flesh. And she sings and she breathes. And gradually the flesh grows fur. And she sings and she breathes, breathes life into the creature. And the creature opens its eyes and stands and starts to walk. It prances right out of the darkness of the cave. And whether by leaping and prancing or whether by a flash of sunlight or a splash of water, that creature becomes a laughing, dancing human being.

So if you are lost and wandering in the desert maybe La Trapera will find you and will sing you one of her songs (The main source is Pinkola Estes 1992: 27–28).

I start with this South American myth mainly because in the figure of the old woman – the healer crone – we see an entirely different value system from the one prevailing in Western culture. The old woman is everything that Western women spend a great deal of money not to be – fat, hairy, a crower and cackler. However, they do share with her one feature – that they are often still secret and private and their sacred space is also secret and not public. It shows how what is devalued in one culture may be valued in another – that value systems are purely social constructs. If we have constructed them we can also deconstruct and rebuild them. This is what Wisdom calls us to do.

In this chapter I will examine the history of the prevailing value systems in Western culture. In doing this I will start to problematize the dualisms that have characterized Western society and give signposts to a more integrated way of being. In my earlier writing (Boyce-Tillman 2000a) – based on the work of the philosopher Foucault (Foucault and Gordon 1980) and the work of anthropologists like Gooch (1972), I built a notion of subjugated ways of knowing. These are ways of knowing that are not validated by the dominant culture of the time. Geertz defines a culture as:

> [A] historically transmitted pattern of meaning embodied in symbols, a system of inherited conceptions, expressed in symbolic forms by means of which human beings communicate, perpetuate and develop their knowledge about and attitudes toward life (Geertz 1973: 89).

The trick of the controllers is to make these meanings/values seem fixed and given, when, in fact, they are mere illusions of truth. Meaning is constructed by having a property of sharedness especially by those who hold positions of authority:

> Each society has its regime of truth, its 'general politics' of truth: that is, the types of discourse which it accepts and makes function as true; the mechanisms and instances which enable one to distinguish true and false statements, the means by which each is sanctioned; the techniques and procedures accorded value in the acquisition of truth; the status of those who are charged with saying what counts as true (Foucault and Gordon 1980: 131).

Many writers have identified the role of myths in the maintenance of the apparent truth of the dominant values, which suggest a fixed version of a value system that transcends temporality (Barthes 1972, Midgley 2003). They represent a sort of pattern or grid that gives meaning to a range of experiences (Pollock 1984). Writers have explored the way the myth of debt plays out in the maintenance of a capitalist culture:

> This is a carefully cultivated myth...Colonialism, development ideology, dependency and debt crisis are structurally linked and operate as different shades of a single mechanism to promote the drainage of wealth from the poor to the rich (Joseph 1991: 11).

Peter Selby sees these established orthodoxies 'as powerful and pervasive as were the orthodoxies of religious empires'. Critiques he sees as the equivalent of heresies (Selby 1997: 84). For the market has been assigned the characteristics once ascribed to a Divine creator in the myth making of contemporary society. We regularly hear phrases like 'The market will not like it' in phrases similar to those ascribed to a vengeful God in the Hebrew Bible. This process has theological implications:

> Humankind....would become the product of a creator. But this time, it would no longer be the Creator who is the cause. It would no longer be monotheism, it would be polytheism, except that the creators would be companies. Monsanto, or Novartis would do the programming (Virilio and Lotringer 2002: 117).

Derek Bunyard goes on to see the dangers of these myths, warning against the potential for the kind of experimentation on humans like that associated with Josef Mengele at Auschwitz-Birkenau. It could lead to the reconceptualization of forms of being which he suggests using the hyphenated name, *human-experiments* (Bunyard 2005: 295). Berman has a more general critique of the myths of freedom and growth built into the capitalist mythology:

> The trouble with capitalism is that ... it destroys the human possibilities it creates. It fosters, indeed forces, self-development for everybody; but people can develop only in restricted and distorted ways. Those traits, impulses and talents that the market can use are rushed (often prematurely) into development and squeezed desperately till there is nothing left; everything else within us, everything non-marketable, gets draconically repressed, or withers away for lack of use, or never has a chance to come to life at all (Berman 1988: 96).

Gender relations, in particular, are often supported by myths. In analysing the role of the Ramayana in Indian culture, Anna Bonisolialquati (2005) writes:

> The *Ramayana* has models for the divinity of kings at its core (Pollock 1984), and exemplifies the traditional ideal of masculinity. ...This project has implied a selection of the features proposed to make characters, such as Rama, or the Pandavas, vehicles and incarnations of a kingship, respectful of the *status quo* (and in particular of the Brahmans' privilege) (Bonisolialquati 2005: 1).

These include physical, professional and psychological attributes:

> First of all, the physical appearance of the king has to conform to the aesthetical canon of the handsome man...and richness of ornamentation of garments and jewellery. This aspect is connected to the theme of the king as lover and husband of the earth, his bride. He is in this way both the attractive young conqueror and the fertilizing male power.

> The king is a skilled soldier, in particular a bowman on a chariot...The king must show purity and religious piety, underlined in connection with the idea of the king as the protector of the Brahmans' heritage and of all his devotee-subjects (Bonisolialquati 2005: 2).

She goes on to show how these powerful representations of masculinity represented a subordinated role for women (Bonisolialquati 2005: 3).

Michael Kirwan, in reworking mimetic theory, sees the possibility of transformation of the dominant value systems by means of reworking literature:

> ...the liberating dissolution of the distinction between fiction and reality. Not that reality becomes dissolved in the fictional, but that through literature and myth we are able to break through and have access to what is real...and be redeemed (Kirwan 2004: 123).

Here we can see that the fragmentation of reality and fiction and the consequent devaluing of myth and literature may have cut off one of the main streams for society's renewal. What we need is 'in place of a transcendent myth, any emotionally satisfying narrative that speaks to our humanity; we have created a materialistic religion that leaves us, as people, empty of an emotionally satisfying, shared purpose' (Clark 2002: 233). The absence of such a myth Clark sees as the deep root of human stress and 'may well be responsible for most fatal attacks on others (murder) and in self (suicide), as well as for the much more frequent instances of lesser violence' (Clark 2002: 306). I tried to set this out in a song with the chorus:

> We'll tell the stories that heal the earth
> We'll tell the stories that heal the earth
> We'll tell the stories that heal the earth
> And bring it to rebirth
> (Boyce-Tillman 2006a: 158–59)

Nowhere is the power of the myth in Western society more clearly seen than in the area of motherhood. Gillian Rye explores this in her paper on Julia Kristeva:

> Mothers are sacred in more ways than one: because of their life-giving functions; because Christianity is formative of cultural memory and the Virgin Mary is a sacred symbol of maternity; because the repression of incestuous desire for the mother is at the heart – or the limits – of our psychic identity; because stereotypes of good and bad mothers police how women are perceived – and perceive themselves – as mothers, so that mothers are, on the one hand, untouchable, inviolable,

cannot be attacked or criticized – and yet, on the other hand, they carry
all the blame and... all the guilt (Rye 2003: 3).

She goes on to identify the phenomenon of 'maternal guilt'
reinforced by myths of 'maternal instinct' starting with such figures
as Jung and his concept of archetypes and supported by:

> ...a whole range of other guilt-inducing discourses for mothers, from
> politics, religion, psychology to feminism itself. Yet newspaper and
> magazine articles continue to attest to women's guilt about being
> mothers while also trying to be women with other interests and
> responsibilities, a career, and so on (Rye 2003: 6).

She sees the feminist theorist Julia Kristeva as offering the
possibility of a guilt-free maternity through her notion of maternal
jouissance – 'this openness of the psyche to the sensual quasi-sexual
pleasure of the mother-baby relationship' (Rye 2003: 7):

> ... the slow, difficult and delightful apprenticeship in attentiveness,
> gentleness, forgetting oneself. The ability to succeed in this path
> without masochism and without annihilating one's affective,
> intellectual and professional personality –
> such would seem to be the stakes to be won through guiltless maternity
> (Kristeva 1979: 206).

This hints at some of the discussion we shall undertake in Chapter
Three, in negotiating a relationship between individuality and
community and the working through of a responsibility without
guilt. Kristeva's solution is the negotiating of identity rather than the
dismemberment of patriarchy or the locating of a space outside it.

Stephen Hunt (2005) explores how the highly popular Alpha
Course is maintaining powerful gendered myths for the Church.
He cites the following anecdote from Rachael, a convert:

> "Since doing *Alpha* we went to do this follow-up course on Philippians
> called 'A Life Worth Living'. I also went along to do the washing up in
> the next *Alpha* course and really enjoyed it." (*Alpha News*, November
> 2003-March 2004: 13, quoted in Hunt 2005: 2).

From this he concludes:

> Leaving such chores to women marks a fairly stringent gender division
> of labour on most *Alpha* courses. ...The matter of hosting the event
> often falls to the women. If the *Alpha* programme is held in a church or
> community hall there will generally be a team of women who are
> responsible for cooking, and the clearing and washing up. Similarly,
> if it is held in the 'neutral' context of somebody's home, it is the woman

who is expected to undertake these duties while her husband leads the course and Bible studies.

While most *Alpha* leaders are male, there may be women in supporting roles, occasionally chairing the small discussion groups on the programme. More often than not, the discussion itself is frequently dominated by the more self-assertive male 'guests' despite their under-representation on the programme. As one female interviewee put it to me:

> "I did not say a word, although I had all the questions to ask. I left it all up to my husband. I was too embarrassed to say anything."

The subservient role of women is also evident on the *Alpha* video presentations (Hunt 2005: 4–5).

The use of morality in this context will be explored in Chapter Three.

And so traditional concepts of gender roles are maintained through the Alpha myth that condemns feminism in its treatment of such issues such as patriarchy, sexuality, and the family.

Kristin Aune also sees how the charismatic movement New Frontiers International (NFI) uses the Bible for the maintenance of myths of masculinity which they see as biblical but, in fact, reflect very conservative views in the wider culture:

> after they had established the central principle that masculinity is about leadership, there were two aspects of masculinity that NFI considered of prime importance for men to develop: responsible fatherhood and heterosexuality. ..... [It] confirms theories about "hegemonic masculinity" (Aune 2005: 2).

Margaret Myers looks at the origin of the myths in the wider society and how they are disseminated:

> The latter day Aristotelians – Schopenhauer, Nietszche, Weininger and in Sweden, Strindberg – were all the rage in the late nineteenth and early twentieth centuries. They were published and republished in cheap popular editions and quoted in daily newspapers and the popular press. Their ideas permeated most educated people's thinking. They were all thoroughly misogynist and denied women all creative and artistic capacity, as had their forefather, Aristotle, whose ideas had survived into modern times because they resonated with the ideas of the Church Fathers.
>
> These misogynist ideas were projected on any woman who embarked on a public, professional career in occupations defined as masculine or creative. Such a woman had to be prepared for ridicule and castigation. She might be accused of being essentially male or essentially immoral (Myers 2000: 206–7). The use of morality in this context will be explored in Cahpter Three.

Power, Patriarchy and Misogyny

Feminists have linked this in Western culture with patriarchy:

> The manifestation and institutionalization of male dominance over
> women and children in the family and the extension of male
> dominance over women in society in general. It implies that men
> hold power in all the important institutions in society and that women
> are deprived of access to such power. It does not imply that women
> are either totally powerless or totally deprived of rights, influence,
> and resources (Lerner 1986: 230).[1]

This was identified by Matilda Joslyn Gage in *Woman, Church
and State* in her remarkable analysis in 1893:

> The difference in civilization between Christian Europe and pagan
> Malabar at the time of its discovery was indeed great. While Europe,
> with its new art of printing, was struggling against the church for
> permission to use type – its institutions of learning few; its opportunities
> for education meager; its terrible inquisition crushing free thought
> and sending thousands each year to a most painful death; the
> uncleanness of its cities and the country such as to bring frequent
> visits of plague; its armies, its navies, with but one exception, imperfect;
> its women forbidden the right of inheritance, religious, political or
> household authority; the feminine principle entirely eliminated from
> divinity; a purely masculine God, the universal object of worship – all
> was directly opposite in Malabar. Cleanliness, peace, the arts, a just
> form of government, the recognition of the feminine – were found in
> Malabar.......under the missionaries sent by England to introduce her
> own barbaric ideas of God and man, this beautiful matriarchal
> civilization soon retrograded and was lost (Gage 1893: 7).

At its most extreme, this is seen in the control of women's
bodies. This has two effects – the first that birth is not valued so
that fewer women are choosing to bear children; and the recent
film *Children of Men* shows the terrifying end of this road where
women are no longer fertile. It also means that children are thought
of as commodities (Haraway 1991: 163).

The Church has been a publicly masculinist organization since
the first few hundred years of Christianity. This has had a
devastating effect on generations of women. The Church has sought

---

1. She links this to the loss of the goddess traditions in the third millennium (Lerner
1986:199-211). The goddess was replaced by a pantheon of gods and goddesses. By
the time monotheism emerges the male gods had come to dominate. (Sophie Drinker
makes a similar linkage in her fascinating book *Women in Music* 1948/1995).

to control, for example, women's creative processes. Elizabeth Stuart Phelps, writing in 1869, describes powerfully the effect that the patriarchal nature of the Western Church had in her experience of church, which is one I can relate to:

> For it came to seem to me, as I pondered these things in my own heart, that even the best and kindest forms of our prevailing beliefs had nothing to say to an afflicted woman that could help her much. Creeds and commentaries and sermons were made by men. What tenderest of men knows how to comfort his own daughter when her heart is broken. What can the doctrines do for the desolated by death? They were chains of rusty iron, eating into raw hearts. The prayer of the preacher was not much better; it sounded like the language of an unknown race to a despairing girl. Listen to the hymn. It falls like icicles on snow. Or, if it happen to be one of the old genuine outcries of the church, sprung from real human anguish or hope, it maddens the listener, and she flees from it, too sore a thing to bear the touch of holy music (Ward 1896: 97–98).

The effect of patriarchy on the place of women in the Church has been explored by a number of writers coming from a variety of positions as we have seen earlier. Carter Heyward in the diagram below shows clearly the effects of patriarchy and shows the variety of those who are likely to become subjugated knowers.

It is the value systems of these people that will become dominant and these groups will put systems in place to see that they remain dominant, like prisons and mental hospitals and redundancy. It is not only women who are subjugated but a range of different people and the natural world. Calls to examine the subjugated ways of knowing have come from many sources. For example, only a certain type of masculinity is valued, which Connell (1987) develops into his idea of 'hegemonic masculinity.' He defines this as the form of masculinity dominant in any culture. In contemporary society this is heterosexual and tightly bound up to the institution of marriage; so homosexual masculinity becomes subordinated. This subordination involves both interactions and ideological warfare. So homosexual men become objects of contempt. He develops this somewhat simplistic analysis (Connell 1995) into four types of masculinity – hegemonic, subordinated, complicit and marginalized – based on how various men negotiate their position:

> There are "relations of alliance, dominance and subordination" within and between masculinities (Connell 1995: 37), and while some men

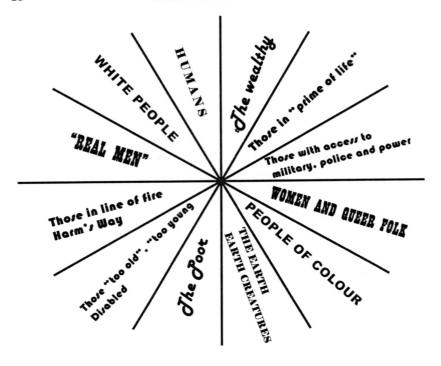

Fig. 1. Carter Heyward

are able to exert hegemony, others are more likely to be complicit – that is, they, I quote, "benefit from the patriarchal dividend, the advantage men in general gain from the subordination of women" though they fail to embody hegemonic masculinity; they are not the "frontline troops of patriarchy" (Connell 1995: 79). Others remain marginalized because of their class or ethnicity yet should be distinguished from subordinate masculinities because they are not (like gay or androgynous masculinities) actively subordinated (Connell 1995: 80–81).

Assertion of hegemonic heterosexual masculinity depends upon the rejection and subordination of homosexuality and femininity (the two are regarded as connected). Men constructing "acceptable" heterosexual masculinity participate in..."a double relationship, of traducing the 'other', including women and gays... at the same time as expelling femininity and homosexuality from within themselves" (Aune 2005: 4).

For Helen O'Grady the answer lies in understanding, which she sees as the axis of change:

Men themselves need to develop a more sophisticated understanding of male experience, one that does not avoid the reality of gender inequality and associated domination and exploitation. Such an understanding could both acknowledge the reality of men's suffering as a consequence of conforming to dominant notions of masculinity and simultaneously recognize that these play a part in perpetuating structures that oppress others (O'Grady 2005: 7).

Because the dominant masculinity is heterosexual, the term often used now for these value systems is heteropatriarchy. The dilemma posed for a variety of people by heteropatriarchy was explored as early as 1850 in Nathaniel Hawthorne's novel *The Scarlet Letter* in which:

> He sees its effects on sensitive men, rendering one dim and the other chilling, and also on relations between mothers and daughters restraining a mother from affirming her perceptions and telling her what she needs to know about men and love. How astonishingly modern this 1850 novel is; as I write, a woman in Nigeria, accused of adultery, is in danger of being stoned to death in accordance with the law of Sharia. An alliance of church and state is solidifying in many parts of the world, encouraging a militant fundamentalism and supported by "an iron framework of reasoning" (Gilligan 2004: 90).

The people in power in a state often resort to violence to maintain their position (as we shall explore further in Chapter Five).

> A state is an organization that has the monopoly of violence. There are two major forms of this. One is against other states, which we call war. The other is organized violence against its citizens practiced by almost all states... There is the development of penal and legal institutions.
>
> In relation to imprisonment by the state, it is worth remembering that this punishment has varied over time. In most traditional civilizations it was too expensive to keep people locked up for 23 hours a day in a cell. So they were punished in other ways: mutilated, sent to be galley slaves, put in treadmills, dispatched to plantations and labour camps. Some were enslaved. Only affluent civilizations have been able to imprison large numbers of their citizens or to keep hundreds waiting on death row. Given the wealth and attitudes in many modern states, there is a tendency for prison populations to grow rapidly as time passes. It is less bother to lock people away than to try either to deal with the roots of crime or to rehabilitate. So the British prison population inexorably creeps upwards and the profits of the increasingly privatized prison service grow. The reputation of politicians who are 'tough on crime' is enhanced. The state tends to

become a prison machine. It can easily become a surveillance state, its public places filled with closed-circuit cameras, its wealthy private citizens living in guarded and walled estates, its police heavily armed. To fight violence, violence of a slightly different kind is used. So we end up with the grim fact that like all species on earth, humans are necessarily violent (Macfarlane 2005: 72–73).[2]

In relation to women Helen O'Grady reworks this as internalized violence:

Unsurprisingly, the lack of value and affirmation associated with the legacy of secondary status is likely to generate varying levels of self-doubt or a diminished sense of worth. For many women this designated role as the caretakers of others. An imbalance between caring for others and caring for self tends to generate a need to please and one vulnerable to feeling never quite good enough. These (and other) factors can contribute to women experiencing uneasy or conflictual relationships with themselves that often are characterized by feelings of inadequacy, guilt, shame or dislike (O'Grady 2005: 2).

The Deviant Other

So we can see that normativity is established by those in power by means of the exclusion of the deviant 'other' who is perceived to be 'deviant' using the norms of the dominant heteropatriarchy. Foucault saw 'deviance' as socially constructed. This was set out most clearly in *Madness and Civilisation* ([1961] 1967) where he saw Western civilization as defining itself over and against 'madness'. He goes further in claiming that the definitions of madness are dependent on who is doing the defining – that is, those who have power at the time. He writes further on how normativity is constructed in sexuality ([1976] 1985), crime and punishment (1975) and health ([1963] 1973). He does not address the subject of women and some of his work is directly misogynist but feminist writers have found helpful concepts in his work, particularly that of creative resistance (McNay 1992a).

---

2. Michael Kirwan in *Discovering Girard* (2004) applies mimetic theory to this problem and reworks theories of atonement, fraught as they are with notions of both Divine and human violence. He sees mimetic theory as enabling 'a structured and responsible reflection on religion in the contemporary world' and as offering a way of reading stories so that faith, hope and love may be challenged, confirmed, nourished, or even called into being (Kirwan 2004: 116).

Constructions of normativity are well illustrated by the way in which disciplines like anthropology were constructed as an examination of the exoticised 'other':

> Ethnomusicologists and anthropologists have become increasingly aware of the power relations implied by the study of a clearly defined Other, be it primitive, tribal, non-Western, nonliterate, nonhistorical – the list could be endless (Jarviluoma 2000: 61).

However, as we have already seen, in *The Archaeology of Knowledge* ([1969] 1972), Foucault sees the 'other' not as a single discourse (as the dominant value supporters may do) but as consisting of multiple discourses, some at variance with another. In my model these various 'others' become 'subjugated ways of knowing' and the people practising them 'subjugated knowers.' These people are regularly pathologised, criminalized and ridiculed as we have seen above:

> [Foucault] provides the empirical and conceptual basis for treating such phenomena as sexuality, the family, schools, psychiatry, medicine, social science and the like as *political* phenomena. This sanctions the treatment of problems in these areas as *political* problems. It thereby widens the arena within which people may collectively confront, understand, and seek to change the charter of their lives (Fraser 1989: 26).

The effect of the often violent enforcement of Western values on indigenous culture has been devastating.

> Material poverty and social dysfunction are merely the visible surface of a deep pool of internal suffering. The underlying cause of that suffering is alienation – separation from our heritage and from ourselves...there is more than one Indian in this world who dreams in the language of his ancestors and wakes mute to them, who dreams of peace and wakes to a deep heavy anger (Alfred 2002: 42).

Many theorists advocate the revitalizing of local governance and dispute resolution processes that reflect the cultural norms of the people themselves (Sutherland 2005: 44). Otherwise, Alfred argues, 'the whole of the decolonization process will have been for nothing if Indigenous government has no meaningful Indigenous character' (Alfred 2002: 33). Chris Clarke sees that such a process is needed to regenerate Western culture, which is seriously distorted:

> Western notions of the individual which originally celebrated every human being's innate creativity and right to freedom has been overdeveloped at the expense of other equally important human needs

such as for meaning and connectedness...Moreover, unbridled individualism and technological "advancement" has resulted in an insatiable greed and self-absorption even at the expense of harming others and the earth (Clarke 2002: 233).

In the American Commission On Children at Risk,[3] American children's doctors linked youth suicide, crime, emotional problems, and violence to the lack of spiritual meaning in the lives of American youth. They saw human beings as 'hardwired' for moral and spiritual meaning and decided that the void left by the absence of spirituality leads to social pathologies such as violence, crime, addictions, and excessive consumerism. They recommend that spiritual values, pluralism and community need to be encouraged in American families, schools, and youth organizations. So Western cultures experience the same dissonance as we have already seen in indigenous cultures from the subjugation of various areas of culture associated with intuition.

So the regeneration of Western culture lies in re-embracing the values of subjugated groups. There are calls for a change of consciousness to regenerate Western culture. This will have an effect on our entire society:

> Given the global loss of meaning in people's lives, it should be of no surprise that we have consequently lost a reverence for life. Global Action to Prevent War "claims that the last century was the most lethal in human history: over 200 million people were killed in 250 wars and genocidal onslaughts, more people than were killed in warfare for the last two thousand years."[4] In examining current wars Lederach (1997: 4) notes that over one third involve member-states of the United Nations, two thirds involve child soldiers, and "half of the current wars have been under way for more than two decades" (Sutherland 2005: 44–6).

Calls to halt the spread of patriarchal systems come from many sources:

> The very notion of "patriarchy" has threatened to become a universalizing concept that overrides and reduces distinct articulations

3. The Commission was comprised of leading US children's doctors – The Commission on Children at Risk, *Hardwired to Connect: The New Scientific Case for Authoritative Communities* (2003 [cited 15 Nov 2003]) available from http://americanvalues.org/html/hardwired.html

4. Global Action to Prevent War, ([cited 15 November 2003]) available from www.globalactionpw.org

of gender asymmetry in different cultural contexts. As feminism has sought to become related to struggles against racial and colonial oppression, it has become increasingly important to resist the colonizing epistemological strategy that would subordinate different configurations of domination under the rubric of a transcultural notion of patriarchy (Butler 1990: 35).

The implications of this for nature are worked out by Anderson:

> As the hero of Homer's *Odyssey*, Odysseus is configured by Horkheimer and Adorno as the modern male subject whose self-consciousness unfolds in an ironic journey of apparent self-preservation and liberation from the mythical powers of nature. This liberation, which from a feminist perspective is highly doubtful, appears to be achieved through the exercise of Odysseus's subject-centered, calculating reason, whereby the ends justify the means. But this strictly male victory of self-preservation is won at a cost. The victorious domination and control of nature by scientific rationality rests upon a paradox in that the subject-centered reasoning is achieved by man who is also in nature. The implication here is that he must equally dominate and control nature in himself (Anderson 1998: 217).

The first story of this chapter illustrates how these dominant paradigms are culturally specific. My own experience of staying with native Canadians illustrates the differing value systems very clearly:

> I was privileged to spend some time with a native people in North America. I had been present at several sweat lodges at which a particular medicine man had been working. I had also purchased a small hand drum and he had consented to beat the Bear Spirit into it for me. One evening he was preparing for a sweat lodge and said that he needed a powerful woman to help him and sit alongside him. This would usually be his wife but she was unable to be there so would I help him. I was both honoured and terrified; but he said he would help me with the ritual and so I agreed to the role. The first round of prayer took place and he concluded it by saying that now June would sing a song about the eagle and the sunrise. It was here that I thought that I had met an insuperable problem. I knew no songs from the culture. But I remembered that in the songs I had heard how each phrase started high and then went lower in order to bring the energy of the sky to the earth. So I started each phrase high and took it lower while singing about the eagle and the sunrise. It was a powerful experience for me and my voice seemed to come from a place of power deep inside that I had not experienced before. With the prayer round ended we went outside to cool in the night air. 'Great song, June' said the leader of the

sweat lodge. I was about to say that, or course, I had to make it up and then remembered from my previous conversations with some of the women singers that in this culture everything is given not the creation of an individual. So I replied: 'The Great Spirit gave it to me when I was in the Lodge.'

Here I was in a culture where the intuitive way of receiving musical material – construed as coming from a connection with a spiritual source – was the dominant way of knowing, not the individualistic, humanistic way of the individual composer creating an individual song from their own experience in their own personal subconscious. I had previously been in a women's sweat lodge after which the leader had said that she thought the Great Spirit had given her the whole of the song when she was in the Lodge and that previously she had only received part of it. In the West we would probably have said something like we had not yet finished it and were working at completing it.

However, the notion of receiving music in this way from a Divine source would not have been remarkable for Hildegard of Bingen in medieval Europe (Boyce-Tillman 2000b). She composed nothing herself but received everything directly from God. In medieval Europe intuitive ways of receiving material were more acceptable than in contemporary Western culture. As Grace Jantzen writes:

> They were not infected with the peculiarly modern virus whose philosophical symptoms are such terms as "realism, evidence, and justified, true belief" (Jantzen 1998: 5).

The Enlightenment saw a massive swing to a different value system in which the intuitive visionary experience, whether associated with music or not, is at best marginalized and at worst pathologised (see Chapter Six). In Post-Enlightenment culture, reason became regarded as paramount and this has coloured the way in which more intuitive areas like music are regarded. Order and clarity and a desire to see the world as defined by scientific reality – 'as it really it is' – have been the ultimate goals. The chaotic, the imaginary, the obscure have been seen as enemies and indeed requiring of a cure that can be achieved largely by reason. This polarity between reason and intuition is but one example of the polarities that make up the value systems that exist within each person and within any particular culture.

Self-policing

Jean Baker Miller identified the problems encountered by the marginalized:

> Subordinates (in this case women) absorb a large part of the untruths created by the dominants; there are a great many blacks who feel inferior to whites, and women who still believe they are less important than men. This internalization of dominant beliefs is more likely to occur if there are few alternative concepts to hand... Within each subordinate group there are tendencies for some members to imitate dominants (Baker Miller 1988: 11–12).

Part of the answer to this situation is the courage to speak out about what one sees. This was central to Hildegard's life (1098–1179) when at the age of forty-one she receives a vision telling her to speak and write her visions after years of being told to keep silent (Boyce-Tillman 2000b).

Carol Gilligan working with Nathaniel Hawthorne's novel *The Scarlet Letter* sees the need to silence the internal critic based on the internalized violence of the dominant values and speak out:

> In overcoming his adamant, Hawthorne did what Virginia Woolf would do in killing "the angel in the house", he silenced an internalized voice that had kept him from saying what he saw (Gilligan 2004: 83).

Gilligan describes how the novel challenged the framework of Puritanism and enabled the heroine to see it as social construct not a God-given reality:

> The human intellect, newly emancipated, had taken a more active and a wider range than for many centuries before. ... Hester [the heroine] sees that "the whole race of womanhood" and the very nature of the opposite sex, or its long hereditary habit which has become like nature are in reality part of a "system of society" that, built up in one way, could be "torn down and built up anew"...Freeing her sexuality, Hester released herself from the restraints of Puritanism; from this vantage point, she sees "the foundations of the Puritan establishment" as a human construction, neither ordained or natural (Gilligan 2004: 85–86).

Self-policing is developed in childhood as parents endeavour to mould their children into the dominant value systems. Derek Bunyard, in an article examining the commodification of childhood and its role in initiating children into Western values examines this in the area of mess and muddle:

Probably every reader of this essay has had to deal with a small child and its mess. Of course the child was soon cleaned up, the floor swept, and the table wiped. The clothes they wore eventually got dumped in the washing machine and some semblance of order was restored. Day after day this pattern was repeated and eventually a level of tidiness and cleanliness acceptable to adult eyes predominated for longer and longer stretches of time. Each correction or encouragement added to the apparent solidity of the practices of everyday life surrounding the child – adults and other children creating an increasingly well-defined reciprocal to the child's own agency; and so the child grew up.

This process is unremarkable, yet it presents society with two forms of danger. Adults, in wanting the best for their children, perhaps try too hard to shape them according to some image of perfection: children, in wanting love, are perhaps too willing to submit (Bunyard 2005: 292).

And there are potentially more sinister processes as technology joins forces with dominant value systems (see Case Study Three in Chapter Three):

As genetic research makes possible ever more extraordinary therapeutic interventions, we seem to edge closer to the dream of a predictable reproduction; and it does not require much imagination or historical study to recognize that techniques developed to deal with life-threatening circumstances will soon be adapted to more fashionable ends. The genetic enhancement of the embryo is not yet with us, but already the more commercially-minded professionals facilitate forms of genetic selection. Over the Internet it is possible to purchase the sperm of the highly intelligent, and for a higher price, the eggs of the very beautiful (Bunyard 2005: 292).

The challenges to the dominant heteropatriarchy come from a variety of groups with a variety of agendas; but the feelings of the subjugated knowers are often similar. Grace Ji-sun Kim calls it *han*:

Han is not only an experience of women; it is a typical prevailing feeling of the Korean people, for the nation as a whole has endured many defeats and disasters…Han is "the suppressed, amassed and condensed experience of oppression caused by mischief or misfortune, so that it forms a kind of 'lump' in one's spirit" (Kyung 1990b: 30, Kim 2002: 57).

She contextualizes this in the Korean experience of Western theology:

In the past, theology tended to ignore the experiences of non-dominant cultures and make them invisible and inaudible. Korean North American women are seeking ways to make their voices heard and their culture valued. They cannot accept the theology of the past, and they cannot accept uncritically the theological methods arising out of other experiences and contexts. These women are a distinct group of people who need to address theology out of their own unique context and experience. Korean North American Christian women need to be creative in developing a method of doing theology that considers seriously their experiences of oppression, subordination, and *han*, and also draws upon the best of their own Asian religio-cultural traditions.

Han is a prevailing feeling of the Korean people. Hyun Young-Hak, a Korean theologian, wrote "*han* is a sense of helplessness because of the overwhelming odds against, a feeling of total abandonment, a feeling of acute pain of sorrow in one's guts and bowels making the whole body writhe and wiggle, and an obstinate urge to take 'revenge' and right the wrong all these constitute." [Chung Hyun Kyung 1990: 30] People of Korean heritage need a relevant theology that addresses their needs and helps them in their process of liberation (Kim 2002: 1–2).

This links with Helen O'Grady's work on self-policing – how the values of the society are internalized and cause serious distress:

Hearing about the pain of these inner battles that frequently accompany women through the course of their everyday lives (lives that for some women also involve external struggles of violence, abuse, discrimination, poverty, legal injustice, loss etc.,) breathed life into Foucault's claim that policing one's own thoughts, feelings and actions to ensure conformity to commonly accepted ideas and practices is an ingrained mechanism of social control in modern Western societies. This effectively means individuals living their lives as though under constant observation... Women can appear to be coping reasonably well yet nonetheless be engaged in punitive and exhausting inner battles. As already mentioned, these battles tend to be experienced as an inevitable or automatic part of identity. As such they often have women feeling as though they are personally deficient...Exposure of the relationship between individual struggle and socially privileged ideas, practices and structures reflects the link between experiences of selfhood and the broader power structures of society (O'Grady 2005: 4).

She also explores the complexity of the subjugated ways of knowing and how various discourses interact to disempower some women more than others:

Cultural invitations to self-police in line with dominant identity norms are likely to exert less of a hold for women who simultaneously occupy sites of social privilege, for example in relation to class, race, sexuality and health. For women in these categories, the impact of gender enlarged self-doubt is likely to be moderated (though frequently not eliminated) by the sense of entitlement commonly afforded by a middle-class upbringing, whiteness, heterosexuality or good health. Some women may be socially advantaged in some respects – for example in relation to skin colour and sexuality – and disadvantaged in others – for instance in relation to class or health, and so on (O'Grady 2005: 5).

This thinking leads us to rethink notions of therapy (Boyce-Tillman 2000a). Based on Jung, theorists like Isabel Briggs Myers (Myers and McCaulley 1985, Myers 1993) have written that each of us chooses particular ways of knowing. Other ways of knowing will then become subjugated in the self – making up the 'shadow' as Jung called it. So those people who choose the dominant ways of knowing will be successful in a society, but those who choose the subjugated ways of knowing will become pathologised. But, as we have already seen, the construction of this is tightly linked to a self-policing developed from the dominant value system.

> James Hillman helped me to see how my insistence that art therapy works with the 'healthy' and 'non-pathological' aspects of the person as a reaction to models of therapy that classify people according to pathologies. The classifying mind has used pathology in a painting or dream as something sick and negative, we can embrace it as part of the soul's nature (McNiff 1992: 25).

Foucault also offers the possibility of using the idea of subjugated knowledges within the self as well as in society and correcting them:

> There are times in life when the question of knowing if one can think differently than one thinks, and perceive differently than one sees, is absolutely necessary if one is to go on looking and reflecting at all...But then, what is philosophy today... In what does it consist, if not in the endeavour to know how and to what extent it might be possible to think differently instead of legitimizing what is already known? (Foucault [1984] 1985: 8–9).

The Construction of Value Systems

So what values are dominant in Western culture? The model I have developed is a model to identify some of them. Drawing on a wide variety of literatures from music, education, humanistic psychology (particularly Briggs Myers 1985, 1993, and Assagioli 1994), sociology, gender studies and theology, I have identified certain polarities which are in dynamic relationship.[5] This model identifies a number of polarities that are in dynamic relationship within the self and within society.

The model (Boyce-Tillman 2005) presents a way of looking at the health of a society and a person. In a balanced person and a balanced society all the possibilities are held as of equal value, but in most people and societies this is not the case. This will be because of the issues of power identified above and the establishing of a normative dominant discourse and internal self-policing. However, the more dominant one of the pairs that make up the polarities becomes, the more the alternative value system will tend to be projected onto the marginalized 'other'; which will consist of groups who have less power or whose power is tightly constrained.

In the model, these polarities are drawn as having a constant flow between them. Balance is defined as being when that flowing is fluid and dynamic. The subjugated and dominant knowings have to be in dialogue with one another to achieve a wholeness. The dominant culture will validate one of the poles more highly than the other; so effort will be required to keep the flow moving to the subjugated way of knowing. It is part of the search for mutuality at the level of self and society:

> Genuine reconciliation involves transition from systems of domination to relationships of mutuality (Sutherland 2005: 23).

In this model the dominant values are on the right and the subjugated values on the left. The ensuing chapters will look at these polarities and how they have functioned at various times in various Christian cultures both in Western cultures and those cultures that were colonized by that culture, where languages and cultures were deliberately destroyed.[6] We shall examine what

5. There are dangers in what might be seen as a syncretic or 'hybrid' approach to the various disciplines on which I have drawn, but it does serve to make the findings of one discipline accessible to others and in the Introduction I have drawn attention to the anthological nature of the book.

6. This is slightly modified from the model as set out in Boyce-Tillman (2000a). The polarities are now represented as circles to show the dynamism of their interrelationship. Also the number of polarities has been increased to eight to separate out the rational/ intuitive polarity, which was subsumed in other polarities in the previous model. I am indebted to Stuart Manins who shared his work with the Maori people in New Zealand for help in refining the model.

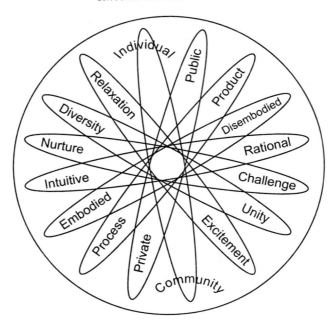

Fig. 2. Model

happens when the dynamism between the subjugated ways of knowing and those of the dominant heteropatriarchy is broken. When the polarities split apart, they become perverted versions of themselves. The answer to these perversions is to trace them back to their original dynamic relationship which produces the good outcome or synthesis resulting from the re-establishment of the dynamic flow. This will be drawn illustrating the process within the self and within society. It is hoped that this will produce greater understanding of the mechanisms that produce both society and the self and how these interact. Therapy and sociology will be seen as interactive and a theology embracing both will be developed:

> For Foucault, the creation of different self-understandings is both possible and desirable in order to enhance the scope for human creativity and generate greater social inclusiveness and diversity. He defines human freedom terms of active participation in the creation of ourselves as other than we are. In his account, freedom is an ongoing practice and one which always takes place in a sociohistorical context (O'Grady 2005: 24).

Resistance Strategies

We have seen how Foucault was taken up in his writings with developing the notion of 'otherness', the unsanctioned meanings, the subjugated knowledges; this led him to the possibility of strategies of resistance. I heard a fine story of such strategies at a personal level. A young woman in the 1930s was destined to work in a tailoring factory. She, however, wanted to be a nurse. She tried a number of ploys such as taking extended breaks, locking herself in the lavatory and cutting the material wrongly. Eventually (paradoxically unwittingly) she was dismissed for failing to provide a sick note that she did not realize she had to provide. Another one, at a cultural level, is provided by Alan MacFarlane in the context of the spread of games via colonialism.

> It is only in the last hundred years or so that the competitive team games in the West have bounced, kicked and batted their way round the world, creating a universal addiction. ...The Indians took up cricket with added zest when they realized that they could beat their white masters at it, and also legitimately stand around in a field for hours without being told that they were being lazy...When games spread they can also be radically altered...In another part of New Guinea they have learnt to play football, but they go on playing as many matches as are necessary for both sides to reach the same score (MacFarlane 2005: 57).

These are inventive strategies – creative solutions to the oppositional dualisms. The feminists of the 1960s and 70s often saw the categories of oppressor and oppressed as fixed, but now there is a move towards 'broader definitions and shifting boundaries' (Isherwood 2006: 9). It would seem that there are three approaches that the subjugated knowers can take to the dominant culture. They can collude with it – play out the roles designated for them. They can keep moving position when they encounter the worse of the oppositional tendencies of those who control the dominant value systems. An example of this is the story of Mary Neal,[7] who, in the early twentieth century when she parted company after a disagreement from her co-worker in the Folk Dance revival – Cecil Sharp – returned to her other philanthropic activities. The third strategy is an overt challenging or subversion of the systems of oppression. Both of the latter might be regarded as resistance

---

7. I am indebted to Lucy Neal OBE for details of Mary Neal's life and work.

strategies. This book contains a number of case studies that illustrate a combination of these strategies and involve negotiation with the dominant culture, rather than a straightforward opposition.

Cyborg theory has been developed as a resistance strategy. It was created by Donna Haraway (1991) as an answer to traditional notions of feminism with its emphasis on oppositional qualities as identity and the loss of a sense of affinity. She used the metaphor of a cyborg in order to construct a postmodern feminism that transcended the limitations of traditional gender and feminisms. Because the cyborg is a merger of human and technology it breaks the traditional models of human, animal and machine, drawing on the Genesis myth. In the Cyborg Manifesto, she writes: 'The cyborg does not dream of community on the model of the organic family, this time without the Oedipal project. The cyborg would not recognize the Garden of Eden; it is not made of mud and cannot dream of returning to dust.' [8] It questions all kinds of concepts like what is natural, what is man-made and what is God-given. This thinking is part of Haraway's insistence that the focus of feminist theory and politics must be to make 'a place for the different social subject' (Haraway 1992a: 95). She looks for the creation of new technologies that are able to disalienate and realign the human connection between or 'technics', material and technical details, rules, machines and methods, with our 'erotics', the sensuous apprehension and expression of love as affinity, (Haraway 1992b: 329). She searches for the position of a 'multiple subject with at least double vision' (Haraway 1992b: 188–98). As post-gendered beings, her cyborgs act in the world differentially, simultaneously, and reciprocally in relation to boundaries. But to do this they need to see the world through different eyes:

> Cyborg imagery can suggest a way out of the maze of dualisms in which we have explained our bodies and our tools to ourselves. This is a dream not of a common language, but of a powerful infidel heteroglossia. It is an imagination of a feminist speaking in tongues to strike fear into the circuits of the supersavers of the new right. It means both building and destroying machines, identities, categories, relationships, space stories (Haraway 1992b: 181).

Many theorists have examined how women have renegotiated their roles in the Church as the surrounding society has changed in

8. http://en.wikipedia.org/wiki/Cyborg_theory, 20 Sept 2006.

its definition of gender roles. Callum Brown identified how in 1960s UK, women 'cancelled their mass subscription to the discursive domain of Christianity' (Brown 2001: 195). This was in contradistinction to the nineteenth-century and earlier twentieth-century when women's adherence to the religion of the day was highly significant in maintaining the structures of society because of their pivotal point in the family. The result of this was that religiosity was clearly defined as feminine; and women's value as woman, wife and mother was based on the maintenance of these religious observances. In the 1960s women started to reject the roles society had defined for them and this resulted in the 'simultaneous de-pietisation of femininity and the de-feminisation of piety' (Brown 2001: 192). Both older and younger women left the Church, as their identity became secularized. Men no longer needed to keep up appearances as an accompaniment to their partner. If before 1800 piety was primarily male while between 1800 and 1960 it was female, after 1960 it became degendered (Brown 2001: 196).

Janet Eccles supports this view in a paper entitled 'Why Are Women Leaving the Church – And Then What Are They Doing?' She describes how women negotiated their position with regard to the Church when there was a paradigm shift in the wider world (Eccles 2005). Outside of Church structures, they developed a different form of piety which they could tailor-make for themselves and which fitted their new position. The Church's monopoly of spirituality was challenged and the link between spirituality and religion was weakened.

Inventive strategies of resistance critique the notion of normativity and even suggest notions of revolution. Matilda Joslyn Gage in 1893 ends her book *Woman, Church and State*:

> Looking forward, I see evidence of a conflict more severe than any yet fought by reformation or science, a conflict that will shake the foundations of religious belief, tear into fragments and scatter to the winds the old dogmas upon which all forms of Christianity are based. It will not be the conflict of man with man upon rites and systems. It will not be the conflict of science upon church theories regarding creation and eternity. It will not be the light of biology illuminating the hypothesis of the resurrection of the body. But it will be the rebellion of one-half of the church against those theological dogmas upon which the very existence of the church is based.
>
> During the ages, no rebellion has been of like importance with that of woman against the tyranny of church and state. None has had

> such far-reaching effects. We note its beginning. Its progress will
> overthrow every existing form of these institutions. Its end will be a
> regenerated world (Gage 1893/1998: 324).

Yet, the suggestion offered by this book is that it is possible to
negotiate a flow between these value systems which are at present
fractured and therefore in a twisted distorted form. This will involve
people from subjugated groups acquiring positions of power, and
also subjugated knowers understanding the way self-policing
strategies work in the self. In analyzing these dominant value
systems it hopes to help to construct a more life-giving set of values
– a call to a form of symbolization that will enable us to re-envision
the Enlightenment values to include a measure of interrelatedness
(Grey 1989). This may or may not be within the Christian church as
it is now represented in its established denominations. This will
depend on whether its own value systems can themselves be
renewed in the light of a Christ who embodies the values of the
Hebrew prophets such as Deutero-Isaiah (Furlong 2000) and whether
such symbolization should embrace elements from other spiritual
traditions. In this sense it is a call to those in spiritual as well as
financial and political power. The prophets of contemporary
Christianity identify the need to engage with geopolitics as opposed
to the privatized spirituality based on the separated Cartesian self
(see Chapter Three):

> Over the long haul of the Enlightenment, Western Christianity has
> been progressively privatized in terms of individuals, families, and
> domestic communities. By and large, out of bewilderment and
> embarrassment, the ecclesial communities have forgotten how to speak
> about national and international matters, except in times of war to
> mobilize God for "the war effort". The inevitable outcome of this
> privatization is to relinquish geopolitics to practical and technical
> analysis...*if the theological dimension drops out of international purview,
> and with it any credible, critical moral dimension, then the world becomes one
> in which might makes right* (Brueggemann 1997: 525).

Rebecca Todd Peters (2004) in her examination of the ethics of
globalization examines four solutions offered by various groups to
the dilemmas posed by globalization. She examines the neo-liberal
paradigm with its model of extending capitalism worldwide and
finding a place for everyone within it. It seeks to globalize
individualism, prosperity and freedom, in fact the globalization of
heteropatriarchy. It sees itself as benevolent and would see our

current Western value system dominant throughout the world. In her second paradigm of social development she describes how the answer lies in social equity liberation. Here the answer lies in addressing issues of inequality. It differs from neoliberalism in its stress on justice and fairness. Although more moral than neoliberalism, it still sees Western values as paramount and simply needing some checks and balances. In the third paradigm which she terms localization, the answer is seen as lying in sustainability; not only does it seek to eliminate poverty and conflict, hunger and homelessness but also the extinction of species, and the pollution of the planet (Todd Peters 2004: 132).

> The vision here is grounded in the reality of human existence and strives to transform relationships of hierarchy and domination into relationships of mutuality and justice. Earthist proponents argue that it is through a vision of the good life as mutuality, justice and sustainability that our world can be transformed into a world of people who care more about the dignity and well-being of other human beings and the care of the planet than about wealth and its illusions of satisfaction (Todd Peters 2004: 132).

This does offer the possibility of a challenge to Western systems but sometimes fails to address the consumerism of the first world. The fourth paradigm sees globalization as neocolonialism and concentrates on the struggle of people's movements for global solidarity. It sees:

> communal autonomy as what constitutes human flourishing...While the exact picture of the good life may differ from culture to culture and community to community, human flourishing requires respect for basic human rights and some degree of autonomy of communities that allows them to participate in the sociopolitical processes that affect the heath and well-being of their people (Todd Peters 2004: 164–65).

She highlights the problems involved in this strategy of resistance and how it needs communities of people who share similar values; she critiques the naivete of trying to withdraw from the world community. She is pessimistic about any middle ground between these last two strategies of resistance and global capitalism.

Various other theorists from different perspectives point to the possibility of a new world order. When the balance is achieved, the self or the society will have developed the new paradigm searched for by such writers as Donna Haraway (1992), Chela Sandoval (2000) and Chris Clarke (2002). bell hooks sets this out, identifying love as a key element:

> Rather than organize black families around the principle of authoritarian rule of the strong over the weak, we can organize (as some of us do) our understanding of family around anti-patriarchal, anti-authoritarian models that posit love as the central guiding principle. Recognizing love as the effort we make to create a context of growth, emotional, spiritual and intellectual, families would emphasize mutual co-operation, the value of negation, processing, and the sharing of resources. Embracing a feminist standpoint can serve as an inspiration for transforming the family as we now know it (hooks 1996: 73).

In the book, *Methodology of the Oppressed*, Chela Sandoval sets out an apparatus for countering neocolonizing postmodern global formations, which she calls:

> "love", understood as a technology for social transformation (Sandoval 2000: 22).

In Part Four of this radical text the author sets out a position entitled 'Love in the Postmodern World' which looks at various forms of dissident consciousness including the principles of political love and desire, love as a political apparatus, the end of academic apartheid, the bases for creating interdisciplinary knowledge, the middle voice as the third voice, the science of technoscience and decolonizing cyberspace. She outlines the role of citizen-subjects as activists in the process of 'decolonizing the social imagination' in the context of the transnationalization of capitalism:

> Love as a social movement is enacted by revolutionary, mobile, and global coalitions of citizen-activists who are allied through the apparatus of emancipation (Sandoval 2000: 182).

These resonate with Chris Clarke's thinking in *Living in Connection: Theory and Practice of the New World-view* in which his starting point is the understanding of:

> This modern world, our own dysfunctional, self-contradictory world, by understanding the scientific ideas which created it (Clarke 2002: 22).

He documents the transformation of eight principles whose roots are in the seventeenth century (Clarke 2002: 23) so that Determinism, for example, is transformed in the twenty-first century to indeterminism (where he explores ideas like some of the thinking in Chapter Four on process and product-based values). He concludes by bringing spirituality and science together and seeing us as 'instruments of shalom':

> We are offering the world an invitation to join with Wisdom...as expressed through the life of Gaia, engaging with the Wisdom of our own bodies (Clarke 2002: 23).

Reconceptualizing the Polarities

So how does my model hope to show and understand the processes of strategies of resistance? How do we avoid the problems of collusion with the dominant culture? We have nowhere else to live at present but in a heteropatriarchal capitalism whether we accept it or oppose it. Here, I draw on Hildegard for a concept that might help us. Hildegard sees the good as indissolubly connected with the evil. Her theology is most carefully worked out in *The Book of Life's Merits* where each virtue is set against its corresponding vice (Hozeski 1994). The vice appears as a twisted, mangled form of the virtue. So, for example, envy is a twisted form of love and the answer lies in untwisting it into its right form as love. Here we see their dynamic relation with one another. These are the words of envy:

> "I am the shepherd and guardian of excess, and I cast out all greenness from men [sic] whenever I want to. ...I draw many to myself and pollute all things that God does. If I cannot have the things that are bright, I value them as nothing. If those who call me night were to sprinkle water on me, I would quickly dry myself. In addition, my words are like hidden arrows and wound the heart of those who call themselves righteous. For my strengths are like the North. All the things that are mine, however, I give with hatred because hatred was born from me and is smaller than me." (Margret Berger 1999: 127).

Love's response shows her untwisting the knots of envy:

> Oh most filthy filth, you are like a snake that attacks itself, for you cannot sustain anything that is stable and honourable...I, however, am the air, I nourish all greenness and bring flowers to mature fruit... I bring forth tears from a good sigh as I also bring forth a good aroma from tears through most holy works. I am also the rain that rises from the dew through which the grass rejoices with rich life. ...God hides no counsel from me. I have a royal dwelling place and all things that are from God are mine (Hozeski 1994: 127).

In her theology it is broken relationship which is the key to this twisting of virtue into vice and this reflects a fracture as the heart of the cosmos. So the answer to the vices lies not in banning them but in unscrambling them so that they can be manifest in their good manifestation.

In my model the fracture at the heart of global society has stopped the flow between the two polarities and caused both polarities to be manifest in a twisted form. The result is that they have become a twisted form of what they should be. The answer lies in establishing the flow between the polarities. This moves the debate away from one of the polarities being better than the other which characterized some of the feminist debates in the 1960s and 70s. This sees both in inextricable dialogue and that both find their true manifestation is by being connected together. Examples of how this might work are given in the case studies in the following chapters.

Summary

This chapter has set out a model of how certain ways of knowing have become subjugated by the power structures of Western society. It has looked at a series of polarities which need to be continually flowing and in interrelationship and has examined the consequences of their splitting by violent reinforcement of the dominant values. It has called for the envisioning of new ways of restoring right relationship between the ways of knowing and the people who have embraced or been forced into particular patterns of knowing. It has drawn on a variety of areas and a variety of literatures as well as personal experience. All of these themes will be further unpacked in succeeding chapters to produce a picture of the Unconventional Wisdom of our society – queering the concept of wisdom.

Chapter Two

WISDOM THEOLOGY

Firmly we believe and truly
God created heaven and earth;
And we next acknowledge duly
Mary gave that Wisdom birth.

And we trust and hope most fully
That God acts within our pain,
Labouring lovingly and deeply
Till our life is birthed again..

We can sense the Holy Spirit
Struggling here creatively
Ev'rywhere and ev'ry minute
For the earth's integrity.

We seek reconciliation
In a world that longs for peace;
We will work for resurrection
With God's joy that brings release.

Glory be to God Creator,
Who transforms our living here,
And the Spirit, our Sustainer
Always strength'ning, always near.

Adoration now be given
In and through the angel throng
To the God of earth and heaven
Through the earth's symphonic song.

(Boyce-Tillman 2006: 26)

This chapter will examine the tradition of Wisdom theology with a view to bringing it together with the ways of knowing explored in the previous chapter. The Wisdom strand of theology in Christianity is like an underground stream surfacing from time to time and then disappearing again into hidden caverns:

> Once upon a time there was Wisdom. There was Wisdom, and she was present everywhere with all the intensity and all the desire of all there was. And once the Word was spoken she alone dived into the spaces between the words, blessing the silence out of which new worlds are born. Now as it was in the beginning, Wisdom is hearing all creation into speech. She alone knows something of the possibilities (Tatman 1996: 238).

Nelle Morton, one of the earliest feminist theologians, used the phrase 'to hear Wisdom into speech' in her seminal text *The Journey is Home* in which she recognizes that 'Wisdom is feminist and suggests an existence earlier than Word' (Morton 1985: 175). In such writings there is a clear link between the silencing of the Wisdom tradition and the subjugated ways of knowing of the first chapter.

Wisdom, or Hokhmah, has its origins in Judaism where it is found most clearly in the book of Wisdom. It may have acquired some characteristics from the cult of Astarte or Asherah, the Queen of Heaven of the Canaanites (Raphael 1999). She was clearly very popular and the Old Testament charts a number of attacks on her such as Josiah's throwing out of her image from the temple in 2 Kgs 23. 6–7. Recent scholars suggest that she was worshipped also by the Israelites, thus posing a real threat to the dominant orthodoxy (Olyan 1988). Drawing on the book of Proverbs, the book of the Wisdom of Jesus ben Sira (written by a Jerusalem teacher about 185 BCE) and the Wisdom of Solomon, Pamela Foulkes writes in summary:

> The biblical figure of Lady Wisdom clearly has the potential to be a powerful and appropriate bearer of divine presence for the women of today's Church. A feminine figure of knowledge and understanding, of strength and insight, nourisher and nurturer. She brings order and justice and balance to all creation. For those who love and seek God, she is there to provide a channel of grace, a pathway to divine immanence (Foulkes 1995: 16).

Joan Chamberlain Engelsman in *The Feminine Dimension of the Divine* (1979) uses Jung's theory of archetypes to see Wisdom's relationship to the Greek goddesses Demeter, Persephone, Hecate and Isis. She sees a growth in her importance as a rival to Yahweh. She also charts her repression in Christian thought, beginning with Philo who at first equates the masculine Logos with Sophia and then substitutes him for her; so phallocentricity becomes the dominant paradigm of Christianity. The Logos now takes over the roles of the firstborn of God and the intermediary between God and humanity. She is now described as ever-virgin, daughter of God and first-born mother. She sees the process continuing in Jesus, who as Christ becomes personified Wisdom. She sees her final demise in the Christological disputes of the third and fourth centuries when her attributes are given to Jesus now defined by masculinist views. Because of her status as less than Yahweh in Judaism she cannot now be linked with Jesus who would similarly become less than God the Father and her repression becomes depressingly complete (Engelsman 1979).

Rosemary Radford Ruether is similarly pessimistic. *Sexism and God-Talk* (Ruether 1983) charts a similar trajectory but claims that elements of the Sophia tradition were kept alive in the traditions of the Holy Spirit. She claims that the female imagery for the Spirit was marginalized and repressed in subsequent history. Schüssler Fiorenza's study of biblical hermeneutics *In Memory of Her* (1990) is more optimistic. She sees the Sophia tradition as an attempt to integrate goddess traditions into Jewish monotheism. In its expression in Jesus she calls early theology – Sophialogy. She sees the early Christians as worshipping Christ-Sophia, now enthroned as a cosmic ruler. The humanity of Jesus was associated with the Sophia tradition. Sophia is depicted in the Hebrew Bible as calling vainly to human beings. In a similar way Jesus' apparent failure to become a king links him with this tradition. In the Gospel of John, in particular, he is seen as having many characteristics of Sophia, like a pre-existent creative form. The modification of the traditional view of Messiah as seen in the Hebrew Scriptures into the Christian concept of Messiah owes a great deal to the integration of elements of the Sophia tradition into early Christology (Cole, Ronan and Taussig 1996: 35–36). This has proved a liberating concept for many Christian women.

Lawrence Cross (1995) in charting *The Redemption of Sophia: A Sophiological Survey from Hermas to Bulgakov* identifies the Wisdom elements in ancient Hellenic thought. He also locates its loss in early Christianity when Justin Martyr argues that Jesus was the incarnation for the Divine logos now seen as divine reason while the Gnostics with their belief in Sophia are designated heretics. He then identifies where wisdom elements then appear in the tradition in theologians such as:

- Clement of Alexandria
- Origen
- Plotinus, who opposed Christianity
- the significant figure, Dionysus the Areopagite
- Hildegard
- Jacob Boehme in the nineteenth century
- the Russian theologian Soloviev.

As this list shows, he sees these as not being necessarily identified only with women although he does identify it as a tradition gendered as feminine.

Barbara Newman (1987) in *Sister of Wisdom: St Hildegard's Theology of the Feminine* describes the suppression of the tradition by the Church Fathers and delineates the characteristics of times when the Wisdom tradition is on the ascendant in European theology:

> Where the feminine presides, God stoops to humanity and humanity aspires to God. ...A more linear understanding of salvation history [is] cast in the form of a narrative beginning with creation and fall, culminating in the death and resurrection of Christ, and concluding with the Last Judgement....The feminine designation, on the other hand, evokes God's interactions with the cosmos insofar as they are timeless or perpetually repeated. Thus feminine symbols convey the principle of divine self-manifestation; the absolute predestination of Christ; the mutual indwelling of God in the world; and the saving collaboration between Christ and the faithful, manifested sacramentally in the church and morally in the Virtues (Newman 1987: 45).

This is a brief survey of the Wisdom tradition very specifically in Judaism and Christianity. I am seeing the subjugated ways of knowing explored in Chapter One as the contemporary version of Wisdom theology – the hidden wisdom of our own culture, which is similarly persecuted as the Wisdom tradition has been throughout Western Christian history. It includes the critiques of the maleness of God. This has happened in the late twentieth century from a number of positions. In academe the spotlight of postmodernism was turned on theology with its single metanarrative and found it wanting. Women from a variety of Christian traditions frayed it at the edges practically by meeting in informal groups, rediscovering material and ideas by women and creating their own material and critiquing the tradition by means of praxis. The ecological movement in the wider society also laid some of the blame for environmental devastation at the door of Christianity. Postcolonial theory also had a number of problems with the alliance of Christianity and colonization.

In doing this I am drawing on a number of strands in feminist theology which is set in the wider context of post-modern feminist discourse and a number of theologians have drawn on the work of secular theorists, even though many of these are critical of the role of theology and the Church in setting up the systems they aim to dismantle.[1] Here we see various attempts to bring together the polarities set out in the model in Chapter One. Grace Jantzen begins by challenging the religious/secular divide in her exploration of the possibilities of a feminist philosophy of religion. She calls it 'a binary constitutive of modernity which calls out for deconstruction [in need of a] destabilization which permits the achievement of new possibilities' (Jantzen 1998: 7). She also points out that although the Continental philosophers on whom she draws use religious imagery, the religious/secular divide remains unbreached by them. She uses Luce Irigaray as a key figure in her construction of a feminist model for 'becoming divine' and reads her using the Derridean strategy of 'double reading'. Marcella Althaus-Reid develops her 'indecent theology' from ideas and methodologies drawn from Marxism, postcolonial theory, Continental philosophers like Derrida, Deleuze and Guattari, sexual theorists like Judith Butler, and Queer studies (Althaus-Reid 2000: 7). Although the philosopher Rosi Braidotti claims that feminist theory does not need to engage with metaphysics she does acknowledge the power of the legacy of metaphysical symbols in her provocative statement:

> God may be dead but the stench of his rotting corpse pervades all of Western culture (Braidotti 1995).

So what are the characteristics of the rotting body of God – the dominant heteropatriarchy – which keeps the Wisdom tradition subjugated despite its attempts to resurface? What are the heteropatriarchal theological traditions? It is necessary to deconstruct the image of the male God. The traditional male metaphysical symbols for God originated in the mind of a male

---

1. This chapter represents an overview of feminist theologians from a variety of traditions. Within these traditions there are differences in emphases (Chopp 1997b).

Trinity in the Middle Ages but moved to the mind of man (and I mean man) in the work of writers like Francis Bacon in the seventeenth century (Bacon 1973: 3). Francis Bacon also sees the Book of Scriptures having precedence over the Book of Creation and so sets the scene for the war between Science and Religion. But this mind of the dominant heteropatriarchy has its origins not in the human mind but in the mind of the male Trinity now dwelling in the hearts of men. The values of triumphalism, dualism, unity, clarity and order are now construed as the highest human virtues and eternal in character. But they did reflect and still do reflect the maleness of God. Without God, who is now reduced to the sidelines, they could now stand freely as an 'objective goodness' – a powerful myth which, as we saw in Chapter One, maintains the status quo by its claims of standing outside temporality. It was no longer possible to challenge these by means of theology (although the notions were born and reared in that discipline) they were now the 'standards of the Academy', peddled as free-standing and objective. The human mind can now aspire to omniscience and power. Grace Jantzen develops this fully saying:

> The result is a series of dualisms characteristic of Western philosophy since Descartes: self-other, mind-body, freedom-nature, and the rest. Even Kant's transcendental reflection succumbs to the noumenal-phenomenal division (Jantzen 1996: 14–15).

Fiona Bowie (1998) notes how the constructions of God have influenced disciplines like anthropology:

> [Anthropologists have been] slower to deconstruct or read across the domains of their own cultures. Cultures..... is what makes the boundaries of domains seem natural, what gives ideologies power, and what makes hegemonies appear seamless. At the same time, it is what enables us to make compelling claims for connections between supposedly distinct discourses. In other words, it is both what makes jokes funny and what makes possible our reading across domains in prohibited ways. Although cultural domains are culturally specific, they usually come with claims to universality, that are seemingly nature-given and/or God-given and are made real through institutional arrangements and the discourses of everyday life (Bowie 1998: 52–53).

The maleness of God and the patriarchal structures of the Church are seen to be crucial factors in the maintenance of a variety of oppressive patterns for many groups like the poor, the 'foreign', the 'unusual' and the natural world, and value systems associated with these groups become subjugated as we saw in Chapter One. The ideas developed from this critique were usually associated with issues of social justice and often with action for social change. The critique was seen as a prelude to action for socio-political change particularly in the American school of feminist theology. There was always an activist wing in feminist theology. There are few areas of theological activity that have not been touched by the feminist debate. It has been an uphill structure critiquing structures that have been in place for 2,000 years and for which Divine authority has regularly been claimed. Although the Christian tradition has at its heart a marginalized person who supported the subjugated groups in his own society, the representatives of the tradition have often aligned themselves with the strong rather than the weak. Also the dominant metanarrative has often been so strong that many voices have been silenced – both in the past and in the present. Much work has been done to make these audible once more and liberation theology has contributed a great deal to feminist debates.

Characteristics of the male metanarrative are necrophilia (Jantzen 1998), dualisms and a biophobia based on a preference for the metaphysical. Although the early theorists used traditional methodologies, gradually the methodologies themselves have become challenged. Audre Lorde drew attention to the difficulty of dismantling the master's house with the master's tools (Lorde 1984a: 110–13). The more radical theologians and theorists declared with Nelle Morton (1985) that 'God' is dead or at least a redundant symbol. One reaction to this was to turn to the symbol of the Goddess and develop a system of thealogy (Goldenberg 1990).[2] Ruth Mantin writes of the liberatory effect this can have:

> In particular, female imagery can help to exorcise from narratives of the sacred the imperialist, colonizing associations of metaphysical, realist expressions of deity. Feminist thealogies can generate such imagery in the construction of a religious symbolic. This was apparent in the responses of the women with whom I inter/viewed. They affirmed the ways in which Goddess myths functioned to counter the debilitating effects of patriarchy and to generate alternative patterns of relation and socio/political structure. The responses also conveyed

2. In a remarkable book by Sophie Drinker, *Music and Women: The Story of Women in their Relation to Music* (1948/1995) she links the loss of women's power in musical traditions in the West with the loss of the Goddess traditions.

an understanding that these myths were not fixed but could travel with them on their own journeys. Goddess-Talk infuses the narratives of the sacred with an openness to plurality and ambiguity. The imagery and mythologies of Goddesses can contribute further to this process by re-membering the connections between the demonisation of female authority and the construction of 'monsters'. A thealogy which affirms the sacrality of monsters might have something to offer attempts to challenge the attitudes which dis-able the different (Mantin 2002: 284).

Wisdom theologians like Elisabeth Johnson see inclusivity as its essence. This sees those who are normally excluded as accepted and beloved and sought after as friends not just tolerated or forgiven. Wisdom establishes a right connection across conventional boundaries (Johnson 1993). She sees the Sophia-Christ bringing victory through compassion and not the sword. The crucifixion thus becomes a struggle for a new creation. It is from these traditions that I draw my own view of Jesus/Sophia.

Many theologians following Elizabeth Johnson, (Johnson 1993: 96–100) see the problem in the translations of *logos* from the original Greek, like Grace Ji-Sun Kim:

> Until recent times, Eurocentric patriarchalism has bound limited and bottled up Christianity. ...This *logos* Christology has some negative consequences, since it perpetuated the male image of God and excluded the feminine dimension of the divine...American feminist theologians have already identified the problem and suggested alternative to classical *logos* Christology. This book endeavors to find a relevant Christology that specifically addresses Korean North American Women (Kim 2002: 3–4).

She goes on to explore the image of a 'marginal Christ, particularly in his birth of an unwed mother far from his home town and sheltered in a manger' (Kim 2002: 4) and in his friendship with marginalized groups such as 'outcasts, tax collectors, Gentiles, women, the poor and oppressed, the lame and the blind' (Kim 2002: 4). Here we get the presentation of the historical Jesus as a member of a subjugated group and as a subjugated knower himself (see Chapter One). 'Christ became the margin of marginality' (Kim 2002: 5).

Mary Grey sets up a dialogue between the two myths of Logos and Sophia. Logos represents a disembodied world governed by rules, whereas Sophia puts the case for those who move at different paces. Sophia knowledge is rooted in the body rather than the logic that resides primarily in the mind. Sophia sets out 'epiphanies of connection' with other human beings and the natural world:

> She is hope for the marginalized community because, as epiphany of prophetic-mystical community, she is revelation for today that the long exile and waiting is over, new voices are heard in the wilderness, and women may safely leave the desert and be the leaven for beloved community (Grey 1993: 143).

Elizabeth Schüssler Fiorenza identifies ways in which this voice is silenced describing them as obstacles in the way of a more general acceptance of feminist theologies. She identifies an increasing problem already seen in Chapter One, even among women, with the concept of 'feminism' from a number of perspectives including a notion that it is necessarily hating of men and also from black and South American theologians who see it as a concept developed by middle-class white intellectuals. They therefore prefer terms like 'womanist' (Cannon 1988,1995) and 'mujarista' (Isasi-Diaz 1996). Secondly, she sees a view that feminist theology is simply for women or as Fiorenza prefers wo/men. Thirdly, she sees a problem with a blanket term that would see women as all alike and deny the diversity among women, as also among men! She does not identify with those theologians who see Christianity as too patriarchal to be redeemed by any amount of rewriting its history and canonical texts. She sees a problem with a divorce of theory from praxis, the Westernization of the Bible (which she restores to its status as a Middle Eastern text), the fundamentalist approach to the status of the Bible and the assumption that a single interpretation of the Bible is a possibility. She looks at a revisiting of methodologies particularly hermeneutics which she asks to be replaced by 'a hermeneutics of suspicion'. Finally, she identifies the emotional investment that is necessary to embark on a feminist critique (Schüssler Fiorenza 2002: 54–57).

These issues will be dealt with in more detail in the following chapters as we explore more systematically the challenge to the traditional values of heteropatriarchal theology using the model of Value systems set out in Chapter One.

Summary

Christianity is a Jewish faith that has acquired a number accretions from various cultures during its history, particularly in the early years, elements of the Graeco-Roman traditions. This has resulted in subjugation of the Wisdom traditions. This chapter has identified figures through whom this has surfaced and sees how this stands in relation to contemporary feminist theologies. These have rediscovered the Wisdom aspects of Jesus/Sophia – humanity, vulnerability, marginalization. Two personal creeds reflect some of these struggles:

Creed One

 We believe in a God who created the world
 And continues to be intimately bound up with it
 like a loving parent
 In all its dimensions – seen and unseen.

 We believe that this God
 Shares our humanity
 In a mystery that is difficult to comprehend
 And is revealed in story, history and myth
 In particular the story of Jesus Christ
 Who was born of Mary in the ancient Wisdom tradition.
 He shared human suffering
 And died a cruel death
 At the hands of the civil and religious authorities of his day.
 But death was unable to hold him
 And we can share in the joy of resurrection
 And through the life of Jesus Christ
 Trust in a God who in a mysterious way
 Is intimately bound up with the vulnerability and strength of
 our humanity and the world.

 We believe in a creative Spirit
 Who is continually making all things new
 Revealed to us through the natural world
 Prophetic voices and the still voice in us all.

 We believe in a community between those struggling
 For their own integrity and that of the world
 And commit ourselves to work with the Spirit in that struggling.

 We believe in the possibility of reconciliation
 And forgiveness between human beings and between God and
 the world

We believe in a connection between the living and the dead,
the material world and the spiritual
We believe in sharing a Christ like quality of life
We believe in the possibility of eternal life today
And that we are called to be co-creators, transformers and
sustainers with God in the life of the world.
(Boyce-Tillman 2004)

Creed Two (A simpler version cutting the above to its essential elements)

I believe in a loving God
Who is intimately bound up
With the vulnerability and strength of humanity
In a mystery that is revealed in story, history and myth.

I believe in the importance of respect
Between human beings, both living and dead,
The natural world,
And God.

I commit myself to work for this with integrity
Within the creative Spirit
Who is continually making all things new.
(Boyce-Tillman 2004)

This chapter has shown some of the dominant themes in feminist theologies. The reworking of images for the Divine and the relationship between the Divine and the material world has delivered a rethinking of many of the traditional values of a theology dominated by the maleness of God. This has resulted in a re-establishment of values subjugated by the dominant culture in both the secular and religious worlds. In an attempt to reestablish a link between the binaries of the dominant culture theologians have sought also to dismantle this divide and see everything as holy. They have also crossed the disciplinary boundaries established in the academy in the use, in particular of the imagination and intuition based on lived experience. Methodologies have been reworked in this process and the interview has become an important tool for a theology rooted in experience. In the intertwining of the divine and human, fluidity and ambiguity have challenged the certainties of heteropatriarchal systems and metaphors of journeying and nomadism abound. Many of the ideas have been developed privately but are now being expressed more publicly in a variety of contexts with a variety of receptions from the dominant culture. Still the relationality of small groups meeting privately for prayer and discussion are significant spaces for the flourishing of a people-centered spirituality. The Wisdom tradition has resurfaced at various times in the history of Christianity. We certainly live in one of those times. The availability of a variety of systems of dissemination has enabled the ideas to proliferate more readily than ever before. It remains to be seen whether in the twenty-first century the Wisdom song can call into being a new world order.

Chapter Three

CREATING IDENTITY

CHORUS
> Sing us our own song the song of the earth,
> The song of creation, the song of our birth,
> That exists in belonging to you and to me,
> To the stars and the mountains, the sky and the sea.

1. Listen! You're hearing the song of the earth,
   They sing it who know of their value and worth,
   For they know they belong with the sea and the sky,
   To the moonshine at midnight, the clouds floating by.

CHORUS

2. It is not one song but patchworks of sound.
   That includes all the pitches that people have found
   That includes the vibrations of earthquakes and bees
   Of the laughing fire's crackling and murmuring breeze.

CHORUS

3. All blend together to make the earth song,
   Fragmented parts separated too long,
   In finding our true notes and colours and beats
   We make sacred spaces where we all meet.

CHORUS
(Boyce-Tillman 2006a: 152)

Society

The relationship between the individual and the community has been expressed in different ways in different cultures. If the role of the community is dominant there will often be a certain conservatism in the society often maintained by the elders and a less clearly

Individual/Community

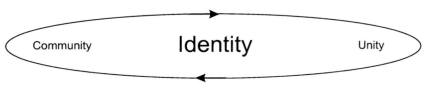

Fig. 3. Identity

defined view of the individual self (Floyd 1998). In societies with individualism prominent there will be a greater stress on freedom and innovation.

The legacy in the UK of the Thatcher years is one of fragmentation and an excessive emphasis on the individual. But it is a process that started with the Enlightenment and its rediscovery of the epic of the heroic journey. Myths have tremendous power over a society as we saw in Chapter One. The male hero narrative (based on *The Odyssey* and *The Aeneid*) is of one who asserts his individuality and 'finds himself' through the undertaking of a journey. This is usually without a permanent companion (although with many temporary travelling associates who are often either embraced or killed). After this, he returns home as a mature person assured of his personhood. The heroic journey was not open to larger numbers even of Western civilization – the poor and women, to name but two groups. Many philosophers and psychiatrists have shown women's patterns are different moving from attachment to continued connection, so that the self emerges within a web of complex relationships. It was also a characteristic of societies colonized by Western culture:

> With us [Pomo Indians] the family was everything. Now it is nothing. We are getting like white people and it is bad for the old people. We had no old peoples' homes like you. The old people were important. They were wise. Your old people must be fools (Macfarlane 2005: 36).

Many women, in particular, sense the need for this connection in the nurturing and rearing of children. For them, the heroic quest was never a possibility and they felt torn apart by a double standard – a society that prized the individualism that characterized the heroic search and their own sense of a deep need for community and stability for the sake of their children or their family.

In a society where the polarity is splitting apart responsibility will start to lose contact with personal freedom. It may be that certain groups of people will be scapegoated for the ills of society or certain people will take on the roles of being responsible. It is often women in the West who suffer from a sense of over-responsibility.[1]

When the polarity is finally split community can only be maintained by the coercive forces of law enforcement and the state and its authorities will be regarded as oppressive of personal liberty. This will correspondingly be maintained by personal rights litigation. So the relationship between the two will be maintained by external forces rather than by the internal maturity of the individuals. Bauman identifies the problems involved in the negotiation of these two polarities when he attempts to define the term identity within the dominant value system. Here he shows the values of individualism and community with a broken flow:

> Yes, "identity" is a hopelessly ambiguous idea and a double-edged sword. It may be a war-cry of individuals, or of the communities that wish to be imagined by them. ... Identity, let us be clear about it, is a "hotly contested concept". Whenever you hear that word, you can be sure that there is battle going on (Bauman 2004: 76–77).

This battle is one example of a blocked flow where the two polarities judder against one another and the polarities are seen as a tug of war rather than in ebb and flow. It also shows the struggle involved in the negotiation of identity. In a society when responsibilities and personal freedom start to be split apart by locating personal freedom in maleness and responsibility in femaleness, both individualism and community appear in distorted form. The law is now called upon to enforce community values and personal freedom rather than by the free choice of individuals or groups.

Self

The individual experiences the pressures of the dominant culture in different ways as we saw in Chapter One. The dominant knowers in Western society will see personal liberty as of supreme importance and abrogate responsibility or see it as not part of their role. The subjugated knowers will be burdened by a sense of over-responsibility and its contiguous guilt, often feeling trapped in

---

1. 'The challenge for men is this: Stop blaming: take responsibility for our life choices; and, in an ongoing way, hold ourselves accountable for our power' (Ellison 1996: 113).

situations that they feel they are unable to escape, often because they are not able to operate a system with any boundaries:

> A sense of boundaries can enable us to be confident of our bodily integrity...Without a boundaried sense of ourselves, we are likely to experience sexual energy as a rush into which we get sucked and swallowed up, or as an addictive commodity that we have to get more of in order to feel good about ourselves. Historically, this has happened to most women. Sexism itself is a structure of sexual abuse, in which women's lives get swept away in currents of male domination, male visibility, male possession, male naming, and male definitions of power, women, sex and God (Heyward 1989b: 110).

When the split of the polarity finally occurs, the dominant knower will become isolated and aggressive sensing a complete loss of any connection with the wider community which deep down s/he knows is necessary for his/her well-being. We see this phenomenon in young people turning weapons on their peers in school. The subjugated knower will lose any sense of boundaries and be overwhelmed by the burden of guilt and anxiety. The result will be pathologized anxiety, leading to self harm.

The Myth of Progress

This distortion is a result of the power of the myth of the heroic journey which has dominated all other archetypes. This myth, based on the ancient Greek and Roman stories of *The Odyssey* and *The Aeneid*, saw this individualized self journeying as these erstwhile heroes had done. Progress dominated the thinking at every level – physical, psychological and spiritual (when this was included in the equation at all as in such areas as the pursuit of a higher consciousness). Progress involved always moving forward (see unity/diversity below) and never staying still, often not even to consolidate. It involved moving house; it certainly involved changing jobs; it involved intellectual advancement and the development of physical prowess that was better than previous generations. It involved the pursuit of innovation for its own sake. This was heavily influenced by theories of Darwinian evolution. Lacan links the worst excesses of the Victorian period with Darwin:

> Darwin's success seems to derive from the fact that he projected the predations of Victorian society and the economic euphoria that sanctioned for the society the social devastation on a planetary scale,

and to the fact that it justified its predations by the image of a laissez-faire of the strongest predators in competition for their natural prey (Lacan [1966] 1977: 26).

Grace Jantzen, comments on how the Church played its part in sanctioning this culture of aggression, in which women were caught up:

> But he [Lacan] forgets that the barbarous predations for which Darwin offered a retrospective secular justification were not performed in a secular world but very much in the name and with the blessing of religion. Slavery, conquest and colonization all appealed to God, the great White Father. Indeed it was precisely within religious ideology that the aggression expressed in such exploitation was baptized. Moreover, the Victorian era was a time in which women – mostly white middle class women – were constructed as heavily subordinated, and were caught up in matrices of oppression in which they were exploiters as well as exploited (Jantzen 1998: 48).

And so we see how this unhappy linking of science with religion caused the subjugation of whole communities in a complex web that damaged the world community on a vast scale. People and situations that remained static were devalued in favour of situations that were dynamic and changing.

Women's Identity

But these concepts sit uneasily with women's concepts of identity. The contract to bring up children or care for a family is not short and it involves a great deal of repetition. There is often no sense of progress. When the washing up is finished, there is another lot of plates being made dirty; when one garment is mended, another is growing a hole, when one dispute is settled another one is brewing. Community building is not a heroic journey; it is the story of women in many cultures and of the poor in most cultures and is often devalued and uncertain in having no returns in financial terms. The process of establishing and maintaining connections between people is a repetitive, circular journey resembling that of Penelope in *The Odyssey*. She is left at home while Odysseus travels the Mediterranean, defeating monsters, loving and leaving women and overcoming the obstacle posed by the natural world. She stays in the same place doing the same thing – weaving her tapestry during the day and unweaving it at night.

Helen O'Grady examines how women internalized these roles from these myths as an ethic of responsibility, identifying how a woman needs to develop 'balance between caring for self and caring for others' (Tronto 1987: 658):

> In the absence of a cultural context encouraging such a balance, the expectation to care for others tends to be internalized as an ethic of responsibility (O'Grady 2005: 31).

Ecology

A concentration on the notion of 'dominance-over' in Genesis 1 combined with the establishment of humanism at the Enlightenment caused human beings to become alienated from the natural world – or indeed superior to it. This resulted at best in a patronizing stewardship and at worst domination and outright rape. This was also linked with establishment of the individual self as distinct from other selves; and this loss of a sense of community with the natural world has resulted in the environmental tragedy that we are now facing. The earth and all non-human life have systematically been raped and pillaged in the interests of an aggressive individualism completely disconnected from its adjoined polarity of community. Other societies, like the native North American peoples, have valued community particularly with the natural world so much that a concept of an individual as constructed in the West is difficult to find. On a trip to Zimbawe I had many fascinating conversations with the Shona women, one of which concerned the 'modernization' of the economy. In the West aid is portrayed as being conditional on the 'modernization' of the Zimbabwean economy. What this meant in 2000 was that all their property was to be put into private ownership. It had all previously been communally owned. The women now lost all the power at a stroke as the land was being put in the name of their husbands. The communities were being broken up and women's power destroyed in the name of westernization euphemistically called 'Reform or modernization'.

The ecological movement has done a great deal to re-establish community between the natural world and human beings. James Lovelock reaffirms our relationship to Gaia as a combinatory living community of interconnectedness and interdependences (Lovelock 1979: 67). He finally sees the power of the Gaian community to readjust its community to the detriment of human beings if that is what is required (Lovelock 1979: 212). David Abrams' book *The Spell of the Sensuous* (1996) calls for Western civilization to consider notions of a common language with the natural environment:

> Human languages then are informed not only by the structures of the human body, and the human community, but by the evocative shapes and patterns of the more-than-human terrain. Experientially considered, language is no more the special property of the human organism than it is an expression of the inanimate earth that enfolds us (Abrams 1996: 90).

A New Identity

Theorists are pointing to the development of a new subjectivity based on strategies of resistance which lie outside the binary configuration of domination and subordination. Foucault does postulate the development of a new kind of citizen-subject who is free from 'the kind of individuality that has been imposed upon us.' He recommends that citizen-subjects recognize that:

> The political, ethical, social and philosophical problem of our day is not to try to liberate the individual from the state, and from the state's institutions, but to liberate us...from the type of individualization, which is linked to the state (Foucault 1983: 216).

To establish an identity we need to know who we are and where we belong.

Theology

Dorothy Soelle in her early text *Christ the Representative* (1967) focused on identity, which she saw as bound up with authority. She followed this with *Beyond Mere Obedience* (1970) which links powerfully with the material in Chapter One on women's identity. She sees our authority lying in both the struggle to love and the resting place between lovers and beloveds:

> For Soelle, God is both the *act* [author's italics] of justicemaking/ lovemaking and *those* who struggle for justice for themselves and others (Heyward 1989b: 78).

Earlier in this chapter, we saw how the archetype of the 'heroic journey' has underpinned Western constructions of the self and how this has caused an alienation of the Western self from a number of marginalized 'others'. In theological terms this has meant a high premium being placed on individual salvation and the relation of the individual relationship to God. Phrases like 'personal time with God' and 'making my communion with God' ran through the training that I received as an adolescent growing up in a Christian home in middle of the road Anglicanism in the UK in the 1940s and 50s. Rita Nakashima Brock draws attention to the contrast between this and the prominence of Paradise in early Christian thought which is communal and includes nature, as seen in the landscapes of Byzantine iconography. It is not the individual salvation of later Christian thought (Brock 2003). Grace Kim writes from an Asian perspective:

> Theology was "Euro-theology" for a long time. This theology tended to pay no attention to the experiences of non-European cultures. Traditional Western theology, with its emphasis on individual salvation and morality, was often disruptive of non-Western cultures, focusing only on the individual with little recognition of community or social context (Kim 2002: 12).

This is highlighted also in *Christianity Rediscovered* by Vincent Donovan (1982) when he sees the nature of community in Masai culture. Throughout the feminist literature there is a high stress on inclusivity in the human community and an acknowledgement of those excluded by the Euro-centric view of individual salvation that was peddled by the colonial powers. This inclusive community will be life-affirming as envisioned by liberation theologians. This is in contrast to Elisabeth Schüssler Fiorenza's (2001) description of kyriarchy:

> Kyriarchy is best theorized as a complex pyramidical system of intersecting multiplicative social structures of superordination and subordination, of ruling and oppression. Kyriarchal relations of domination are built on elite male property rights as well as on the exploitation, dependency, inferiority, and obedience of wo/men.
>
> Greek kyriarchal democracy constituted itself by the exclusion of the 'others' that did not have a share in the land but whose labour sustained society. Freedom and citizenship not only were measured over and against slavery but also were restricted in terms of gender. Moreover, the socioeconomic realities in the Greek city-state were such that only a few select freeborn, propertied, elite, male heads of households could actually exercise democratic government (Schüssler Fiorenza 2001:118–19).

She goes on to problematize certain structural elements in kyriarchy like the complexity of networks of domination that make it up, the different ways in which it has been constructed in different cultures like Rome, Asia Minor or Japan, the role systems of racism, heterosexism, classism and colonialism, the need for a servant class maintained through 'law, education, socialization and brute violence (Schüssler Fiorenza 2001: 122) and finally:

> Both in Western modernity and in Greco-Roman antiquity kyriarchy has been in tension with a democratic ethos and system of equality and freedom. In a radical democratic system, power is not exercised through "power over" or through violence and subordination, but through the human capacity for respect, responsibility, self-determination, and self-esteem. This radical democratic ethos has again and again engendered emancipatory movements that insist on the equal freedom, dignity and equal rights of all (Schüssler Fiorenza 2001: 122).

The structure of many religious congregations illustrates the dilemmas of kyriarchy as set out in the Benedictine Rule. In theory it is based on a notion of koinonia (communion) – mystical communion characterized by 'a kind of flight into mystical interiority' (Dulles 1988: 61). This interiority is expressed by means of a concentration on prayer and worship as the prime acts of Christian discipleship. However, the structures within the convent are unashamedly hierarchical with the Abbot/Abbess holding supreme authority and the nuns/monks committed to obedience to God through obedience.[2] There are also hierarchies with people in positions of authority, which produce strong infantilizing tendencies within the system. These hierarchies – reflecting a controlling God – require people to remain in positions of children forever rather than relationships of mutuality.

Neil Douglas-Klotz reworks a familiar text to see a true relationality of self and others in the commandment to love God and neighbour (Mk 13. 30–1). In so doing, he blurs the distinction between inside and outside the individual and his/her neighbour. To do this he unearths Aramaic concepts for:

- Soul (which would be the same word as that used for thyself in the second commandment).

2. Nuns needing things like dentistry have to wait for the Abbess's permission, for example.

- Love, which pours from the innermost womb of Wisdom.
- Heart, the centre of one's feeling being and intelligence.
- Mind, the instinctual part of the brain.
- Strength, life force or energy.

After this he produces a new version of the familiar text Mk 13. 30–31:

> Let compassion unfurl from your inner womb
> For Sacred Unity
> In the form that impresses you most deeply,
> inside or out.
> Send this love with and through
> your whole passionate self,
> your whole awakening, subconscious self,
> your whole instinctive mind,
> and with all of your life energy...
>
> Give birth to love for the one "next door",
> as you do for your own soul-self
> and the part of it that feels like a neighbour.
>
> Give birth to compassion for the nearest,
> yet unfamiliar, aspect of yourself,
> as you do for the one outside
> who feels like a stranger.
>
> Give birth to the deepest warmth for
> the neighbour, inside and out,
> as you do for your own
> subconscious community
> inside and out (Douglas-Klotz 1999: 116–19).

So individualism is challenged by diminishing the divide between God and self.

The theologian Mary Grey, draws on such Wisdom theologians as Hildegard to develop a theology of relationality:

> Hildegarde presents us with the imagery where God continually bodies forth creation, the cosmic body of Christ, where the further we enter into that synergy which the Sapiential cosmology depicts, the more we know ourselves as encountering the yearning of God, the divine eros, experiencing the power of greening, being transfigured by the Spirit into shining whiteness. If we embody the praxis which this

implies we cannot separate the well-being and wholeness of the least sentient thing from the spiritual, salvific becomings of the human person, and the integrity of the whole of public life (Grey 1992).

This inclusion of the natural world in the wider community means that the definition of community includes the cosmos community which becomes a process not a product (see Chapter Four) and community is that of interconnecting energies as depicted in the visions of Hildegard. The need for relationality with the cosmos links with Hildegard's concept of sin as a break in relationship or wrong relationship. McFague (1993) sees sin as human refusal to accept humanity's right place in the scheme of things. This has been developed by contemporary theologians such as Carter Heyward:

> Sin is our out-of-touchness with the fact that we are in relation – that or lives are connected at the root and that this is the sacred basis of creatureliness, our humanity, our lives together on planet earth....Weakened immeasurably by sin, generation upon generation, we do evil without having a clue that it is evil we are doing – the countless ways we betray one another and ourselves: lying to those we love; turning our backs on the homeless; holding racism and other structures of injustice in place through fear, ignorance or apathy; paying taxes that build bombs and missiles; floating through life in spiritual bubbles that seal us off from shared Sacred 'I' Power to struggle against the systemic violence undergirding so much of our public policy as we enter a new millennium (Heyward 1999: 84–85).

She sees seven qualities in right relation; *courage, compassion, anger, forgiveness, touching, healing, faith*, adding;

> None is a virtue. Each is blessing available to us through the power of mutuality (Heyward 1989b: 139).

Rosemary Radford Ruether saw the need to examine the individual and the societal as she explores a variety of relationships in a concept that clearly links with Helen O'Grady's work in Chapter One:

> Sin as distorted relationship has three dimensions: there is a personal-interpersonal dimension, a social-historical dimension and an ideological-cultural dimension. It is imperative to give due recognition to all three dimensions, and not only to focus on the personal-interpersonal aspect, as our confessional and therapeutic traditions have generally done (Ruether 1988: 71).

Carol Christ (2003) links this with freedom and flow:

> But what if relationship and freedom are connected? Like two sides of the same coin? Process philosophy offers a social view of reality in which all individuals in the world, human beings among them, are connected to others, to their immediate environments, to social worlds, and in a larger sense to the whole world and all beings in the web of life. For process philosophy, creative freedom is co-creative, always in relation to someone or something. Individuals with creative freedom are embodied and engaged in a web of relationships. Creative freedom makes new relationships and makes existing relationships new (Christ 2003: 74).

As the notion of community expands, the traditional division into the sacred and the profane becomes problematized. The division of the community into these categories is part of the dualisms that were addressed by the model set out in Chapter One and has perpetuated the oppression of others like women, the poor, the 'foreign.' and the 'natural'. Many theologians call for the envisioning of new symbols. Braidotti claims that new images have the 'capacity to offer us ordinary access to extraordinary thinking' (Braidotti 1994: 8). The use of a new symbolization of the Divine has been taken up by many theologians as well as the reworking of traditional symbols (McFague 1987).

This leads to a radical reworking of traditional ecclesiology. Radical women have had a problem with traditional ecclesiology for generations but when Professor Mary Daly was asked to preach in the Chapel of Harvard University on 14th November 1971, she invited women to leave the service, claiming that the patriarchy of the church both in its Protestant and Catholic forms was irredeemable. This thinking led her into the post-Christian position expressed in her seminal text, *Beyond God the Father* (1973).

Other theologians like Monica Furlong (2000) and Carter Heyward (1999) have struggled to survive within the traditional structures. The four pillars of the traditional church were:

- Unity
- Holiness
- Catholicity
- Apostolicity

Drawing on the work of Elisabeth Schüssler Fiorenza (2000)[3] and Robert Goss (2002), Tiffany Steinwert reworks these as they might

---

3. In this text Schüssler Fiorenza develops her notion of the basileia/commonweal of G*d in first century Christianity and links it with her concept of kyriarchy.

appear in 'queer' base communities. Unity is transformed from doctrinal uniformity (expressed traditionally in creedal statements) to solidarity, a concept central to the thinking of liberation theologians. Holiness ceases to be individualized piety and becomes justice-seeking (another important aspect of liberation theology). Catholicity traditionally worked out in a form close to Roman imperialism both in the so-called Roman Church and the Protestant traditions especially in their colonial enterprises, is about radical inclusion, accepting difference (drawing on the diversity of the representation of Jesus in the four Gospels). Apostolicity ceases to be about a male lineage but a working out of what it means to be an apostle – in other words, committed action (Steinwert 2003).

So feminist theologies see community and relatedness as central to their understanding and see themselves committed to forming communities of relationality. June Osborne (2006), Dean of Salisbury Cathedral, shows clearly how Jesus negotiated this polarity in the story of the feeding of the five thousand. She describes how by this time Jesus had captivated the ordinary people and convinced the religious establishment that they should plot to kill him. At this point the people begin to look like a frenzied mob and Jesus realizes that he might become the victim of their religious fervour. She sees this based in three threats to their dignity:

- 'There's need: the people are hungry, they live under occupation, their taxes support local despots and a distant emperor, and the religious establishment is insecure and large self-interested. It's harder to keep your dignity when you're needy.
- There's powerlessness in the face of that need: their choices are limited, their scope for a better life, for public reasoning also limited. They don't make the essential decisions about their life. In that situation what makes impact? The angriest voice, the extreme slogan seems to be a better option than what generates understanding.
- So thirdly, there's always the temptation to violence: fuelling enmity, wreaking revenge, the potential of religious fervour mingling with social resentment and grievance.'

She sees Jesus' technique in handling this potentially explosive situation of mob violence as getting people to see themselves as a collection of hungry individuals and not a crowd. He then 'demonstrates that as well as being individuals they're also a community' as he gets them to sit down quietly. He then turns a tribal community into a universal community by blessing the bread and distributing it to everyone. So she demonstrates how effectively Jesus uses the dynamic movement between these two poles.

Case Study One: Renegotiating Ecclesiology

A new identity for the Church means a reworking of ecclesiology; but first we must unpick the doctrine that has underpinned traditional ecclesiology as doctrine and ecclesiology are intertwined. The doctrine of the Trinity is interesting in this context as it is a model that combines both individuality and community – one in three and three in one.

Various models of the doctrine have surfaced over Church history. Here are three from different sources:

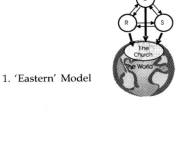

1. 'Eastern' Model

2. 'Western' Model

3. 'Ecological' Model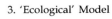

Fig. 4. Models of the Trinity[4]
Creator (C), Redeemer (R), and Sustainer (S)

4. I am grateful for the help of Revd David Billin and Revd Carol Rowles in developing these ideas as part of the Southwark OLM course.

The famous Rublev Icon with three figures seated around a table with a central cup (Fig. 5), reflects model one (the Eastern Model) showing the Trinity as a shared feast into which the church, and through it the world, are drawn:

Fig. 5. The Icon of the Holy Trinity

There is a painting in the Rohan Book of Hours in the Bibliotheque Nationale Paris (see http://campus.udayton.edu/mary//resources/bkhours.html), that portrays the death of Jesus. In this picture God the Father looks on at his dead Son and the two are linked by a backdrop of wings suggesting the action of the Holy Spirit.

In this – the Western Model – we see the intervention of the three persons of the Trinity in the world – three different functions of God. Here a Creator God looks on at the death of Jesus linked by the wings of the surrounding Holy Spirit. There is a measure of distance between God and the world. This is the Augustinian Model (Knox 2006) supporting kyriarchal church structures based on lines of authority through priest and bishop to God.

The third model – the 'Ecological' – is based on Hildegard's three pictures of Cosmic Humanity which visualize the world and God as interdependent.

In three pictures drawn from her visions Hildegard (1098–1179), wrestles with images for God's relationship to the cosmos. The first picture depicts a person in sapphire blue, surrounded by various rings of colour, which she entitles *The Trinity in the Unity*.[5] Here a bright light designates the Father, while the figure in sapphire blue 'without flaw of obstinacy, envy or iniquity' designates the Son (Hart and Bishop 1990: 161). The glowing fire is the Holy Spirit.

> The second picture [see next page] entitled "Cosmic Humanity" shows God the Father [who] bears the great wheel of creation in his breast. It is supported and embraced by the figure of flaming Love [the Spirit]. In the middle of the universal wheel stands a human being, projecting beyond the tiny earth into the realms of universal forces with their various elements and rays. The human figure seems to hold the universal network or system in its hands, thus accepting humanity's task of creative commitment to the world (Schipperges 1997: 75).

A third picture – On the Articulation of the Body – sees the cosmos as a network of inter-relationships within the energy of God portrayed here as an enclosing fire within which the cycle of human activity is portrayed as a series of vignettes of country life.[6] This reflects an interdependence between God and the world – a mutuality of relationship. Both Creator and creation are in a

---

5. This picture is portrayed in Boyce-Tillman 2000b: 32.
6. This picture is portrayed in Boyce-Tillman 2000b: 98.

relationship of mutual love. This interpretation suggests that there is a creative Will that generated the universe using the energy of the Spirit, the wisdom of the Son/Sophia and the infinity of the Father/Creator and is continually working within it, making all things new. Love is being continually worked out in relation to creation and the universe.

Fig. 6. *Cosmic Humanity*, reprinted with permission of the Abtei St Hildegard, Eibingen, Germany.

This model (my preferred one) manages to bring together notions of individual and community to produce an identity for the divine that is inextricably bound up with the universe (within which the Church has to find its place).

> We are asking whether one way to remythologize the Gospel for our time might not be through the metaphor of the "world as God's body" rather than as the king's "realm". ... When the world is viewed as God's body, that body includes more than just Christians and more than just human beings (McFague 1987: 61–71).

A measure of transcendence is retained, for in the second Hildegard picture God's head and feet are beyond the world. The world is contained within God's body:

> The critique provided by feminist theologies such as those of Ruether and McFague, and the attempt to conceive a non-dualistic or 'panentheist' spirituality in the work of writers like Fox, have a considerable importance in alerting us to the distortion to which the classical doctrine has fallen victim – God as monarch, God as imposing alien meanings, God as supremely successful manipulator of a cosmic 'environment'. But a simple, undialectical affirmation of God's identity with the cosmic continuum (an uncritical maternal image to replace an uncritical paternal image?) will not serve – as Ruether and McFague appear to be aware. Authentic difference, a being-with, not simply a being-in, difference that is grounded in the eternal being-with of God as trinity, is something which sets us free to be human – *distinctively* human, yet human in co-operation with others and with an entire world of differences... Being creatures is learning humility, not as submission to an alien will, but as the acceptance of limit and death; *for* that acceptance, with all that it means in terms of our moral imagination and action, we are equipped by learning through the grace of Christ and the concrete fellowship of the Spirit, that God is 'the desire by which we all live', the *creator*. "I am the Giver...Trust me" (Williams 2000: 78).

This is the position of the mystics. There is mutuality between God and creation experienced by many Western mystics like Hildegard of Bingen:

> Just as the creator loves the creation, so also does the creation love the creator. Creation was designed to be beautifully enriched, to be lavished, to be richly endowed with the love of the creator. The whole world has been hugged by this kiss (Boyce-Tillman 1992).

So the new ecclesiology depends on a notion of God intimately bound up in creation – loving it and generating it. It is a real community held together by love.

Vincent Donovan in *Christianity Rediscovered* (1978/1982) re-envisions traditional ecclesiology in ways we saw in Kim (2002). He examines traditional missiology and problematizes individual conversion which he sees as exiling people from their community roots and looks at the difference between hierarchical organization and real community. He revisits ecclesiology.

> It by no means leads one to come automatically to the form of the Western, Roman church we know, nor to the parish church we live and work in...It is the white European response, with its Roman-Byzantine face...this is the church we know...We have come to believe that any valid, positive response to the Christian message could and should be recognized as church...Their acceptance, their response, whatever it might be, is the church (Donovan 1982: 83).

This led him to challenge the Western concept of individual salvation as simply inappropriate for the communal nature of Masai people in favour of lived community. He draws this conclusion because in the Masai he finds real living community and feels that he can only relate to them as a group and not individually.

> Finding a real community among the Masai, I was able to teach them as a unit, to dialogue with them as a group, because there was a similarity of feeling and reaction among them (Donovan 1978/82: 86).

In his critique he shows how the idols of the Western church – individualism and organization – have become substitutes for real community, dominating the use of language:

> For these Africans the purpose of words is not to establish logical truth, but to set up social relationships with others (Donovan 1978/82: 28).

Donovan goes on to describe his mission to whole community. This does not preclude individuals taking particular roles and he identifies people with priestly characteristics although he draws back all the time from a Western notion of priesthood – looking at how these models would be inappropriate. 'He made no mistakes. He was eloquent. That is why he is the speaker' (Donovan 1982: 96). 'Ordination would be simply the recognition, through imposition of hands, on all of the functionaries of the community, of the reality that is accomplished in them by baptism the authorization in unity with the church everywhere, to use the power that is in them' (Donovan 1978/82:157). We see him here working towards a theology of mutuality growing out of the tradition of the Masai. So we have a model of Church based on the mutuality of God and creation that affirms existing natural community as God-given.

Case Study Two: Renegotiating Priesthood

The notion of priesthood was taken over by Christianity from Judaism. The long line of priestly families stretches back behind the first non-Jewish members of this tradition in the early Church. Paradoxically, Jesus was not born into this line and indeed could not have exercised the ministry that he did if he had been. It was the oppressively hierarchical nature of the ministry particularly of the high priests that he attacked so strongly culminating in the final symbolic event of the time of his death of the rending of the Temple veil – the veil through which only the man at the apex of the hierarchy was allowed to pass. It could be, and indeed has been, argued that it is exactly this same hierarchy that the followers of this anti-clerical leader have created in his name. Interestingly, contemporary Judaism has abandoned the notion of priesthood in its concept of leadership in favour of the notion of teacher or rabbi. Here the concentration is on the knowledge of the Torah – symbolically handed to the newly trained rabbi at his/her ordination.

The early Christian priests would have been familiar both with the Jewish tradition and Jesus' critique of it. As members of a radical and oppressed minority their leaders – the early priests, deacons and presbyters – appear to have been elected from within communities – natural leaders growing from within rather than chosen by external hierarchies in the way that characterized the tradition when it became accepted by political authorities.

The oppressive nature of the priesthood in her day was well set out by Matilda Joslyn Gage in 1893:

> That ecclesiastical pretense of divinely-appointed power has ever made priesthood arrogant, coarse and tyrannical; the male laity dependent and dissimulating; woman, self-distrustful and timorous, believing in their duty of humiliation and self-sacrifice...Today, as of old, the underlying idea of monasticism – of "brotherhoods", "sisterhoods"

and their ilk even in Protestant denominations – is the divine authority of some priestly superior (Gage 1893/1998: 58).

It is, however, clear that a worshipping group of people needs a number of roles to be fulfilled in order to function efficiently. Some of these are practical, others to do with the psychology of the group, others to do with their understanding and others to do with spiritual well-being. Before Vatican II, Roman Catholic priests were first ordained into minor orders. These may well be codifications of important tasks in the early church. (It is clear that there were at least three ordained ministries – presbyters, deacon and bishops and that women were able to hold these positions.) I will use the titles of those orders to indicate some of the necessary roles required within a community of Christians.

- Cleric: The cleric is called to present their body in Christ's service. It was the traditional moment of the giving of the tonsure. It marks a real commitment to take responsibility to represent Christ. It is best illustrated by the Quaker distinction between members and enquirers. It marks a transition from being a consumer of a community to being an active member in its creation.
- Door keeper: This was clearly an important role in a persecuted church. It is a role of protecting the community from dangerous interlopers and literally keeping the door. As such in the contemporary church it is subsumed into the role of sidesperson and welcomer. This role can be extended to include the pastoral care of the community like that of a pastoral auxiliary. It could be extended another way to include the role of building manager.
- Reader: This function has been retained in the Anglican tradition. It concerns the role of teaching and training for it involves study of theology and biblical exegesis.
- Exorcist: This is the healing function. This was an important part of early ministry but went into decline. It is now being revived and the ministry is open to both clergy and laity.
- Acolyte: This is the function now fulfilled by the sacristan who ensures that everything required for worship is available.
- Subdeacon: This function was marked by the giving of various vestments. The closest role to it now is that of server. It marks the transition to the overtly dramatic roles in the liturgy. Here it is worth looking at the liturgy as an act of performance with various performers in various roles. Here the vestments are

important signifiers of these roles. There is a sense in which every sharing of food is a Eucharistic act and the distinctiveness of the liturgical celebration is its dramatic quality. The Last Supper is seen to be re-enacted ritually in public. The use of vestments links the Christian tradition with many other religious traditions. When the appropriate vestments are put on, the person wearing them takes on the persona of the part they have to play. The concept of role here is very different from a role in a play where the portrayal of particular character in a particular situation is the focus. In the drama of the liturgy, the players take on a role on behalf of a particular community. In one sense they cease being John or Jane, and become the subdeacon/ deacon/priest on behalf of the assembled group. It is much closer to dramatic traditions like Japanese Noh theatre with highly ritualized and traditionalized approaches to its narratives.

- Deacon: This function here is to serve the priest during the Eucharist, sharing some of the role, but under the direction of the priest (for a further discussion of the diaconate see below).
- Priest: This function is to understand the nature of sacramental acts, to know the traditions of the rituals and be able to carry them out effectively.

This theology grows out of a non-kyriarchal view of church favoured by more radical theologians. It is ecclesia rather than kyriarchy. Few contemporary denominations have explored such a systematic review of the priesthood of all believers. I saw something like it in the Hildegard Community in Austin, Texas. This alternative worshipping community loosely attached to the local American Episcopal Church was systematically working out a new form of ecclesiology. It was deeply democratic and people on joining were linked with a soul friend and into various groups. They welcomed those excluded from mainstream Christianity and consciously developed the use of the arts in new forms in their worship. Here, when people joined their talents were identified and printed on a metal tag which was then attached to a banner which was ceremonially used in a dance by the priest at the end of each service. The banner and dance celebrated what each had to offer to the community – the priesthood of all believers.

The problem with the notions of minor orders was not its helpful identification of these functions, but its placing of them hierarchically with the priest at the apex – also the implication that the priest should be able to fulfil all these functions. Although this has never been so overt in the Anglican Church, there is still a feeling that the stipendiary priest in particular should be able to embrace all these roles. A more functional approach to ministry would not require a priest necessarily to be a teacher or a pastoral visitor. In this model, the priest's expertise should be in the understanding of the sacraments. The leadership of the Church could rotate around those carrying out all the functions. All of these functions should be recognized by some public ceremonial – a commissioning, for example.

Robin Greenwood in his book *Transforming Priesthood* (1994) suggests a role of the priest as gathering the community. This would seem to be a significant role that links together some of the roles discussed previously (although his treatment of it is somewhat hierarchical). The priest gathers the community, so that communion, *koinonia*, may be established; and so that the community may offer itself and its life in response to Christ's offering.

The notion of a priestly hierarchy draws its justification from a model that sees Jesus (who was not a priest) 'ordaining' apostles to whom all the church orders can be linked. The Apostolic succession has been, and still is, a minefield for the combined enterprises of theologians, church historians and canon lawyers. It is a central issue for the Roman Catholic Church, but the Anglican Church makes some (disputed) claims to it. This doctrine supports the kyriarchal model of church, for the power of consecration comes down a line through history passed from those at the top of hierarchy to those further down it. It does not allow for the community itself to ordain its own priests.

There are real dangers in the clericalism arising from this view and these have played a significant part in Church history. The rise of clericalism marked an increasing removal of power from the laity. So, for example, rites of marriage and death were originally ceremonies conducted in domestic situations, before being 'clericalized'. Sacramental confession grew out of pastoral support in the community and has been criticized for the control over the most private parts of people's lives that it gave to the clergy. The greater the strength of clericalism, the more the laity will be disempowered. It was against this phenomenon that Jesus directed his strongest criticism. (This notion of an exclusive elite is not only a religious phenomenon but also one that has developed in other areas such as the health services and therapeutic professions.)

It was as an antidote to this phenomenon that at various times in Church history the notion of the priesthood of all believers has been explored. Most notably this was at the Reformation with Luther and the other reformed theologians, and at Vatican II in the Roman Catholic Church. In traditions, like the Congregationalists this meant a real return to congregational control over the ordination of ministers; and it was this characteristic in Congregationalism that enabled the first woman to be ordained in the UK. It needed only one congregation to make that decision for it to happen. Nevertheless this theology drawing on the Epistle to the Hebrews has never been explored in any depth by any of the mainstream churches, who have clung quite tightly to institutional control over who is ordained to the priesthood or ministry.

Case Study Three: Renegotiating Normality

The church's relationship to 'the normal' has been interactive. It has both shaped and been shaped by the dominant culture as we saw in Chapter One. Ethics is an area where community and individualism interact very powerfully. Ethics traditionally maintain group solidarity. Chris Clarke distinguishes between ethics and morality and describes how our values are linked with our world view. He defines ethics as 'publicly shared values that derive from a common world view'. Morality he links with 'a code imposed by an authority, rather than living out a vision of the world' (Clarke 200: 190) and thus more related to the dominant values:

> I will use the word *ethics* to mean a system of publicly shared values that derive from a common world view. Thus for me ethics is not a matter of the social conventions that a society may adopt (either through debate or 'social selection') to further its survival, but a matter of the living-out of a world view by society or within society.
>
> I will use *morality* as a rather more general term, which may include following a code imposed by an authority, rather than living out a vision of the world. Code and vision may be two sides of the same coin. For example, in principle it might happen that leading members of a socially dominant religious authority derive a code from a view of the world which they then impose on others by fiat. More often, I suspect, people usually impose moral codes largely in order to further their own power without any rationale based on a world view.

Apparently arbitrary codes may also be imposed that have the effect
of reinforcing the feeling of identity of the followers of a particular
religion, making them feel part of a group that is bound together, and
distinguished from neighbouring groups, by their practices. (Clarke
2002: 190).

He refers to food prohibitions as an example of such codes that
are used to define groups of people. He develops an 'ethics of
connectivity' drawn from quantum theory (Clarke 2002: 195). He
draws on an unpublished talk of Isabel Clarke to present the
relationships that make up the world view on which we draw:
* Relationship with the people, who are important to me.
* Relationship to our ancestors, to those who will come after us;
  to our tribe.
* Relationship to the whole human race.
* Relationship to the other than human species.
* Relationship to the environment.
* Relationship to the ultimate – to God, or however we understand
  it (as this relationship literally 'passes understanding' (Clarke
  2002: 196).

But in our increasingly secularized society on what basis will
ethical decisions be made? Without the shared belief in a Christian
God, an absolutist position based on a fixed spiritual frame is no
longer a possibility for public morality, even if it can still form the
basis of some people's private ethics:

In open, democratic societies, however, it is impossible to impose, let
alone to police moral systems that are based on traditional principles
that are no longer accepted (Holloway 1999: 106).

In his book *Godless Morality* (1999) Richard Holloway reworks
an absolutist view of God in favour of one using the image of God
as jazz improviser constantly reworking traditional themes in new
contexts (Holloway 1999: 33–34):

If we reject the role of God as a micromanager of human morality,
dictating specific systems that constantly wear out and leave us with
theological problems when we want to abandon them, we shall have
to develop a more dynamic understanding God as one who
accompanies creation in its evolving story like a pianist in a silent
movie. We can opt for a series of fixed texts that wear out and have to
be constantly changed, or we can choose the metaphor of the jazz
session that constantly makes new music by listening to what's
happening around it and applying the best of what is left of the

tradition to the current context. The genius of improvisation seems to be a better metaphor for actual human moral experience than struggling to apply a single text to every situation. God invites us to join the music, to listen and to adapt to one another, to keep the melody flowing. Part of this versatility will involve us in listening and respecting themes we ourselves do not choose to follow; and part of it will encourage us to find common themes in which many of us can participate (Holloway 1999: 33-34).

Holloway's view is a fluid one as the polarities of respect for individual difference and the views of the community are reworked. It possibly can produce the possibility of a more fluid view of normality in the area of humanity. But as we saw in Chapter Two notions of God started to die out in the Enlightenment. It was reworked in a form that saw those properties once ascribed to God as those that are distinctively human. Mary Warnock, drawing on Aristotle, bases her work on these values that are distinctively human (Warnock 2001: 113–14) which would include 'the possibility of altruism, or unselfishness, ...central to morality (Warnock 2001: 162). So ethics are now constructed as human. On the one hand, this may appear to be individualistic. But how can we be sure that these universal values are not those of a particularly powerful group or simply an exploitation by those who know how to operate the market? Morality has traditionally been used by the dominant knowers to control the subjugated. However, let us examine this picture:

At an evening dinner party in 2069, we should not be too surprised to find ourselves sitting next to a mermaid or a centaur at a dinner hosted by a 159 year old human with thin diaphanous wings and insect eyes. We might sit there and laugh at the irrational behaviour of our predecessors who fell in love, lost their tempers, experienced jealousy, collected stamps, got ill, lived for only 80 years and on occasion were discontented or unhappy. We might alternatively be incapable of imagining what such things were (Woolfson 2004).

This story raises a vast range of questions about how each age constructs its own notions of normality. In the area of health, for example, the notion of hip replacement, a possibility unheard-of two centuries ago, has now become a 'normal' procedure. However, the story poses considerable questions about:

- The nature of humanity.
- The role of suffering in that construction.

- The nature of responsible and irresponsible choice.

These questions are raised most powerfully by the Human Genome Project particularly in the area of pregnancy and childbirth— areas traditionally controlled by women. However, it is not yet clear whether the project's ability to cure illnesses in an unprecedented way will keep pace with its capacity for diagnosis and this will raise problems of normativity particularly in the area of the termination of pregnancy:

> This undoubtedly will lead to more requests to genetic clinics for diagnoses at molecular level, and for carrier detection, and also for pre-natal diagnosis. This brings mixed blessings to patients; the real benefits will come only when a cure can be offered as well, or at least effective treatment for the condition. Unfortunately this is not an immediate sequel to gene identification, for that is a far more a long-term prospect. If the genetic disease is severe, it is of little help simply to know that one has the mutation, although some people do find a comfort to put a name to the disease that afflicts them. What they really need is to be relieved of the symptoms of the disease. Thus the present application of the new genetic knowledge to patients needs to be identified but no cure, in the short term, there will be an increase in terminations of pregnancy for those diseases (Seller 2003: 39).

So does the Human Genome Project in an age without a transcendent God to resort to for guidance, threaten our view of what it is to be human and leave this in the hands of multi-nationals? Bronislaw Szerszynski (2003) argues that the Human Genome Project threatens to destroy the concept of human being by reducing the surface differences and deep unities that have traditionally defined it to a *mathesis* consisting of chromosomes. Having reduced human beings to a collection of chromosomes the way now lies open for manipulation and control, as we saw in Chapter One, by large corporations.

Who will control the decisions that are made? As we saw in Chapter One, this is linked with power. The debates resonate with the figure of Thrasymachus, one of the participants in Plato's dialogue, *The Republic*, who enunciated the view that justice or morality, was nothing but the interest of the stronger, a system imposed on the weak to keep them in order (Warnock 2001: 171). Not only do the strong decide on the frames in which the decisions will be set but also who will have access to the technologies.

Closely linked with the notion of power is the question of where is it decided? In the Middle Ages it would have been in the hands of Church authorities, and still is for practising Roman Catholics who are regularly controlled by documents from the Vatican. However, as we have seen above, there is a difference between private ethics and public morality. The latter will be controlled by legal frameworks generated by politicians for whom expediency may well be the governing force. Legislators must in general be consequentialists having regard for the benefits over the harms, based on nineteenth century John Stuart Mill's Utilitarianism (1851) but the 'greatest happiness' principle is now discredited because of the fracture of the flow between community and the individual. The language of rights increasingly colours the thinking of legislators particularly since the Universal Declaration of Human Rights which postulates drawing on a higher authority than simple expediency:

> However, it is sometimes argued that, apart from the positive laws which currently create rights, there is a higher law from which higher rights may be derived (and this might include the higher right of all children to equal treatment, educationally, not granted them in the pre-1972 legislation (Warnock 2001: 89).

Yet, in discussing this trend, Mary Warnock warns against absolutist tendencies here, especially in the area of a child's inherent right to life whatever its quality (Warnock 2001: 93–4). She cites the UNICEF charter of children's rights: 'every child has the inherent right to life.' But does this mean that absolutely every baby that is born, however slim its chances of survival, however poor will be the quality of its future life, while it lasts (Warnock 2001: 93–4)?

As we have seen, it is likely that while the frameworks for ethical decisions in this area will be enshrined in legal frameworks, it is medical authorities who will turn these into practical actions and definitions of health will play an important part in these. This will be done in collaboration with the parents who will have to make that decision on behalf of a child who may oppose that decision when they are able to choose for themselves. The literature is often more concerned, however, about the control of the area by the market (Clarke 2002: 204). All writers stress the need for proper regulation – that the twisted form of community offered by the market will not override individual choice and potential. Will it be possible to have a centaur-shaped child as the opening story postulates? Watson (2001: 208) discusses the possibility of raising human intelligence as a justifiable aim for parents for their children. It is a short step from this to the so-called 'designer babies' where parents can make a child have all the characteristics that they would desire in their child.

Various writers give examples of how a flow between the polarities might be negotiated. Messer (drawing on the theologian Bonhoeffer) gives us some guidelines on which choices may be made by linking 'therapeutic' choice to legitimate 'penultimate' choices that are in line with God's will for humanity and 'non-therapeutic' manipulation to 'ultimate' choices that are part of human pretensions to be divine (Messer 1999: 1–16). Is there a clear distinction between the therapeutic and the non-therapeutic in the area of parental choice?

> Elsewhere I have drawn on Bonhoeffer's distinction between the 'ultimate' and the 'penultimate' to argue that *therapeutic* genetic interventions can be considered a legitimate part of the 'penultimate' activity to which humans are called by God; *non-therapeutic* manipulation or genetic 'enhancement', on the other hand, risks becoming part of a grandiose project with 'ultimate' or divine pretensions (Messer 1999: 1–16).

But the distinction is often not clear, as illustrated by a recent case where a second child was needed to help a first child with a genetic disease. This description also raises issues of the 'sovereignty' of God. Should 'nature' be allowed to take its course in issues surrounding the termination of pregnancy? How far is this perceived as a process emanating from God and how far are human beings in their role of relieving suffering doing the work of God?

But all of these raise the issue of normativity – a distorted form of community. With the resources of the Human Genome Project will everyone choose to 'normalize' their offspring into alpha males? Here we come to the place of suffering (or disease) in Christian theology. It is interesting to reflect, as Neil Messer (2003) does, that if the Human Genome Project had been available in the first century, would Paul have written the glorious message of 2 Cor. 12. 7–10 in which, in dealing with his own 'thorn in the flesh', he hears God saying:

> "My strength is made perfect in weakness" So I will boast gladly of my weaknesses (*NRSV*)

Karl Barth, whose theology is based to a large extent on the experience of Paul notes:

> Health means capability, vigour and freedom. It is strength for human life. It is integration of the organs for the exercise of psycho-physical functions (Barth 1961: 356).

He relates sickness to sin and death. Although rejecting it as God's punishment, he sees it as an opportunity for showing God's miraculous cures as in Jesus' healing miracles. So we are required to resist sickness. This view is critiqued by feminist and womanist theologians who see this as a position generated by people in a position of power and not by subjugated peoples (Cannon 1988).

> However, his second view is more helpful here. He stresses the temporal and limited nature of sickness and sees the possibility of discovering through it that 'Christ will be our consolation' (Barth 1961: 373). His two views represent a paradox which is implicit in 2 Corinthians 12 and the dilemma of balancing the needs of the community and the individual.

Medical authorities have wrestled with this as they produce various definitions of health. Boorse defines disease as an abnormality in relation to the norms of the species, but distinguishes it from the more serious condition of illness which has the following characteristics:

- Undesirability for its bearer.
- A title to special treatment.
- A valid excuse for normally criticizable behaviour (Boorse 1976: 62–63).

Any definition necessarily raises problems for 'disabled people':

> It would be possible to use a medical model of health-as-normality to legitimate our fear of diversity and of those who are different from us. This becomes all the more important in the light of the fact that molecular genetics offers a powerful set of tools with which society could implement 'quality control' of children and eliminate 'abnormalities' from the population (Messer 2003: 99).

How are notions of normality linked with medical views of health? The World Health Organization's definition of Health in 1948 was:

> Health is a state of complete physical, mental and social well-being and not merely the absence of disease or infirmity. [7]

7. http://www.who.int/aboutwho/en/defintion.html, 26 April 2002.

Some writers see this as a fine description of biblical concepts like *shalom* (Wilkinson 1998: 11–13, 19). However, others see it as too narrow an understanding of human well-being (Messer 2003: 100) which is obtainable without physical and mental well-being, as in times of physical illness. The Church has traditionally seen physical disabilities or suffering as having various roles:

- To enhance the merits of the just through their patience.
- To safeguard virtue from pride.
- To correct the sinner.
- To proclaim God's glory through miraculous cures.
- As the beginning of eternal punishment, as in the case of Herod (Tempkin quoted in Turner 1984: 68)

A variety of scholars from different backgrounds have developed these themes. Hauerwas develops a theory of the learning generated for the wider society by children with severe learning disabilities who:

> Force us to recognize that we are involved in a community life that is richer than our official explanations and theories give us skill to say (Hauerwas 1988: 211–17).

John Hull follows a similar line in reflecting on his own blindness and Isa. 42. 16: 'I will lead the blind by a road they do not know, by paths they have not known, I will guide them. I will turn the darkness before them into light, the rough places into level ground'(*NRSV*). He sees here that God accepts blind people and how other's behaviour is modified to accommodate them (Hull 2001: 108–9).

Many writers see the problem as resting with the wider society not the person, rebalancing normativity by means of individual case studies. In a powerful article, Gelya Frank describes how a 35 year-old American woman, born with quadrilateral limb deficiencies, resisted attempts to make her body 'normal' by the use of prostheses:

> From childhood, Diane DeVries's attitude toward her body when healthy and free of devices has been remarkably positive (Frank 1986: 195).

Her sense of being different was imposed on her by others:

> Certain things could happen during the day to make me sad or mad, 'cause I could go…weeks without it bothering me at all, because nothing happened. But something *could* happen, like once when I was

a little kid I was in a wagon and we were in this trailer park, and some kid came up to me with a knife. He said: "Aw, you ain't got no arms, you ain't got no legs, and now you're not gonna have no head." He held me right here, by the neck, and had a little knife (Frank 1986: 195).

If Diane has moments of alienation from herself or feelings of regret about her body, she has not conveyed them to me. A more relevant focus for an individual like Diane may be to protect herself from the attitude so easily taken by the non-disabled that her body is flawed and unacceptable (Frank 1986: 195–96).

Virginia Mollenkott in her book *Omnigender* describes the anger of hermaphrodites at the surgical procedures used to make them 'normal.'

It disturbs me to know that so many intersexual children are mutilated by well-meaning doctors who think surgery is necessary to prevent parents or other people from treating them like outcasts (Mollenkott 2001: 49).

The view of the 'disabled' may be completely different from that of the wider community showing a fracture of the relationship between the individual and community:

The videotape [*Hermaphrodites Speak!*] features ten intersexual people at the first international gathering of intersexuals as they talk about the lies and mutilations they have suffered at the hands of the medical and psychological establishments. All agree that they would have preferred to have been left alone, "not helped so much". The one person to have "somehow avoided surgery", Hida, spoke of her good health and her love of her body. She emphasized that her only problems came from "society's need to polarize gender and the pressure to conform." Hida stressed that "the problem is not the child but the attitudes toward the child."

It disturbs me to know that so many intersexual children are mutilated by well-meaning doctors who think surgery is necessary to prevent parents or other people from treating them like outcasts. It disturbs me that intersexuals are often brought up in secrecy that makes them feel freakish, shameful, and isolated. It disturbs me that "expert" doctors continue to make the decision that no one can be allowed to remain intersexual, instead of listening to the voices of adult intersexual people who feel they have been seriously harmed by medical intervention... The vast majority of intersex surgery involves normal little girls whose clitorises are deemed too large by doctors, often because the doctors fear the girls will grow up to masculinized lesbians (Mollenkott 2001: 49).

In this case and that of Diana DeVries the decisions will be taken by parents and only later will the child's own view of how they were treated become apparent. This raises a further issue of how far these decisions, made during pregnancy and in infancy, should be revealed to the adult.[8] The notion of the rights of the child and the responsibility of the parents are tightly intertwined in this area.

Nancy Eisland has developed very fully a theology of suffering, basing it on the central image of Christianity as being a broken body (Chopp 1994: 11) and goes on to see disabled people as calling the Church:

- to repentance and transformation (Eisland 1994: 75);
- to see the truth of the incarnate God more clearly (Eisland 1994: 99);
- to see that 'interdependence is the fact of both justice and survival' (Eisland 1994: 103).

It is remarkable in the face of the woundedness of the central figure in Christianity that the Church has failed to enable the flow between the disabled and the views of the wider community.

> The most astounding fact is, of course, that Christians do not have an able-bodied God as their primal image. Rather, the Disabled God promising Grace through a broken body, is at the centre of piety, prayer, practice, and mission. Indeed the centrality of the Disabled God to Christian symbolic logic is a powerful image of resistance to oppressive constructs of "normal embodiment" and an image of transformation for all persons created in the image of God. As Eisland suggests, the disabling theology of most Christian traditions has equated disabilities with sin. From codes of purity to acts of Jesus' healing, the implicit theological assumption has equated perfect bodies with wholeness of spirit. And, as if to ensure the quest for purity, physical afflictions become elevated to virtuous suffering when, and only when, they can be spoken of as trials of obedience. Such teachings allow either one of two options for those with disabilities: miraculous healing or heroic suffering (Chopp 1994: 11).

And yet if this flow could be established in this area the Church could teach the wider community a great deal:

> The disabled God is God for whom interdependence is not a possibility to be willed from a position of power, but a necessary condition for life. This interdependence is the fact of both justice and survival. The

---

8. This could be seen as similar to the issue surrounding the identity of fathers who donated sperm.

disabled God embodies practical interdependence, not simply willing to be interrelated from a position of power, but depending on it from a position of need. For many people with disabilities, too, mutual care is a matter of survival. To posit a Jesus Christ who needs care and mutuality as essential to human-divine survival does not symbolize either humanity or divinity as powerless. Instead it debunks the myth of individualism and hierarchical orders, in which transcendence means breaking free of encumbrances and needing nobody and constitutes as somebody in relation to other bodies (Eisland 1994: 103).

I enjoy this thinking. What will happen to the notion of a 'wounded' God when, one day human beings are apparently suffering-free? How does a soteriology based on the Crucifixion sit in such a world and what are the possibilities for a Christian community to find its way through the issues posed by the Human Genome Project? It is Celia Deane-Drummond (2003: 236–47) who attempts to establish a flow within this complex area by developing the theme of Wisdom as a way of 'integrating strands in deontological, consequentialist and virtue ethics, while remaining theocentric in orientation drawing on a Sophianic theology of nature' (Deane-Drummond 2003: 225). She develops[9] it by deconstructing Wisdom into its component parts; to construct a virtue ethics, she then applies these to the Human Genome Project. She shows how the question: *What shall I do?* in a virtue ethic becomes *Who am I? Who shall I become?* and *How am I to get there?* She starts with Prudence basing her ideas on Thomas Aquinas (Porter 1994). She follows Josef Pieper (1959: 11) in identifying various attitudes within it:

- Humility of the silent – to contemplate the truth of a given situation by 'unbiased perception'.
- Trueness to memory – to include past experiences in the decision, including the dangers of eugenics in the philosophy of the Nazi regime.
- The art of receiving counsel – the ability to listen to a variety of points of view including those of scientists, governments, theologians.
- Alert composed readiness for the unexpected – being prepared for sudden advances like the cloning of Dolly the sheep.
- Purity, straightforwardness, candour and simplicity of character.

9. This is not unlike the way worked out by Hildegard in the twelfth century and the motivic view of morality set out in Holloway (1999) above.

- Standing superior to the utilitarian complexities of mere 'tactics' – challenging the mission of the scientist and the politicians' need for public support.
- Justice, 'the habit whereby a person with a lasting and constant will renders to each his due.' (Aquinas, trans. Gilby 1974 2a2ae Qu.58.1) – the embedding of natural law in laws and regulatory frameworks like the Human Fertilization and Embryology Authority.
- Fortitude, a correct evaluation of things and a willingness to suffer – associated in the Christian frame with the question of the availability of the technologies to the disadvantaged.
- Temperance – concerned with self-restraint governed by reason.

She sees Wisdom as being distinct from scientific knowing and based on a relationship of love and faith with God. She includes peacemaking within the concept of Wisdom which she relates to the bringing together of differing views and also hope, which is for a right relationship between God and humanity and other creatures. This brings us back to some of the ideas explored at the opening of this case study.

The Human Genome Project poses very special questions about the relationship between the individual and the community. We have seen how various disabled individuals have operated strategies of resistance by utilizing a different identity by that imposed by the wider society, calling communities to rework their understandings in the process. A many facetted Wisdom theology can give some guidance for developing a contextual theology in this area.

Case Study Four: Renegotiating Self-policing – The Witnessing Project

We saw in Chapter One how subjugated knowers learn from the dominant culture a powerful inner self-policing mechanism. The individuality of members of subjugated groups is threatened by community pressure. Helen O'Grady describes a therapy developed in Australia and New Zealand to deal with the negative effects of this on women:

One therapeutic approach compatible with a feminist exposé of self-policing is narrative therapy. Narrative therapy develops out of collaborative work of Australian and New Zealand family therapists Michael White and David Epston during the 1980's. Significantly influenced by Foucault's thought, feminism and cultural anthropology, this approach is concerned about the ways in which various taken-for-granted therapeutic assumptions inadvertently may be reproducing oppressive practices and structures of the broader society and this contributing to the very problems people are seeking to address. These include a predominantly individualistic approach to therapy which obscures the social context in which problems develop and prosper. Such an approach tends to ignore the link between personal identity and experience and the broader power structures of society. Conversely, narrative therapy is interested in the degree to which problematic experience is caught up in the taken-for-granted cultural assumptions and structures of inequality (White 1995: 115).

We have seen in Chapter One how the feeling of 'han' develops in subjugated knowers if their inner self-policing policies stay unchallenged for too long:

Self-policing practices are characteristics of many women's self-relationship. These include surveillance of one's thoughts, feelings and conduct, ongoing self-judgement, self-criticism, insidious comparisons with others and personal isolation. Such practices tend to be experienced as a given part of psychic make up which makes it difficult to subject them to critical scrutiny. Yet their disabling effects render this important. Foregrounding self-policing and examining the context in which it prospers undermines its seemingly inevitable status. In turn, this increases possibilities for developing a different type of self-relationship and for active participation in broader questions of identity (O'Grady 2005: 41–42).

Many people designated as clinically depressed by the psychiatric services are further pathologized by services which actually reinforce the values of the dominant culture, by whom they are, after all, employed. For example, an able and intelligent woman in a psychiatric hospital was told: 'You have a husband and two children. What more do you want?' The concentration is mostly on enabling the individual to accommodate to the surrounding culture, whether by means of medication or various talking therapies. The Witnessing Project aims to develop strategies of resistance:

The charting of a history of personal resistance indicates the extent to which the problem has not got the better of people (often a surprise), and provides encouragement of ongoing resistance. It also offers clues to their preferred values attributes and aspirations which provide the basis for an alternative self-description. The latter is authenticated and enriched by "outsider witnesses". Rather than reflecting the recovery of an innate self, re-authored narratives always evolve in relation to the sociohistorical context. The idea of relational identity encourages individual creativity and leaves open the possibility of further self-making (O'Grady 2005: 60).

Narrative therapy offers a path towards:

> The idea of woman as an active social agent capable of instituting radical change at the micro-political level (McNay 1992b: 115).

This enables an identity to be formed that is self-critical and contextual. The individual sees him/herself as both an individual and related to a context and sees how the subjective and societal interact powerfully. This empowers them to renegotiate their identity in relationship to the dominant culture:

> Drawing on aspects of Foucault's later work. I argued that an emphasis on the type of ethical relationship we have with ourselves provides a way of redressing an imbalance in many women's lives between care for the self and care for others...I suggested the usefulness of hooks' notion of structuring relationships around the principle of love [hooks 1996: 73] and Lugones' concept of playfulness [Lugones 1990: 401] (O'Grady 2005: 97–98).

Here we see women using strategies of resistance by means of narrative therapy to renegotiate identity in relation to themselves and their relationship to their surrounding community.

Summary

We have seen how a flow between community and the individual can result in a sense of identity and how a negotiation of a relationship of mutuality between God and the world may reverse traditional ecclesiology and notions of priesthood that could reflect this mutual, non-hierarchical relationship. Developments in medical science highlight the dilemmas in negotiating the flow in the face of a market ready to exploit notions of normativity. Finally, the Witnessing Project represents a determined effort to renegotiate mental illness by dealing with internal self-policing.

Unity/Diversity

1. It was dark in the dawn of time
   When the waters of chaos seethed.
   Darkness was brooding across the abyss
   Till the Spirit gently breathed.
   Slowly she hovered across swelling waves
   Till the world from the chaos emerged.
   Then the rest in the dark was transfigured with light
   As the Spirit worked out her plan.

2. It was dark in the rocky cave
   Where the body of Jesus lay.
   Resting down deep in the heart of the earth
   Till the stone was rolled away.
   In the still night he'd stayed hidden away
   In the cold of primeval gloom.
   Then the rest in the dark was transfigured with light
   As the Spirit worked out her plan.

3. Mary sank down deep into grief
   When her Master was crucified.
   Deep in the darkness of sadness she lay
   Till her love she recognized.
   Waiting she stayed all alone in the night
   In the chaos of loss and despair.
   Then the rest in the dark was transfigured with light
   As the Spirit worked out her plan.

4. It is dark in the moistened earth
   Where the seed for a season lies
   Buried down deep as a dry pregnant husk
   Till the earth is pushed aside.
   Nurtured by warmth, it has waited alone
   Till the time to spring up has come.
   Then the rest in the dark was transfigured with light
   As the Spirit worked out her plan.

5. It is dark in the sheltering womb
   Where the baby for nine moths lies,
   Curved like a moon near a warm woman's heart
   Till the waters roll aside.

Water of life kept the child safe inside
Gently folded, enclosed in love.
Then the rest in the dark was transfigured with light
As the Spirit worked out her plan.

6. It is dark in the heart's deep cells
Where the Spirit of Wisdom lies.
Firm are the strong rooms and bars of the mind
Till the barriers are rolled aside.
Yet her idea in the dark has been formed
Till the time for release should come.
Then the rest in the dark was transfigured with light
As the Spirit worked out her plan.
(Boyce-Tillman (2006a: 42–43)

All descriptions of creativity (and especially its processes) include a measure of chaos or darkness – a time when the whole appears to fragment before it re-establishes itself again in a different configuration. The Cartesian view of the unified, separated self has been central to the project of Western rationalism. It posited an 'essential' self to which various attributes like gender and race could be attached. It was attached to a notion of a steady march towards wholeness which was often equated with the 'light' both of the Christian Scripture and the Enlightenment project as a whole. It perpetuated the more violent aspects of social policy. It characterizes neo-colonial enterprises, such as the spread of multi-nationals like McDonalds and the enterprises of performing groups of Western origin, like orchestras and rock groups. Notions of equality were based on this notion of enforced unity and postmodernism has encouraged moves beyond this to the valuing and respect for 'difference'. This has called for a challenge to the socio/political implications of the fictive unity of the self.

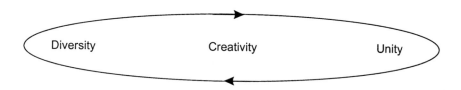

Fig. 7. Creativity.

Society

The tolerance of diversity is an important element in the way a community defines itself. The tightness of the boundaries established by a particular society is a product of the degree of threat that is seen either from without or more significantly, from within. And yet, it is by the admitting of diversity that new societies and new ways of conceiving society have emerged. When the two poles of unity and diversity are balanced in a society, it can grow and change creatively. The process of readjusting this balance has been seen in a post-apartheid South Africa or Australia's struggle to acknowledge the rights of its indigenous aboriginal population. In the West we have placed a high value on unity. Indeed, in the follow-up interviews to my piece *The Healing of the Earth* (Boyce-Tillman 2001a), which saw many diverse musical elements brought together, the children aged 9–11 did not even know the meaning of the word diversity. They live in a world where unity in the form of normalization is taking control with standardized testing for all children regardless of race, economic class, gender and all the factors that make children various rather than the same. The excessive concentration on this normalizing process has split the binary apart and we see it in many parts of UK society – the divide between rich and poor in health care for example, and the increasing number of people who are pathologized or criminalized. The end of the binary split is Fascism which is a perfectly unified society, obliterating diversity, sometimes by means of destruction. This links back to the progress myth that we examined in Chapter One:

> To bring freedom or knowledge or health or prosperity to a people *in order that* they become Christians is a perversion of missionary work. But what of a system [of missionary activity] that would bring them progress and development for its own sake? Is that not as bad? Nazism will stand forever as the ultimate indictment of progress for its own sake (Donovan 1982: 12).

The risk of the supremely tolerant society is that it will slip into anarchy. As the music educator, Murray Schafer (1973) said after a school principal had experienced one of his classes where the children had been creating their own pieces, in response to the question: 'Where does it all lead?' 'Anarchy, anarchy, total anarchy, a totally creative society is totally anarchic.' The free flowing between these polarities produces a creative and innovative society but when tolerance and normalization start to split apart the ultimate end is either fascism or anarchy.

Self

At a personal level the pursuit of the integrated self and the perception of the journey as being a straight and steady progress have resulted in a certain internal fascism, which we may describe as rigidity or indeed, obsession. The pattern of the self is a cyclical exploration of deintegration and reintegration and this is health. Because of the high premium placed on integration, deintegration is frequently pathologized. A classic example is the grieving process. A loved person, animal or object has been part of the integration of a particular self. When they disappear, the self has to deintegrate in order to reintegrate with a previous part missing. In former times days were given for this process to happen and people were protected from the demands of ordinary life to give them time to grieve, which is the process of deintegration. Now with the requirement that life go on as normal (when it clearly is not) the self has no time to reintegrate naturally. The process is then pathologized, with the result that the person is now sick for a longer time and the self has huge problems in reintegrating, which it would do quite naturally, given time and support.

Other cultures have a greater degree of diversity within their cosmology which enables a greater degree of multiplicity within the self. Spirit possession and shamanistic cults have this because of the belief in a number of spirits which can possess the self. The notions underpinning shamanic and spirit possession cults have a way of explaining diversity within the self by reference to another world which interacts with the everyday world.[10] So the self goes through a pattern of deintegration and reintegration. When these start to lose touch with one another, the person either disintegrates or becomes rigid.

---

10. This world is explored safely by musical means. The training of shaman involves the concept of a difficult journey using a supporting drum beat into intuitive areas, which is where the healing songs are to be found. The healing itself is also accompanied by musical as well as ritual elements (Boyce-Tillman 2000a).

Valuing Diversity

Notions of identity that include ideas of diversity are now beginning to emerge in many literatures. Anthony Giddens hints at this in the Reith Lecture on Tradition, suggesting that the growth in the therapy and counselling industry in the contemporary world is part of a search of personal identity in a society that no longer provides that identity within its own structures.[11] He suggests that it is part of the process of globalization in which we all have a greater range of choice than before and that the self is dynamic and fluid (Giddens 1999). Postcolonial theorists, like Elizabeth Spelman in her book *Inessential Woman* (1990), chart how nations of essential 'womanness' can be as oppressive as that of the generic 'man' was to cultures other than of the West (Spelman 1990: ix). Haraway writes:

> Identities seem contradictory, partial, and strategic. With the hard-won recognition of their social and historical constitution, gender, race, and class cannot provide the basis for belief in 'essential' unity. There is nothing about being 'female' that naturally binds women. There is not even such a state as 'being' female, itself a highly complex category constructed in contested sexual scientific discourses and other social practices (Haraway 1991: 155).

Dawkins' (1978) notion of 'the selfish gene' also includes a notion of multiplicity; this time at a molecular level. He postulates that identity is created and caused by a re-assembling of the replicating genes.

> Individuals are not stable things, they are fleeting. Chromosomes too are shuffled into oblivion, like hands of cards soon after they are dealt. But the cards themselves survive the shuffling. The cards are the genes. The genes are not destroyed by crossing-over; they merely change partners and march on. Of course they march on. That is their business. They are the replicators and we are their survival machines. When we have served our purpose we are cast aside. But genes are denizens of geological time: genes are forever (Dawkins 1978: 37).

The shift from a self defined by society to one that is more varied has been reflected in two ways in the literature. The literature arising from psychotherapy has concentrated on the ebb and flow within

---

11. I come from a family where the women had been in service for a long time. In my grandparents' generation I would have little choice other than to become a servant. Education has given me the possibility to construct my own identity. This has been done by making a series of choices.

the individual; it has looked at it from the inside out. The postmodern philosophers have looked at it more the outside in with notions of performativity.

Drawing on Lacan's concept of the Name of the Father, Irigaray ([1974] 1985) and Grosz (1990), Grace Jantzen describes the notion of the post-Enlightenment subject as 'heavily masculinist and heterosexual' (Jantzen 1998: 8). Judith Butler in her groundbreaking book, *Gender Trouble* (1990) challenges the essentialist ideas of 'woman' that underpinned much early feminism. She sees an association between violence and the assumption of a universal basis for feminism; it is against this notion of normativity and its problems for cultural otherness that she develops the notion of the self as performative. Rebelling against the unified self of the Enlightenment, she claims that 'Gender... [is] an identity tenuously constituted in time, instituted in an exterior space through a *stylized repetition of acts*' (Butler 1990: 4). This opens up the possibility of a multiplicity of identities and gives far greater possibilities for freedom in the self as explored in carnival traditions. People encountering these ideas in my workshops experience a deep sense of freedom. 'You mean I can be many things?' is a comment expressed with great joy. Women, in particular, are often aware of having to be multiple. I, for example, often wondered in my experience whether the mother who was hunting for her son's lost trainer was the same person who a quarter of an hour later was standing in front a class a giving a lesson.

Drawing on the work of Deleuze and the image of the rhizome, the postmodern philosopher Rosi Braidotti (1994) develops the notion of a nomadic subject:

> The nomadic subject as a performative image allows me to weave together different levels of my experience...There is a strong aesthetic dimension in the quest for alternative figurations (Braidotti 1994 : 4–8)

She too links the notion of unified self with violence, saying that 'gesture that binds a fractured self to the performative illusion of unity', is an act of violent force. She develops the notion of a non-phallocentric nomadic community in which the ancestors are included as in Levi Strauss's 'cold' societies (Levi-Strauss 1970: 18). They are also primarily orate which enables them to contextualize the stories of their peoples, allowing a connection with 'dangerous memories'.

The psychotherapeutic community concentrates on the inner journey and embraces diversity, chaos, darkness. Notions of identity based on unity in the work of Adorno (1948/73) have been associated with a repressive imperial force and he looks to art to deal with darkness:

> Art is able to aid enlightenment only by relating the clarity of the world to its own darkness (Adorno 1948/1973: 15).

The creative process is seen (Wallas 1926) as including various phases (which are adjusted, fine-tuned and restructured by later writers). These include preparation (the exploration of possibilities and generating of ideas) incubation (which involves less conscious activity), illumination (the 'eureka' experience) and elaboration (the working out of the project in a tangible form). The incubation phase can be likened to a descent into a personal underworld, chaos or darkness.[12] Importantly, a descent into the personal unconscious or subconscious with its somewhat chaotic nature is seen as an important component of the incubation phase. Particularly creative people have strategies for handling this phase and whereas it is possible for all to enter into the process (particularly the idea generating first phase), how far they proceed is often limited by their level of skill in handling it (Hindemith 1952). Arthur Koestler (1964) developed a theory of bisociation as central to this process in which two previously unconnected domains of the mind come together to produce the new outcome. The process is seen as part of the flow of living and important for growth and change. It involves a degree of courage on the person who needs to be free to enter playful processes in order to achieve what is seen as a re-ordering of personality. The result is a sense of empowerment, which can be nurtured by encouragement and an environment that encourages acceptance and spontaneity. Philosophers and psychologists have linked creativity to states of ecstasy and transcendence, although creativity always involves some bodily action.

Psychologists like Michael Fordham (1986) and Joseph Redfearn (1992) have challenged the notions of unity that underpinned Jung's concept of integration, while Assagioli (1973) develops his notion

---

12. I have explored this in my performance *Lunacy or the Pursuit of the Goddess* (2002) which involves three descents to the underworld with underworld goddesses.

of subpersonalities from Jung's notions of archetypes. The work of the philosopher Gillian Rose includes the notion of working in what she calls 'the broken middle' and has within it the necessity of living with the contradictions:

> Her work seeks to retrieve the experience of contradiction as the substance of life lived in the rational and the actual...In the middle of imposed and negated identities and truths, in the uncertainty about who we are and what we should do, Gillian commends that we comprehend the brokenness of the middle as the education of our natural and philosophical consciousness. She commends us to work with these contradictions, with the roaring and the roasting of the broken middle, and to know that it is 'I' (Tubbs 1998: 34).

The theologian Mary Grey (2001) in her Winton Lecture links this with religious ideas of the Underworld. In dealing with the story of Psyche and Eros she sees the problems Western society has with facing real life death and dying – the mythical underworld:

> Psyche returns from the Underworld – she has not conquered death in the way that Christians interpret the Resurrection of Jesus – but she has found a way of seeing in the dark, of living with death and destruction (Grey 2001: 62).

Currently, it is the discourse of science and technology that is supplanting theology. It, like theology, assumes a universalizing stance towards its objects; it is this one-dimensionality which should be questioned (Harding 1991). Haraway's own critique starts by pointing out that science's notion of objectivity rests upon the specific observations and interpretations of individuals. (Haraway 1989: 3–5). She calls for a recontextualizing of truth from multiple perspectives:

> So, not so perversely, objectivity turns out to be about particular and specific embodiment, and definitely not about the false vision promising transcendence of all limits and responsibility (Haraway 1991: 190).

The notion of diversity as opposed to unity allows for the contextualization of truth (Hill Collins 1998: xix). It values rather than devalues syncretism as part of the process of inculturation rather than seeing it as a 'watering' down truth. It acknowledges the existence of multiple truths. Patricia Hill Collins raises the problem of relativity and highlights the role of power in the validation of truth or truths (Hill Collins 1998: xix). She raises further issues with notions of authenticity when a number of different groups need to 'break' silence 'often striving to be the most oppressed or the most different' and how authenticity can rest only with a representative of particular cultures (Hill Collins 1998: 53–54). She draws attention to the problem of the commodification of knowledge in a capitalist economy and what that means for black women, highlighting people who 'make careers from black women's pain' (Hill Collins 1998: 55) including the appropriation and analysis of their work (Hill Collins 1998: 53–54).

The origin of the term 'womanist' lies in a desire to establish a plurality among women's voices establishing both an identity different from white feminists and one that includes a 'softer' attitude to black men (Hill Collins 1989: 61–63). Indeed, Hill Collins highlights how the movement has highlighted differences between individual black women, especially in the area of sexuality. The task Patricia Hill Collins suggests is a balance between heterogeneity and shared concerns from a common location in the web of US social life and its economy. She emphasizes the need for collectivity and of confronting power in the public sphere as a way of confronting social injustice. She looks to postmodernism to deconstruct reality and reconfigure the relationship between scientific knowledge, power and society. However, she sees the less linear, more circular writing of postmodern academics as potentially disenfranchising those who have not had access to 'the new logic'. There are interesting possibilities here. I think that the postmodern citizen belongs to a number of different communities, which operate rather like a series of interlocking frames. This notion of the intersectionality of communities gets away from the potential danger of the deconstructionist approach that we are all completely separate individuals, sharing no history. The idea of multiple selves is linked with a number of interlocking communities (into none of which we fit completely, as we might have done in former views of society.)

If truth is multiple then so is the methodology used to approach it. Subjugated knowers are often eclectic in their approaches to the various disciplines and cross the boundaries set up by the dominant structure. Feminist researchers have deliberately embraced diverse methodologies rather than the unified approach to truth of the dominant paradigm. In Beverley Diamond's study, *The Interpretation of Gender Issues in Musical Life Stories of Prince Edward Islanders,* she deliberately uses two methodologies; one is based on an essentialist position that looks for:

> sameness and pattern, ways in which 'groups' are constructed as if they share attitudes, values and lifeways. This lens reveals some of the ways in which a gender dichotomy between male and female is socially asserted though differently reinforced in various musical worlds. Although this analysis is certainly motivated by my political belief that such essentialisms must be revealed as constructed (not natural) and hence mutable, I also recognize and respect the strategic uses of essentialist positions by many consultants. The constructionist lens focuses not on pattern but on flux, change, and disjuncture. These moments in the musical life stories reveal the contingencies of gender identity and the strategies by which we negotiate with the world and assert individuality. Neither story is truer than the other. Both lenses are needed to understand the ways in which concepts of gender operate in relation to the musical worlds we create and perform and to which we respond (Diamond 2000: 105).

Patricia Hill Collins writes of the difficulties of the multi-disciplinary approach, both in its execution and its acceptance because of dominant orthodoxies:

> I try to take the best from positivist science, Marxist social theory, postmodernism, North American feminism, British cultural studies, and other intellectual traditions...Keeping multiple intellectual traditions such as these in mind, I invoke theoretical and methodological tools from different disciplines when they seem relevant to the goal of fostering economic and social justice... All around me I hear lip service to interdisciplinary research...I want to remind readers that actually doing this type of work on a daily basis over a period of years remains extremely difficult (Hill Collins 1998: xviii).

To summarize, notions of the controlling unity of the Cartesian self have been challenged on a number of different fronts, both within a single society and within the self. The notion that the self is multiple and performative is part of postmodern thinking and this has been reflected in performance projects. Psychotherapeutic literature has also highlighted the need for a rhythm of de-integration and reintegration. Normative discourses often use violence to enforce a fictive unity. Only when this is in touch with diversity can either the self or society be creative.

Theology

The Christian Church in Europe has put a high premium on unity and the dominance of a single metanarrative. Early in Christian theology, unity was associated with God and diversity with creation. Robert Govaerts writes of the seventh century Maximus the Confessor, showing how notions of unity are seen as Divine and notions of multiplicity as human or cosmic:

> With the earlier orthodox writers, Maximus affirms God to be utterly simple, devoid of any division or multiplicity. Creation, on the other hand, is distinguished from God exactly in the fact of it being a multiplicity. The created multiplicity forms an entire spectrum of beings that range from the inanimate, the animate, to the rational beings that include ourselves and the angels. ... For St. Pseudo-Dionysius, a sixth century monastic writer, probably from Syria, there was this spectrum of beings. Thereby, Maximus believes that there is a correspondence between the Creator and His creation. All the created beings reflect in their own manner the characteristics of God who is the source of goodness, of wisdom and beauty.
>
> Moreover, all beings that come into existence are moving. Everything is subject to change. The created universe is dynamic in every aspect. The object or goal of these creaturely movements is the attainment of a dynamic rest that is reached within the divine unity, so that the creature is no longer subject to change (Govaerts 2005).

This theology reflects the phallocentricity of traditional theology. Indeed, very early in Origen (c. 185–254) that diversity was defined as sinful and a fall from the divine unity, the result of human beings becoming embedded in matter. As such, his view upon the material creation was rather negative. Feminists such as Grace Jantzen show how the notion of the signifier Phallus moves in Lacan's writings (1982) from being a dominant signifier to being a universal signifier, a modern reconstruction of a male metanarrative. This enables him to reinforce his silencing of women (Jantzen 1998: 51). These dominant values have gone alongside a concern for order and the privileging of order over chaos which has been demonized in such hymns as:

Thou whose Almighty Word
Chaos and Darkness heard
And took their flight.

Here we see the images of order, light and truth inextricably linked in the images presented. Feminist theology has problematized such thinking (Ward and Wild 1995b) following in the steps of postmodern and postcolonial theorists who see such thinking as linked with all great colonial enterprises. Liberation theologians have also been taken up with the process of inculturation or interculturation that Christianity must necessarily go through which is not aided by a single view of the nature of the Gospel:

> Bosch [1991] realizes that Western Christianity has domesticated the gospel in its own culture. This resulted in the gospel becoming foreign to every other culture and assumed that the Western Gospel was a fully indigenized, universalized, and completed product (Kim 2002: 31).

The advent of theologians from postcolonial countries has opened the idea of theological truths being multiple and needing to be reworked in various different cultures. The expansion of symbols for God/Goddess has led to the discovery of new metanarratives of the sacred that are characterized by ambiguity, flux and plurality.

Grace Jantzen (1998) draws on Daly's work on 'God the Verb' (Jantzen 1998: 257). She does not go as far as Daly in rejecting God Talk altogether or moving towards Goddess the Verb, (Daly 1984) but this possibility opens up a whole new range of possibilities for envisaging the Divine, which we shall explore in the next chapter.

Marcella Althaus-Reid in her book *Indecent Theology* (2000) deconstructs the Divine from the perspective of 'the crossroads of Liberation Theology and Queer Thinking' (Althaus-Reid 2000: 2) contextualized in Latin America, particularly Argentina. She is primarily concerned with the complicity of theology in the construction of 'otherness' and how this regulates the borders of ecclesiological, theological, political and amatory structures in Latin America. She draws her imagery from carnivals, especially such figures as transvestites and drag queens. From this position she is able to offer alternative divine images or per/versions. One of these is the Bi/Christ, who 'helps to problematize the 'either/or of monopolistic economic and affective relationships.' She sees these as potential alternatives to the binaries of Western culture, welcoming their ambiguity:

> Bi/Christology walks *like a nomad* in lands of opposition and exclusive identities, and does not pitch its tent forever in the same place (Althaus-Reid 2000: 119 [italics mine]).

She too arrives at 'process' models of the Divine, drawing on John's Gospel, where the Divine is described as 'dwelling among us as a tabernacle' (Jn 1.14):

> The beauty of this God/tent symbolic is that it can help us discover Christ in our process of growth, the eventual transformations through unstable categories to be, more than anything else, a Christ of surprises (Althaus-Reid 2000: 120).

As can be seen from this brief overview of a little of the literature breaking open older imagery and re-establishing new images, there is an abundance of life-affirming images that can be drawn on to give a very plural view of the nature of God.

Postcolonial liberation theologians (Kwok 2002b) argue for the acceptance of the multiple identities of women. This leads her to the nature of the self as 'fluid'. She sees this particularly in Asian Americans whose sense of identity is 'multiple, transversal and hybridized.' This opens up the way to a challenge to the Cartesian fixed view of self and identity, which is intricately bound up with the plural nature of the Divine. Many feminist theologians now are critiquing the Enlightenment paradigm of a single self or subject which we saw in the philosophers whose work was outlined in Chapter One. Grace Ji-Sun Kim takes her starting point from the biblical notion of pilgrimage:

> A praxis for justice and reconciliation as an essential dimension of the sacred pilgrimage to which we have been called. [Lee 1987: 96]. Like Abraham we too are in the wilderness, and our wilderness is called *marginality* (Kim 2002: 6).

The goddess thealogian, Naomi Goldenberg, also argues for multiple identities from the point of view of the encouragement of non-violent ways of relating:

> The world needs more people who can feel several loyalties, several affinities, several identities (Goldenberg 1990: 64–67).

Here it is important to remember the differentiation set out at the opening of the chapter between de-integration and disintegration. Although the concept of fluidity in the self allows for this process of deintegration it does not mean the identity does not and cannot exist. The process of disintegration that many women experience at the hands of a patriarchal culture can be differentiated from a process of deintegration lived through in an atmosphere of relationality and seen to be connected with the processes of deintegration that characterize the cycles of the earth. This process, entered into a climate of relationality, can truly be linked with a life-giving process of re-membering oneself. This can be particularly true during the process involved in the loss of a loved one. Carol Christ's work exploring feminist spirituality describes a process running through – Nothingness – Awakening – Insight – New Naming (Christ 1980). These processes are aided by storytelling and mythology (as we saw in Chapter One) as for example, Brigitta Loewe's thesis, *Storytelling – An Act of Liberation* (2003). Although there appears to be something of a steady progress towards integration here, when she describes it, it is more like a spiralling movement that expects no destination in unity.[13] So we can see that there is considerable stress laid on diversity in notions of the Divine and the construction of the self in theologians from a variety of traditions (Mantin 2002). Christopher Duraisingh shows how the flow between can be established:

> What [is needed] is not a liberal co-existence of plurality nor an innocuous pseudoequality of viewpoints...but rather, in letting the plurality of the voices speak, [to address] creatively the deep structural issues of social life in solidarity and, in the midst of the brokenness of relationships [to point] to possibility of liberated and liberating life for all (Duraisingh 2001: 353).

The result will be an inclusive Gospel.

The distinctiveness of the Christian message for the Masai was its inclusiveness:

> This young lady's difficulty lay in extending the obligation of love not to me and my white faced tribe, or to the brown-faced Indian traders, or to people of hostile, alien tribes surrounding her own. Her difficulty lay within her own tribe, towards people of another clan who lived three miles down the road...that was the chasm impossible to cross. That was the testing point of Christianity (Donovan 1982: 48).

So, theology has challenged the violence in a unity unconnected with diversity both within the Divine and the human and has offered a variety of solutions to the dilemma of negotiating between the two polarities.

---

13. In her *Odyssey with the Goddess* she described it as a 'serpentine path' which 'does not ever come to a point', laying stress on the journey (Christ 1995: 163).

Case Study One: Renegotiating Creativity

I have written elsewhere on how music can play a significant part in the bringing together of unity and diversity (Boyce-Tillman 2000b, 2001b).[14] Janet Wootton identifies the struggle in the process of hymn writing:

> Because if you do send it back to yourself again and again, as I send [hymns] back to writers who write and send things in, and say, "This isn't *yet* – you haven't quite got it *yet*. Go into battle again with the idea and struggle again." And I don't think – the other difficult thing about a hymn is saying, "Right, now it's finished," because there's always the temptation to go back and *just get that last bit right*, so that eventually the struggle has to end and you have to say, "Well, now that is the hymn," and then there's the immense pleasure of hearing people sing it and hearing the words come to life. And the enormous pleasure of working with composers who are obviously undergoing a similar creative struggle, and when a composer writes something which is perfect for the words you've written, then – then it's hugely satisfying[15] (Wootton 2003).

This struggle can be seen an act of re-shaping the personality. The artist/composer descends into his or her personal underworld or unconscious to refashion the elements in it. The ability to enter that chaos, with tools for handling it, would seem to be what differentiates the experienced composer from the less experienced musician.

> What we need is to fumble around in the darkness because that's where our lives (not necessarily all the time, but at least some of the time, and particularly when life gets problematical for us) take place; in the darkness, or, as they say in Christianity "the dark night of the soul". It is in these situations that Art must act and then it won't be judged Art but will be useful to our lives (Cage 1978 quoted in Malcolm Ross 1978: 10).

---

14. I have explored this in Harvey 2001 where I examine music as a transformative process like a religious ritual such as the Eucharist or a shamanic rite. It is evidenced in such phenomena as Smetana's (1824-1884) second quartet which transforms his experience of tertiary syphilis into a piece of great beauty. It is from such phenomena that the subtitle of my book on musical healing is *The Wounds that Sing (2000a)*. Also the practice of music therapy has developed ritual like elements within this practice (Agrotou 1993).

15. Interview at Union Chapel 2003.

If we look at the accounts of musicians of their creative processes we see notions of confusion, madness and dreaming:

> I forget everything and behave like a madman. Everything within me starts pulsing and quivering; hardly have I begun the sketch when one thought follows another (Tchaikovsky 1878 in Vernon 1970: 58).

Researchers like Professor Tony Kemp see the act of composition springing from a 'personal need to create order and wholeness.' (Kemp 1996: 216). Most musical forms allow for a degree of repetition and contrast. This is a reflection of the flow between unity and diversity. Music allows for juxtaposition and simultaneous combination of ideas; it therefore can accommodate difference and differing degrees of unity. It allows for things to stay separate or to be recombined into new ideas. Some composers have left us some records of this process, like Beethoven and his sketchbooks. The process is one of moving from deintegration to reintegration. Perhaps we see it most obviously in the slow movement of the fourth piano concerto with its powerful orchestral passages answered by the softer more vulnerable passages from the piano. Here we see Beethoven bringing together two very different aspects of himself. It was written at the same time as the Heiligenstadt Testament. In this letter he wrote about his realization that he is going deaf and how nothing can stop the process and about his anger against God for taking away from him the one sense he really needed. The music provides some resolution by bringing the aspects musical relationship. It can also provide a similar journey for the listeners (Boyce-Tillman 2000a).

There is much literature supporting the claim that there is no creativity without a descent into chaos – nothing originally creative came out of total order. Psychiatry – handmaid of the dominant culture – does not handle creative people well. The increasing diagnosis of bi-polar disorder and its treatment via powerful medications that 'even-out' the emotional state of the client may well be blocking the most creative people in Western society.[16] Helping them to manage periods of disorder – disunity, apparent fragmentation – may enable them to fulfill their creative potential. So, the creative process is, in itself, a flow between the two polarities.

---

16. The marginalization of the arts therapies in favour of the therapies using medication reinforces this trend.

Case Study Two: Renegotiating Self

In their position as subjugated knowers, women increasingly have to renegotiate self. It would seem that women have always had multiple identities. In my performance *Juggling* I present the notion that we are not a single self but that the self is multiple and consists of performances which are learned, following theorists like Judith Butler (1990) and Rosi Braidotti (1994). It presents multiple identities which interact with one another. Each of these has a visual symbol in the show which is associated with a catch phrase. Each of the audience is given a symbol with one of these on it. When this symbol is held up, the person is asked to say the catch phrase and at the end these visual symbols are attached to a large cape in which I circle demonstrating the variety of roles I have played. The performance uses story, song and mime. It has had a powerful effect when performed to a variety of groups. One woman who had to say the pupil's phrase: 'I'm a good girl' said that as she said it so many times she thought that she had been a good girl all her life and now was going to stop. The housewife says 'wash, sweep, mend, clean'; a counsellor of women who had been abused said that he simply could not say this phrase as it had been said to so many of the women that he counselled.

In a paper appropriately entitled 'The "Hellish" Task of Negotiating Multiple Identities: The Case of a Christian/ Mother/ Wife/ Teacher' (2005) Anna Halsall, Jayne Osgood and Marie-Pierre Moreau in a project arising from a European Social Fund Project at the Institute for Policy Studies in Education, London Metropolitan University, examine the case study of Rebecca which highlights how she has negotiated in a conservative context the areas of vocationalism and deference:

> The analysis arises from an ESF funded project conducted with approximately 75 women teachers in 15 case study schools throughout England, including both Roman Catholic and Church of England denominational schools. Using a feminist lens the authors seek to explore the complex relationship between gender, work and faith in the context of both church and educational equal opportunity discourse, to highlight possible issues faced by women teachers in denominational schools. Broadly this study highlights the difficulties faced by women teachers with relation to career progression and the impermeable structural inequalities that continue to exist. This paper highlights additional and often complex tensions that some religious women encounter within this context.

Rebecca, a well educated wife of a missionary, negotiated many dilemmas. In Africa, while her husband took leading roles in the community, she undertook some teaching in the college, taught English to school students, and for the last four years of their time away taught her own children at home. She undertook supply teaching in the UK to support her husband's ordination training and then gradually worked herself up to the position of Deputy Head. Through the narrative of her career they identify many themes. She holds deeply religious views of a conservative evangelical kind, which colour her view of her husband's career. She holds a 'directive, possibly patriarchal/paternalistic view of God.' And decisions that might be difficult to her are rationalized as God's call.

> But I think that for us, being Christians, the whole thing about praying about something and thinking is this the right path, is this what God wants, that is probably the overriding thing.

Throughout the interview religion and gender interact powerfully, raising issues of 'control and paternalism, which are found within some contradiction, complexity, and struggle within her narrative,' as she negotiates the roles of wife, mother, and career. Her faith presents her with paradoxes that she has to negotiate as 'she both enunciates women's rights in a forceful way, and concurrently articulates a gendered view of women as more passive and self-doubting.' Her description of her own career is dominated by her husband's career. Within her reflections on her own career, Rebecca primarily expresses willingness to 'subvert/sacrifice her career for her husband'. Yet at times she also comes out with moments of 'rebellion' and regret for what might have been:

> If I'd not had children, not married, I might be a Head now.

In the interview there are real signs that she negotiates that polarity of individual and community:

> I accepted when I married him that somebody has to give.

Her frustrations are sometimes apparent; what can be seen is that feminist aspirations are quickly 'corrected' in her narrative (recalling aspects discovered in the Alpha Course mythology in Chapter One). Her chosen domesticity is legitimated through her religious views. It is her faith that enables her to contain her rebellion and make sense of the decisions that she is forced to make.

This links clearly with the self-policing that was drawn attention to in the work of Helen O'Grady above. So carefully had Rebecca internalized the view of her conservative evangelical tradition that the locus of all her power is now outside herself firstly to her husband and those decisions are legitimated by God. Her own sense of vocation characterized her pre-married life:

> I haven't talked about this for years, I suppose I felt that I'd had a privileged, I hadn't had a privileged background, but I felt I was so fortunate that I'd gone to Oxford and that I should do something with my life that was giving something to people who were much less privileged.

Tensions arise from the fact that she felt she was doing the job of Deputy Head before she actually got the job. She doubts if a man would have behaved like that but this is quickly converted into the view that she is grateful for the opportunity. Here we see how self-policing helps to rationalize feelings of injustice. The writers conclude:

> Rebecca's multiple identities and positions entail a polyvalence of discourse (Foucault 1990: 95) that is strongly evident in her narrative here. As emphasized by Foucault (1990), this can give rise to resistance and 'counter-discourse', which are also both evident in Rebecca's narrative. Her narrative also echoes Foucault's (1991) idea that where there are power relations/domination there is also resistance.

For the purposes of negotiating this polarity Rebecca finds in her religious views a way of negotiating her varied identities without complete collusion with the dominant value systems.

Despite the experience of women, in particular that their identities are multiple, we cling to notions with a strange nostalgia that the self may be one. And we now have a well-developed pathology of multiple personality disorder. But if we examine the most extreme examples of a particular phenomenon, we can also understand the general principles underpinning the lives of the 'normal, a point made by William James in his Gifford Lectures (1903). In a society that clings tightly to a notion of a unified self rather than one that is sometime united and sometimes more fragmented or diverse will have less examples of extreme cases such as exemplified in those diagnosed with multiple personality disorder. A website devoted to ways of managing the disorder offers the following case study:

Rose, by the very nature of her unique experiences and adjustments, provides just such an opportunity. She has much to teach us and we have much to learn. I would add that there is much still to discover, for there are indications that the picture given here is incomplete in some important particulars. The core personality is split into four parts, Happy, Sad, Big and Spooky, which relate closely to each other. The last two possess what, in the context of the strange world they inhabit, can best be described as paranormal abilities.[17]

What is interesting here is that some of the personalities have paranormal abilities, a characteristic not valued by the dominant culture (see Chapter Six), which has played a part in splitting apart the various facets of the self in this case.

In a society where people are increasingly mobile across national boundaries by choice, mischief or mischance, the business of creative negations of a variety of national identities becomes of great importance. Music can play a significant part in holding diversity and unity in creative flow. The ready availability of a variety of musics from many world traditions are a mark of the diversity implicit in the search for identity in the twenty-first century. Music creates identity for the creators and the receivers. Cultural mixes help others to make sense of their own multiple identities. Andrew Blake shows how syncretic forms are developing in Handsworth, Birmingham, such as 'Bhangra' North Indian folk-music driven by the rhythms and technologies of European/American dance music (Blake 1997: 117). Such intercultural mixes legitimize the intercultural knowing that makes up our twenty-first century identity. Many children in our schools have been very successful in the building of bi-cultural identities – speaking a different language and embracing a wholly different culture in the home from that in the school and the wider society. Malcolm Floyd's (Floyd 1999) research on the Masai and Samburu in Kenya, shows that they are having to develop a triple identity:

- As Masai/Samburu.
- As Kenyan, an identity that includes poles they would traditionally have fought.
- Global.

This is often expressed in terms of location. They spend six months in their village and six months working in Western contexts. If they

---

17. http://www.spiritrelease.com/cases/multiplepersonality2.htm, 9 August 2006.

were not developing this multiple identify the Masai/Samburu culture would be wiped out by the expansion of Western culture via globalization.

In a paper entitled 'Negotiating the Identity: Between Romary Creams and Oreos' (2005) Maria Frahm-Arp charts the way African women are renegotiating identity in the new South Africa:

> They explained to me that if you were modern, successful and black, you could either be an 'Oreo' (black on the outside and white on the inside, the classic coconut) or a 'Romary Cream' (a biscuit that is chocolate outside and inside). On the surface both looked the same but their values and relationship to African culture were different (Frahm-Arp 2005: 1).

These women wove together elements of African culture and art with others from Western culture (largely American). So the:

> "Oreos" did sometimes go to Soweto because shebeens (township pubs), "shack chic" and township culture were currently trendy (Frahm-Arp 2005).

She found the 'Romary Creams' at Grace Bible Church where the membership and leaders were all black:

> While there were several "Oreos" the culture was one of "Romary Creams". These "Romary Creams" looked very much like "Oreos", they too were well dressed in the latest fashions, had been to predominantly white schools and spoke English well and African languages poorly. They were also successful in the commercial world, drove expensive cars and lived or aspired to live in the suburbs; but their attitude and values were different. As Venon explained, "It's about remembering where you come from...My wealth is not just for me alone." While they rejected ancestor veneration they supported the idea of the community and the extended family. People were encouraged to uphold lobola, attend weddings, funerals and other family gatherings. They want to sanitize their own involvement with African culture but not discard it (Frahm-Arp 2005).

They found that women did move between the categories. They might be an 'Oreo' in their teens and twenties but become more like a 'Romary Cream' in their thirties. The paper illustrates two strategies for reaching:

> a de-mythologized form of African culture that could be proudly South African and could be upheld in the global market and each of these constructs was contributing something to the emerging South African identity (Frahm-Arp 2005).

She saw how the Pentecostal-Charismatic churches had helped women in these negotiations as good education and movement from the shacks and shanties of Soweto became possible for them. They chose various strategies and the churches helped them to gain social and cultural capital as well as maintain family structures. They also boosted their confidence and gave them a sense of purpose.

Case Study Three: Renegotiating Liturgy

There has been a strong sense in the designing of liturgies that they must be 'all of piece' which often means a similar style of music, in one language, with a unified theology. As our communities become more diverse and more people within them are negotiating diversity within themselves, there is a strong case for rethinking these concepts. Often a single parish church faced with the dilemma of accommodating the tastes of a diverse congregation, manages it by means of a variety of services at different times each using a single style. This may avoid the real issue of the incarnation of Christ in a diverse world. Liturgy is a corporate incarnation of Christ's body – it is the manifestation of the Church as incarnation.

God has often been (and still is) incarnated by Anglicanism in liturgy as a Victorian gentleman and this aspect of Church history is often illustrated in our hymnody. A wonderful example problematizing the practice of sending old hymn books to the 'Mission field' in the mid-twentieth century was found in Central Africa by the Director of the Royal School of Church Music:

> In meadow and field the cattle are good
> And the rabbits are thinking no evil.
> The anemones white are refined and polite
> And all the primroses are civil.
>
> Oh, once in a while we obey with a smile
> And are ever so modest and prudent,
> But it's not very long before something is wrong
> And somebody's done what he shouldn't.

(J. G. Crum original edition of Hymns Ancient and Modern)

Cathedral Evensongs in many places keep the 1662 prayer book alive and intact – nothing can be changed. In a cathedral evensong I wanted the University choir to sing a setting of an inclusive language Magnificat and Nunc Dimittis by a graduate student. A chapter meeting decided that only the 1662 texts could be used, even though this one was from the New Zealand Prayer Book. As the student herself was going to conduct her own piece in this context and I was sure that this was in line with incarnating Christ, we did sing at least the Magnificat, re-titled *A Song of Praise*, as the anthem, where there is no canonical text. It was a good example of negotiation with and resistance to the dominant culture.

However, we are now exploring services attempting to embrace a notion of Christ's incarnation in a multi-cultural, multi-style service. The inauguration of the Right Revd John Sentamu was one such event in November 2005. The variety of elements used included:

- The tradition with Judaism: the hymn: *The God of Abraham Praise.*
- The Celtic tradition: the hymn: *Be Thou My Vision, O Lord of My Heart.*
- The Roman tradition: the hymn: *Veni Creator.*
- The evangelical tradition: the hymn: *The Servant King.*
- Women's music making: The Luo Singers and Dancers (Uganda), a Mothers' Union Group from St Matthew's Stratford, East London, sing a Luo Song of Praise.
- The Archbishop's African origins: the hymn: *Siya hamb' ekukhanyen' kwenkhos* and a dance of rejoicing and thanksgiving to God, the Bwola, from Archbishop Janani Luwum's homeland Gulu, Acoli, Uganda was performed.
- The affirmation of servanthood: The Archbishop washed the feet of three children and then placed a cross from El Salvador around the neck of the children who had taken part in the service. The words of Oscar Romero were inscribed on the back of each one of them. 'Peace will flower when love and justice pervade our environment'.
- Liberation Theology: the hymn: *We Shall Go Out with Hope of Resurrection.*

In the same year in the Carol Service of the University of Winchester we attempted a similar diverse elements held together by the structure of the traditional carol service:

- Theatre beyond words: a mime questioning the behaviour in Church but maintaining the notion of faith including music.
- Christmas hymn: *Angels From the Realms of Glory.*
- Ghanaian dance and song with drums including: *O Come Let Us Adore Him.*

- *One Moment in Time:* a secular song used to express religious ideas.
- Dance expressing the doctrine of the incarnation.
- Philippine dance/song partly in Tagalog expressing issues of peace and justice and the call of faith.

Twenty-first century liturgy needs such strategies of resistance to dominant notions of unity twisted into notions of uniformity so that it can express an incarnation theology that includes both unity and diversity in a creative flow. This may be more truly an accurate reflection of the body of Christ and may, incidentally ask diverse congregations to deal effectively with their differences by means of mutual respect.

Summary

This chapter has examined how the polarities of individualism and community and unity and diversity have became separated and twisted into perverted forms of themselves. We have looked at six examples of strategies of resistance that have attempted to bring the polarities into right relationship. It has looked at how reworking the Trinitarian doctrine can contain notions of individualism and community and leads to a new ecclesiology and how this would be reflected in re-examining notions of priesthood. It sees how re-examining ethical issues leads to revisiting notions of normality. It examined a project to reverse the negative effects of self-policing. It has looked at work in the areas of the nature of creativity, reworking views of the self, and reshaping liturgy.

Chapter Four

AN INTEGRATED MANIFESTATION

1. Share the silence, feel the strain,
   Sense God's nurture hold our pain,
   Fire within, we can begin,
   Hoping in our sadness, entertaining gladness

CHORUS

   Following the vision, we will move forward
   Following the vision we won't look back,
   Following the vision we will move forward,
   Our resolve will never slack, never, never slack.

2. Share the anger, feel the pow'r
   Make the Spirit in us flow'r,
   Fire within, we can begin
   Overcoming weakness, questioning our meekness

CHORUS

3. Break the silence, voice the shout,
   Use God's strength to end our doubt
   Fire within, we can begin
   Speaking of our outrage, moving on with courage.

CHORUS

4. Break the bread and lift the cup
   Now God's joy is lifted up
   Fire within, we can begin,
   Celebrating glory in a woman's story.

CHORUS

   (Boyce-Tillman 2006a: 150–51)

Public/Private

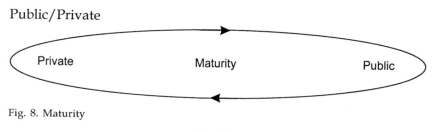

Fig. 8. Maturity

Society

The construction of this domain has had important significance for women's position in Western society. The binary of male=public, female=private (domestic) has been much discussed. The notion of privacy, particularly in relation to the press, is part of the daily discussion in the press itself. The British Royal Family struggle with it, particularly in relation to their children. In Western culture we are now in a situation where certain people (so-called celebrities) are always public (even the most intimate parts of their lives), while certain people are completely private – for example, the homeless, the differently abled, the criminals, to name but a few.

Camila Batmanghelidjh,[1] leader of the powerful and respected drama project, *Kids Company*, in a powerful interview on Desert Island Discs describes the making of a criminal privately for nine years. 'Where was society when they were being created?' She laments the small number that Social Services are able to follow up of the cases reported to them that concern the welfare of children; private abuse ends up in public criminality. Her conversation with politicians reveals a similar discrepancy between the private and the public. Privately, some politicians see prison as an unsatisfactory way of handling young people who commit criminal offences but publicly, she adds, they have not the courage to act against the weight of public opinion. Society is, in her opinion, as responsible for criminality amongst the young as the youngsters are themselves. Her project shows how compassion and love develop internal control for the young people in her project. Her own choice not to bear children is a similar reversal of the public and the private. Her public work is very much associated and concerned with children. Therefore she does not want to have children (even her own) in her private space. This is a reversal of the 'norms' of the Western family and shows a new model of family.

1. Desert Island Discs, BBC Radio 4, 27 October 2006, 9am.

So public and private are often fragmentary and contradictory. Those 'in the public' eye will be valued by means of high salaries; the others may receive nothing. These latter have a hard time getting their experience known at all. They cannot express their thoughts, feelings or indeed the details of the difficulties of their lives. Repressive regimes regularly use methods of surveillance, which make the private public. 'Bugging' was a regular part of Soviet Society. A society that loves publicity inserts cameras onto the most intimate parts of people's lives as the growth of surveillance cameras shows. The nightmare of the Big Brother of Huxley's *Brave New World* is becoming the basis of a well-loved reality television show that some people want to take part in. Television shows now use this film as entertainment. I am reminded of a certain group of aboriginal Australians who considered that to be photographed was to have their soul removed. How many souls have been lost in Western society? So dominant is the value of the public that people seek publicity for its sake without realizing how it might imbalance their lives. So we have a society where in some situations like therapeutic ones, confidentiality is absolute. In situations that are abusive or inappropriately coercive in some way, this becomes twisted into an enforced secrecy and people are deliberately silenced. Free expression is often prized as an important value system of the West, but out of balance with an appropriate privacy, it leads to enforced or indecent exposure.

Groups of subjugated knowers regularly seek alternative public spaces where they can share views and also 'publicize' them. The tight boundaries which the media invent as news worthiness – that it is dramatic, of interest to humans has a human angle – often ignore notions of ethics in the pursuit of audiences. 'Good news,' including ethical action, struggle to become public alongside more dramatic events. So a carol service involving Catholic and Protestant children in Belfast at the height of the troubles in Northern Ireland was not reported as the children were mixed together and there was no disturbance. The Internet has provided an alternative public space and protesters have been inventive about using public spaces – like the American protesters pouring their blood down the side of the Pentagon as a protest against US policy in El Salvador. Women singers have started their own record companies and small presses have been started by minority groups. There is a dilemma here, for many of the feminist presses were taken over by larger publishing houses in the late twentieth century. It was felt by many feminists that the job was done. But in a time of cutbacks, the lists of gender studies are often the first to be cut. So there are dangers when confidentiality – the private sphere – loses touch with expression. Then the private becomes an unhealthy secrecy and public an equally unhealthy exposure.

Self

Within the self there are introvert and extravert tendencies, even if one may appear dominant. A knowledge of when it is appropriate to speak and when to be silent is a sign of maturity. The introvert who fails to keep in touch with his/her extravert self becomes phobic; while the continual extravert can lose all touch with the more hidden part of his/her self. The slogan of feminists in the 1970s was that personal is political and this became a powerful rallying cry linking the private struggles of many women with wider socio-political issues. Books like Susie Orbach's *Fat Is a Feminist Issue* (1990) formed powerful linkages between women's private, often very carefully hidden struggles, and the wider society. The notion of confidentiality has been much developed in therapeutic work in the West. This concept is very foreign to other societies where for example, healing rituals are carried out publicly and the wider community is seen to be both part of the problem and part of the healing of the problem. I have argued elsewhere that music could be particularly useful here because it is 'veiled' medium, it is on the one hand public but also private, because its meaning cannot be easily interpreted[2] (Boyce-Tillman 2000a). There is now a raft of public chat shows making television out of people's desire to self-reveal. The effect of this on individuals can be devastating, for the revelations cannot be taken back and many of the situations would be better dealt with privately. So each personality has both introvert and extrovert tendencies which need to be managed maturely. When the flow is fractured the introversion becomes phobic and the extraversion becomes shallowness.

2. Music is a language by whose means messages are elaborated…Since music is the only language with the contradictory attributes of being at once intelligible and untranslatable, the musical creator is a being comparable to the gods, and music itself the supreme mystery of the science of man. All other branches of knowledge stumble into it, it holds the key to their progress (Levi-Strauss 1970: 18).

Finding a Voice

In many societies, public roles have often, indeed usually, been denied to those embracing subjugated ways of knowing. Throughout the world the hiddenness of women is identified, as in Kim in her writing about Korean women (Kim 2002: 59) and Mary Grey describing the 'hidden women of Rajasthan':

> They have no faces within contemporary culture (Grey 1995/2001: 61).

Patricia Hill Collins draws on theorist, bell hooks, to identify three interrelated components in the process of black women finding a public voice:

- Breaking silence about oppression.
- Developing self-reflexive speech (dialogues between women sharing the same standpoint).
- Confronting or 'talking back' to elite discourses (Hill Collins 1998: 48).

She draws attention to the hidden or private knowledges of subject peoples:

> For oppressed groups, such knowledge typically remains hidden because revealing it weakens its purpose of assisting those groups in dealing with oppression... Ironically, in fulfilling the emotional labor of caring for the whites, males, and/or the affluent these same mammy workers gain access to their private, usually hidden knowledge. Thus access to both public and hidden knowledge on both sides of power positions [enables] African-American women and other groups similarly situated to develop distinctive standpoints on hierarchical power relations (Hill Collins 1998: 49).

In terms of space, she highlights the value of the marginal space following bell hooks' writing about it as potentially dangerous and potentially creative. She sees how the space has been defined by core/periphery relationships and centre/margin metaphors that were generated from unjust, hierarchal power relations (Hill Collins 1998: 127–28).

Various versions of the feminist agenda (Humm 1995) have seen women's entry into the public space differently. Liberal feminism has been part of the mainstream for a long time from the early work of Mary Wollstonecraft [1792] (1975). The roots of women's oppression are here seen as a lack of equal civil rights and educational opportunities. It sees the need for women to be allowed into the public spaces as they are. It works from freedom for sexual strictures in the workplace and fair access to public services. It is about accommodation to the dominant structures. Socialist feminism is more radical, seeing the most oppressive aspects of patriarchy lying in the economic system. It asks for economic reform of the public space of capitalism, so that women are not exploited and have a right to own the means of production. It looks at reforming the public space and to a certain extent certainly the economic aspects of the private space. It encourages economic strategies of resistance. Radical feminism calls for a complete rethinking of the way in which public and private is conceived in terms of gender and class. It argues that the problem lies in the definition of women as 'the inferior sex' on the grounds of gender. It aims at rooting out patriarchy in both private and public spaces, claiming that all forms of oppression are the result of male supremacy. Based on 'the personal is political' it looks towards a 'woman-centred society' and calls on strategies of subversion.

The case of music shows how these ideas have developed in the twentieth century. The notion of music as self-expression became a valid exercise after The Enlightenment. With the growth of the new concept of creativity, human beings gradually acquired the central position formerly occupied by God. The hierarchy that had come to be associated with God (mediated largely through the hierarchical structures of the Church) also broke down and the way was open for the establishment of creativity as a universal attribute. The movements in music in the 1950s, 60s and 70s saw more and more children at least able to make their musical voice heard publicly. This arose from the growing literature democratizing creativity.

This mounted a challenge to whose voices might be heard in the public sphere. An area previously limited to those who could fulfil the performed role of 'genius' could now be opened up to a wider range of people. The fruits of this are now seen in rock bands proliferating and small individually run record labels that artists create for their own works, some of them women. The great stress was on the effect that this would have on people's general well-being. People need to be heard publicly and this process was, by definition, beneficial. The conclusion to be drawn from such writing is that the end of the process of fostering creativity is not to create geniuses but more integrated people. The creativity of the 'ordinary' people is in terms of entry into a process not the production of a product.

However, such notions did not penetrate the classical canon which is now still securely based on the notion of genius and 'masterwork'. But, the rise of community music making and self-made groups of various kinds is starting to denude concert halls of audiences and represent the penetration of this thinking on creativity into the wider society. The world of classical music has had real difficulty in admitting more people to the already-established canon – among them black composers and women. The situation is not a lot better in rock and pop traditions, as writers like Mavis Bayton (1998) have pointed out. The roles women play here are often clearly defined, and although people can point to examples like Madonna, Susie Quattro and the Spice girls, the notion of image is so all pervasive here that it is difficult for people who don't fulfill the stereotypes of society to find any acceptance in the market.

To summarize, Western culture prizes the public highly and devalues the private, which often has no economic value at all. While publicity is sought by many, there is a clear line between those whose lives are almost totally public and those that are completely hidden. To enter the public arena in some artistic way is seen as beneficial and the movement towards democratizing creativity has opened up the public space to more people. Debates about women's positions in both spheres have ranged from those who are happy to enter the public sphere as constructed by patriarchy and those who look for a radical redefinition of both spheres and how the two are balanced in a culture. In music (including liturgical music), women have been very active in private and smaller public spaces (unpaid) but have been less apparent at the top of any musical hierarchy, particularly in the generation of music for worship.

Theology

Thus, during the ages, the church through its "Fathers" and its priests has devoted itself to a discussion of the most trivial questions concerning woman, as well as to the formation of most oppressive canons against her. And although, as shown, she has found an occasional defender and even claimants for her superiority upon certain points, yet such discussions have had no effect upon the general view in which the church has presented her, as one accursed of God and man (Gage 1893/1998: 311).

So wrote Matilda Joslyn Gage in 1893. Elizabeth Schüssler Fiorenza draws such a radical view out in her reading of the Hebrew Wisdom texts:

Her voice is a public, radical democratic voice rather than a 'feminine' privatized one:

> Wisdom calls aloud in the streets,
> She raises her voice in the public squares.
> She calls out at the street corners,
> She delivers her message at the city gates (Prov. 1. 20–1).

> Like a prophet or street teacher, Wisdom is found where the economic, juridical public life of the city takes place (Schüssler Fiorenza, 2001: 77).

Neil Douglas Klotz carries this further (echoing the thoughts of Camila Batmanghelidjh above) in seeing the need for the testing of outer codes by the inner test of one's inner motivation. He draws on the Gospel of Thomas and sees the bringing together of public and private as the standard of holiness:

> Do not lie. And do not do what you hate. For all things are manifest before the face of the Universe. For there is nothing hidden that shall not be revealed and there is nothing covered that shall remain without being uncovered (Saying 6. 1–5; Douglas-Klotz 1999: 58–59).

Grace Jantzen (1995) talks about the attempts to privatize spirituality in the twentieth century as a private, personal, individualized relationship with the divine, critiquing such figures as William James (1903). This fracturing of the relationship between private prayer and public action skews the traditional relationship between mysticism and action for social justice shown throughout history in figures like Hildegard of Bingen. She links this with the Churches' attempts to silence women and make the personal private rather than political (see Chapter Six).

Debates in this area have often centred on the public authority of women, with such issues as women priests (as seen in the opening song which was written for the Catholic Women's Ordination conference in Montreal). Support for the case is increasingly coming from scholarship about the practices of the early church (Torjesen 1990). This was started by Schüssler Fiorenza in her influential text, *In Memory of Her:*

> The marginalization of women is not to be understood as an authentic presentation of historical reality but rather as ideological construction

reflecting early Christian patriarchalism which defeated "more egalitarian" tendencies. With this understanding in mind, Schüssler Fiorenza maintains that the few early Christian texts which show that the early Christian movement was inclusive of women's active and equal participation in this life, even in leadership, do not speak about rare exceptions to the rule but rather hint at much wider female activity. Based on these observations, she delineates a new reconstruction of Christian origins, where a special emphasis is laid on women's contributions, on the one hand, and in their suppression by patriarchal views and structures, on the other (Marjanen 1996: 6).

Antti Marjanen, drawing the material from the Nag Hammadi Library including *The Gospel of Mary*, sees an early struggle about authority among the disciples:

> Mary Magdalene.... assumes a leading role among the disciples as a receiver, an interpreter and a transmitter of the teachings of the Risen Jesus...A conspicuous tension prevails between Mary Magdalene and the male disciples of Jesus. Peter in particular experiences her as a rival who threatens his and other disciples' authority (Marjanen 1996: 4).

She goes on to describe the process that made the current New Testament as canonical texts and the marginalization of texts some of which were authored by women.

And yet resistance in the churches to women's ministry has been considerable and women have achieved ministerial authority in many traditions relatively late:

- 1950s acceptance of women ministers in white US Methodism (although the black churches had women ministers earlier).
- 1976 Acceptance of the American Episcopal Church of women's ordination.
- 1992 Vote for women's ordination in the UK Anglican Church (by two votes).

At the time of writing, the Anglican Church in the UK has women priests but no bishops and the Roman Catholic Church will not admit women to the priesthood. A similar pattern has been followed in religious music although this has seldom been a subject of debate for theologians. Indeed, faced with a hostile reception by journalists in a debate about women priests, before they were allowed to be ordained in England, I raised the subject of musical leadership and participation. I received the following comment:

> 'You are not going to take away our choirboys as well, are you?'

In Anglican cathedrals there is, at the time of writing, no female organist in charge and very few assistant organists. In many circles, the boys' choir is still held to be superior to those who have girls' choirs.

Debates about women's authority whether it concerns priesthood or musical leadership reveal a variety of opinions in these groups. In terms of priesthood, some would want to abandon the notion of ordained priesthood altogether in favour of a priesthood of all believers model as seen in Chapter Three. Certainly, even when women priests are present, the model of women's liturgies is one of shared authority, consecration of the elements by the group, for example. The symbols of bread and wine are often avoided in favour of food like hazelnuts, apples, or honey to avoid a clash with public liturgical practice.

The wider debate is concerned with the reception of feminist theological thinking in general by the established 'public' authorities; the story of this is not very encouraging. Roman Catholic theologians have lost positions in theological teaching institutions for their position on liberation theology and attitudes contrary to the Papal opposition on abortion and birth control set out in Humanae Vitae.

The result is that many of the debates have gone on privately and covertly and only when a critical mass of support for the ideas is gathered will ideas be shared in the public arenas. The Catholic Women's Ordination Movement is one case in point (Wijngaards 2001). Small cell groups of women in various countries have gradually gained strength since Rosemary Radford Ruether's book *Women-Church* (1985). The gathering of Catholic Women's Ordination Worldwide organization in Dublin in 2000 was a huge example of 'going public' and caused the leaders of the movement to enter into often confrontational dialogue with the Rome authorities. The expansion of the World Wide Web has given immense scope also for the publicizing of such ideas and the building up of webs of support more cross-culturally than ever before. Women have been illicitly or illegally ordained in central Europe and America into the Roman Catholic Church and Elizabeth Stuart has been consecrated as Bishop in the Liberal Catholic Church.

There has, however, been a considerable growth in private meetings of women for worship in many countries especially Roman Catholic women. Diann L. Neu writing of ecofeminist liturgy (and

many of these groups would locate themselves in this position)
describes the following principles. Ecofeminist liturgies:

- Value women's bodies and nature as holy vehicles of divine
  revelation, and honor women and nature in all their diversity
  as imaging the divine and as enjoying divine activity.
- Use symbols and stories, images and words, gestures and
  dances, along with a variety of art forms that reflect the
  interconnectedness of creation.
- Use music that identifies with the earth community.
- Are celebrated in environments that reflect the sacredness of
  the earth.
- Image the Divine as the source of life that sustains all creation.
- Motivate participants to sustain a balanced and diverse earth
  community, to resist its oppressors, and to lament the violence
  and abuse that has been done to it (Neu 2002: 23–9).

Many of these gatherings show a concern to make visible lost
women from the Christian tradition.[3] Janet Wootton describes this
as the origin of her inspiration as a hymn writer:

> It can come from reading the Bible. A Bible story – I've written a hymn
> about Leah, for example, and that just comes from looking at somebody
> – *Here's someone who there isn't much written about.* I want more hymns
> to be written about people – about their stories in the Bible. That's
> another characteristic, perhaps not of music but of the writing words
> that women write, is that it's important to tell the stories…And that
> those stories are accessible to people – worshipping congregations –
> when they won't come across them through the lectionary
> readings…you have to develop the tradition and, therefore, to write –
> to use that tradition to tell new stories, or to tell old stories that haven't
> been told (Wootton 2003).[4]

These groups are important staging points between the public
and the private and their existence has been alternately accepted
and rejected by authorities. The story of the Hildegard Community
in Texas and the Brevard Episcopal Mission in North Carolina has
been chequered in relation to the Church authorities. The story is
often one of initial acceptance for those groups set up within a
particular church structure, which then appears to be reneged on

---

3. Susan Ashbrook Harvey writes about hymns in early Syriac Orthodox tradition,
which put words into the mouths of women who are silent in the biblical texts (Harvey
2000, 2001).

4. Interview at Union Chapel, 2003.

by the initially supportive authorities. The debate is often about critical mass. While the groups remain private and small there is acceptance when they become more public the confrontations with the authorities on such issues as sexuality, women's authority in Eucharistic rites and inclusive language start. Public challenges to the prevailing order can also provoke these and some groups took deliberate decisions to remain private and not engage in this way. The St Hilda community in London for example, received negative attention from the church authorities when they allowed a woman priest to celebrate the Eucharist before this has been officially sanctioned by the Anglican Church.

These groups also sometimes have a limited lifespan, as in the case of Women in Theology in the 1980s and 1990s in the UK. When the ideas have found a wider public acceptance the groups disappear. Schüssler Fiorenza (2001: 80) puts these small groups into a wider context of the creation of participatory democracy. This is certainly my experience as a regular participant in women's liturgies taking place in general in domestic or private spaces since the 1980s. They have been bridges between the private divine discontent and the more public expressions of these ideas[5] and represent an important part of the flow between public and private.

Case Studies

Case Study One – Women's Church Roles

The association of women with the private and men with the public has had a distinct effect on women's religious involvement. In *Bloody Women and Bloody Spaces* (2003), Joan Branham links this with heteropatriarchy's fear of the menstruating woman. Feminist theorists highlight the need for understanding the diversity and complexity of women's roles. Mitchell has suggested that there were four structures influencing the nature of women's social formation: production, reproduction, sex, and the socialization of children; and her conclusion was singular:

---

5. We will see in Chapter Five the dilemmas posed for example, by the use of inclusive language in the regular public worship of the Church. In such private groups it would be accepted practice.

The lesson of these reflections is that the liberation of women can only be achieved if *all four* structures in which they are integrated are transformed. A modification of any one of them can be offset by a reinforcement of another, so that mere permutation of the form of exploitation is achieved... A revolutionary movement must base its analysis on the uneven development of each, and attack the weakest link in the combination. This may then become the point of departure for a general transformation (Mitchell 1984: 43, 45; author's italics).

This illustrates clearly some of the strands in feminism which illustrate a variety of relationships with the dominant capitalist culture. Whereas radical feminism and liberal feminism have recommended working within the dominant culture and have concentrated on power and equality in the area of production, socialist feminism sees the need for a reworking of society to enable this freedom and equality. Such a reworking would require not only a rethinking of women in the area of production but also the other three areas – reproduction, sex and the socialization of children. Here feminists have found classic Marxism wanting (Bunyard 2005: 293).

As women have found their way into the area of production and into the economic sphere previously monopolized by men, women's relation to religion is also changing. (Richter and Francis 2005). Theories of women's greater religiosity in the past have focused on the 'structural location' of women primarily in the domestic sphere – the private and in lower levels in employment (Kay and Francis, (1996: 11–13). This analysis concentrates on men's economic role (Hobson 2002). Women with their families are located in the (subjugated) sphere of the family with a prime responsibility for the socialization of children, which includes moral training. Greeley (1992) confirmed this in his survey of the 1991 British Social Attitudes survey, which found that 'women's devoutness and religiosity are more like those of men . . . *before* they acquire a spouse and children.' So, the responsibility of caring (as we saw in Chapter Three) encourages a religious attitude (Greeley 1992: 62). With women less represented in the production/economic sphere it was also argued that women are likely to be less secularized than men, because they participate less in the modern secular world. A corollary of this is that the private sphere is less social than the public, with the workplace providing a greater opportunity for social contact than the home. In response to this women turn to the Church as a form of community and a place of social support.[6]

It is interesting to reflect here that women often initiated and ran a number of church organizations that were primarily social in their function like sewing circles, Mother's Union, playgroups and so on. They did, of course, have more disposable time to dedicate to this (Kay and Francis 1996: 11–13). However, to return to Mitchell's analysis of the complexity of women's roles, as women play a greater part in the area of production – the economic sphere – many of their reasons for religious engagement will be removed. They will have less time and will become more secularized. The responsibility for the socialization of children will be handed to other organizations – most of them secular such as child-minders, nurseries or older family members. It is interesting to note in one South London congregation how it is the grandmothers that are often bringing the younger children to Church. As life becomes more complex for women it is likely that their relationship with religious institutions will change. They are in the process of renegotiating their religious roles. The availability of ordination to the priesthood or the ministry in some denominations will also mean that the positions they hold within the organization are renegotiated and when they take a role of greater authority in the liturgy, they will be less visible in the traditional women's groups.

So women have been in the process of renegotiating their traditional place in their Church as their place in more public positions in the secularized world changes. As their place in the area of production changes, their relationship to reproduction and the socialization of children is renegotiated and this affects their participation in religion. As they can take a more public part in worship, their more private roles in Church structures also change.

6. It is interesting to reflect that the technologizing of domestic tasks and the establishing of the Protestant nuclear family destroyed traditional women's communities associated with communal washing places, carrying water, communal cooking and so on, while leaving the men's social contact in the work place untouched. Women's communities were therefore, broken up and women experienced a greater degree of isolation than men. This is still often true of a woman's experience after the birth of their first child. The absence of a social grouping and the assumption that a small baby can provide all the socialization that a woman needs has played a considerable part in the phenomenon of post-natal depression.

Case Study Two – Renegotiating Women's Clothing

> The Countess Godiva, who was a great lover of God's mother, longing
> to free the town of Coventry from the oppression of a heavy toll, often
> with urgent prayers besought her husband that, from regard to Jesus
> Christ and his mother, he would free the town from that service and
> from all other heavy burdens (Roger of Wendover quoted in Ellsberg
> 2006).

The upshot of this is that an eleventh century countess makes the
private public by stripping off her garments, letting loose her hair
and riding through the streets of Coventry. By turning convention
on its head she gets justice for the common people. But women
have been very much subjugated knowers in the area of which parts
of their body can be made public and which remain private. Visiting
countries like Italy in the 1960s meant for women, the carrying of a
large scarf to cover whatever parts of their anatomy the cathedral
authorities required covered. What is appropriate has been much
more proscribed by the dominant culture for women than for men.

Women's dress and fashion have often been analysed in terms
of their symbolic nature and representation (Roach and Eicher 1965)
or their communicative function (Davis 1992). Social psychology
has provided some further suggestions in terms of situated bodily
practice, with a simultaneous understanding of the body as socially
constructed (Entwistle 2000: 11). There has been much discussion
recently in the UK of the Islamic veiling of women. It is interesting
to reflect that there is far less discussion of the ways in which men
cover their own bodies and it excites far less fervour than women's
clothing. Women's dress and hair styling has for a long time and in
many cultures signified her status within that culture. Hair up means
married, hair loose and down means available–whether unmarried
or a prostitute. I remember how in the 1960s with the advent of the
mini skirt, girls' schools got girls to kneel and measured the distance
of the hem of the skirt from the floor. There are male uniforms
associated with religion – liturgical dress and monks' habits – but
never have there been the disputes and controversies around these
that have surrounded women's clothing. This concerns most
powerfully how much and which parts of a woman's body can be
public and which should be private. As women in the West appear
to have a privatized choice about how much of their bodies are
public and how much private, the West appears to transfer its
interest in this area to Islam. So it can set up its own identity by

means of identifying the hijab as a deviant 'other'. The hijab becomes an object of strange attraction with qualities of beguilement. Indeed, a male friend of mine remarked recently that he found veiled women, more seductive as relics of an ancient and authentic piety associated with an exotic civilization-a real exoticized other. Scholars argue about where veiling sits in *Qur'anic* injunctions. While the male colonialists of the nineteenth century oppressed their women at home, they liberated women from the perceived oppression of the veil in the lands that they colonized and so set them on the road to 'progress' in line with the Darwinian myth we saw in Chapter One. But it can also be seen as an act of appropriation, indeed of sexual conquest – an assimilation of the Other into the culture of the Same.

Maha Azzam suggests several reasons why women veil. They fall into several categories:

- Religious.
- Cultural (counter Western).
- Sexual.
- Economic [avoiding fashion trends] (Azzam 1996: 225–26).

Other theorists have added a political dimension (Smith 1984: 98) as it also provided a cover for smuggling weapons and other materials in struggles like the Algerian War of Independence (Lazreg 1994: 135).

Alia Imtoual (2005) sees the experience of Muslim women in Australia as different from their counterparts in the UK, showing how the personal and societal interact. She defines discrimination as the *active* disadvantage experienced by *individuals* on the basis of one or more of their markers of identity and taking the form of such behaviours as:

- the refusal of employment,
- failure to provide equal pay for equal work,
- the prevention of individuals from performing religious or cultural duties, devotions, ceremonies, or worship,
- the refusal to provide adequate housing or medical care to these individuals.

She sees discrimination as being an individual act which frees the wider society from responsibility and that regardless of whether racism is intentional it is still harmful; she argues that understandings have ignored the effects of racist attitudes. She draws on interviews conducted with young Muslim women in South Australia about hostility and violence. Despite the fact that the number of women who wear full face covering would be far less than one per cent, one woman told her story of being asked by the media who were filming her to replace her coloured hijab with black face covering so that only her eyes were visible; she was told that this was because people wanted to see poor oppressed Muslim women not happy and smiling ones, which are not sensational. The way in which public and private interact in the media here is very clear.

Public sites like airports were seen as 'sites of emotional and psychological trauma and vulnerability' because of Australian legislation and guidelines. There are narratives of petty harassment and hostile treatment. Even innocent belongings were misconstrued as threats. In the area of employment women talked of problems with hijab and were unlikely to lodge complaints about their treatment. Another woman delayed wearing the hijab because of the narrow mindedness of the world of business and accounting. It caused her considerable distress that she could not fulfil the obligations of her religion. She is therefore suspicious of initiatives based on cultural initiatives to overcome fear which put the onus on the Muslims rather than the perpetrators of the fear.

It is interesting to compare the Islamic veil with the religious habit of Western society which in most European cultures is accepted and respected. Marta Trzebiatowska, in her paper 'Habit Does Not a Nun Make? Religious Dress in the Everyday Lives of Polish Catholic Nuns', compares the situation in the UK with Poland where the nun's habit is still ubiquitous after Vatican II (1962–5) and by a series of interviews examines the role of the habit in establishing an identity for Polish religious. It concerns the public meaning of private choices. This is a very helpful framework, for in the paper she looks at identity in the area of the nuns' self-image, the place of the habit in social interaction and then on actor-network theory and its understanding of society as heterogeneous networks (Law 1992).

All the communities she examined were apostolic carrying out practical work, very often of a charitable nature. Symbolically the habit represented the sacred and divine, signifying a relationship to God as a 'marital' status:

> It implies that they possess a stock of knowledge on the topic of the divine which may or may not be verbally articulated depending on the personal abilities of a given individual (Trzebiatowska 2005).

She identifies how the meanings can be read differently, sometimes as deserving of privilege and sometimes of abuse because of the perceived abuse of the Roman Catholic Church (and we can add to this the use of the habit in cross-dressing parties). She found that the sisters wanted to be noticed as people like other women rather than merely their habit. They found that the public did consult them on spiritual matters. Younger sisters found this particularly daunting and appeared to be surprised that despite their youth and consequent inexperience, the public still trusted them. They also function as a check on morality. The habit also legitimated certain gestures and actions like making the sign of the cross and praying the rosary – actions that they might otherwise have felt uncomfortable to perform in public. She sees power in the habit which becomes 'an *actant* in its own right.' The habit possesses agency.

The comparison between 'habit' and 'habitless' religious orders further illuminates 'the contingent relationship between a woman's sacred status and her attire.' Both groups claim that their position facilitates their religious vocation. Sometimes the arguments for a habit are practical and it is seen as a liberation from bodily self-censorship. Here the public and private interact powerfully. The habitless communities may have more individuality and diversity but run the risk of being designated too flamboyant or provocative.

> Guidelines for habitless orders recommend that the clothes be modest, ordinary and feminine. In practice, this may often translate into loose jumpers and skirts in neutral colours. One of the crucial points of the religious mission of habitless orders commends not drawing attention to oneself and blending into the lay crowd...It could perhaps be described as a deliberate lack of individual style. Habit sisters, on the other hand, resemble each other in their attire to the point that any external expression of individuality becomes virtually unattainable. Sister Samuela summed up the uniform identity of the whole order in one sentence: 'Here, we all look the same- we become one because of our habits. People can't tell us apart!' (Trzebiatowska 2005).

This links with claims for fashion that it simultaneously pushes individuals towards conformity with and differentiation from others. But their reflexive project is orientated to the soul rather than the body. The uniform frees them from the dilemma of choice in the area of the body.

> It could be argued that for habitless communities, it is the 'unity without uniformity' which is at the heart of their identity...Habitless nuns retain more scope for individuality and distinction, however risky their judgment of what is appropriate may be. Here, freedom of choice may pose a problem – in the case of habit nuns the decision is made for them (Trzebiatowska 2005).

She sees all the nuns as rejecting societal notions of femininity and the necessity for feminine masks to gain approval and acceptance. In Judeo-Christian traditions female bodies have been seen having the power of sexual temptation which means that there are 'hegemonic discourses of modesty and respectability' (Tseelson 1997). However, as celibate religious they necessarily challenge the concept of femininity as involving an appeal to men. Their ideal is somewhere between the 'masculine' and the 'provocatively feminine':

> Moreover, despite their stated unwillingness to attract attention, for some nuns the habit meant that they were complimented by men in the street, often for the first time in their lives. Popular discourse on nuns construes them largely as asexual non-women, yet at the same time their visibly stated sacred status strengthens their femininity in the eyes of other people.

This links to the beguiling nature of the Islamic hijab. So here we have three examples of how various groups of women negotiate the public and the private in terms of dress.

Summary

So women are renegotiating their roles in relation to the public/private spaces. Often this is a question of authority and concerned with priesthood and roles in leadership. This has resulted in a decline in their participation in traditional church roles. Women's clothing often has a religious connotation. It is often concerned with public and private areas of the body. How this is managed is often in the control of the dominant culture and men in positions of authority. Male clothing has not been controlled in the same way but women have used a variety of strategies for negotiating this polarity including the roles they take in Church and the way they dress.

Product/process

> CHORUS And we'll all go a-godding
> To bring the world to birth.

1. New life is calling;
   Help set it free.
   And we'll all go a-godding
   With a song of liberty.

CHORUS

2. Hunger is calling,
   Find food to share;
   And we'll all go a-godding
   To give out abundant care.

CHORUS

3. Hopelessness calling
   Lonely and drear;
   And we'll all go a-godding
   In warm friendship drawing near.

CHORUS

4. Warfare is calling.
   When will it cease?
   And we'll all go a-godding,
   In our arms, the flowers of peace.

CHORUS

5. Justice is calling
   Scales in her hand;
   And we'll all go a-godding,
   In her strength we'll take a stand.

CHORUS

6. Wisdom is calling;
   Search out her ways;
   And we'll all go a-godding,
   To the ending of our days.

CHORUS

(Boyce-Tillman 2006a: 97)

Fig. 9. Manifestation

Society

The sphere of work will tend to reflect the values of the dominant culture. Capitalism deals only in products. Those who are too old, too young, too ill or not skilled enough to produce products have no value and often little means to support themselves. This value system validates de-humanizing forms of production and the rape of the earth for the materials of production. A silent Charlie Chaplin film shows him working on a production line into which he finally falls and out of which he emerges the same shape as the product he has been making. Factory farming and sweatshop labouring are two examples of the phenomenon. Once this was part of the working life. People knew that at work they were required to turn out particular sorts of things, whether it were the cars of industry or the academic papers and books of academe. Non-production means redundancy. In many areas this means a literate process carried on by means of written words in the form of email communication and reports and documentation of various kinds. Schools and exams are commodified:

> The task of education was to instill truth in young minds through repetition. There was no questioning, just some explanation, elaboration, leaving out of obscure meanings.
>
> This tendency was reinforced as wealth increased. There were more priests and teachers; the ability to pass examinations on the texts became ever more important as the key to power and status; the period of education became ever longer...Mental worlds were, if anything, increasingly closed. Truth was asserted and given sanction by being written down...there was nothing new to be said or thought. The aim was not to lose any accumulated wisdom. The knowledge and thinking of the charismatic founder – Confucius, the Buddha, Jesus, Muhammad – was distributed to his followers who earned a reasonable living interpreting it and passing it on to their pupils (MacFarlane 2005: 141).

The workplace is increasingly literate and the oracy[7] can find no place in it:

> Knowledge has been passed on through most of history by word of mouth. This does not allow much criticism. Nothing is written down, so different versions cannot easily be compared. There is no "external truth" or "way" providing an orthodoxy from which there can be deviations (MacFarlane 2005: 140).

Leisure activities are often much more concerned with process. The culture becomes more orate with conversation – whether over meals or in the pub – playing a significant part. In leisure we rebalance the demands of the work environment. So increasingly sedentary work is balanced by the gym and the treadmill. We don't do in leisure what we do at work.

But leisure time is increasingly eroded for those at work. So we have one group of people for whom work consumes their entire life and one group who have no work at all. So the split opens up between the unemployed and the workaholics. And those in work are increasingly spending their time in the controlling structures of bureaucracy rather than having space for creativity and ingenuity and time and effort are taken up in operating rules and systems:

> The system becomes ever more complicated with more and more rules, rather than leading to openness and transparency (which was the original intention). This leads to a situation where a highly trained specialist (professional bureaucrat) knows how it works. There is, as a result, more space for corruption...there is also a loss of personal incentives...One unexpected effect of over-bureaucratization is the spread of cynicism...Cunning, cheating, deviance and learning the real rules behind the rules are what it is all about, a phenomenon found in all over-centralized bureaucracies (MacFarlane 2005: 178–79).

The division explored above into public private can also be seen as a process/product split. The home (the more private sphere) can be seen as a process space where relationships are continually negotiated usually through the spoken word and we can 'do nothing' legitimately.

7. Following the usage of Ong (1982), the words literacy and oracy refer to processes of communication. The terms literate and orate refer to societies which use either the written word or the spoken word as the prime means of communication.

And yet the commodification is now entering these spheres as well. Human beings are invited to package themselves with branded names and lifestyles that make them a certain sort of product. Image makers are paid to support this process. Advertising offers a range of options in terms of image whether it is terms of dwelling place, domestic gadgetry, sports equipment, plastic surgery or a typology of children. The advertising industry now presents us with sets of products in terms of images that we may or may not like to become.

The devaluing of process has done women no favours. The cyclical nature of a woman's experience rooted in her own bodily processes means that she fits uneasily into the male constructs of the world of product-based work. The Western working structures with their patterns of reward and promotion have meant that women have been forced into bearing children later and later in their lives when the processes are much more difficult. Men too can play little part in the process of bringing up their children because of the paramount demands of production. The advent of women in the workplace required a radical rethinking of the work structures of Western society which enabled the production based workplace to be balanced effectively with the process based domestic sphere. It would lead to:

- More flexible patterns of working including the privileging of job share as an employment strategy.
- Freeing up educational processes to enable child rearing to take place younger.
- The re-establishment of networks of people such as the extended family and kinship groups to enable child rearing to be a communal activity.
- The valuing of part-time working in career advancement.
- The reduction of ageism in employment practices.

Such a process would enable men and women to both 'be' and 'do' effectively. However, leisure with its association with oracy loses contact with work associated with literacy, the rhythm of life is lost. We have now unemployment (permanent leisure) out of touch with workaholicism where there is no leisure at all.

Self

For the self there is ideally a balance between process and product, between freedom and containment, between the vastness of the ideas of the head and the manifestation of them in some material form – the unmanifest needs to become manifest. When being and doing become too split in a life or one gets left out altogether then the system goes out of balance. Christopher Robin returning from his first day at school is asked by Pooh Bear what it was like. His reply is that he thinks he will never be allowed to do nothing ever again. School is an initiation into the doing, the product based world of work. The end of it is burnout when the self finally rebels against the constant demand to produce, and what's more to produce perfection. The idle person has regularly been condemned in the West, which has similarly condemned colonized cultures with a greater degree of 'beingness' in their value systems as wasters and idlers. The controlling clock tower of Western time that controls the factory output was often the first symbol of colonialism to be erected. Current trends in itemizing the amount of time spent, for example, by social workers and health visitors has prevented these people from actually 'being' with their clients in any meaningful way. Human beings are in general process-based creatures who function better when process and product are inextricably intertwined. The area of leisure allows us also to reconstruct ourselves and our relationships orally. Being and doing need to be kept in contact or being will become idleness and doing burn-out.

Valuing Oracy

The call to more process models within our society comes from many sources. Studies of leisure look at its role in rebalancing the self (Wilensky 1960: 32–56). Studies of health and healing call out for process models (Helman 1994, Boyce-Tillman 2000a) linked with the concept of the multiple self. Many of these involve interpersonal contact in some way – a sense of community (often as a counterbalance to a predominantly individualistic work culture).

The notion of the value of oracy in a society that is becoming more and more literate in its calls for accountability and permanence is expressed in David Abrams' book *The Spell of the Sensuous*. He looks at the complexity of spoken embodied language:

> If, for instance, one comes upon two human friends unexpectedly meeting for the first time in many months and one chances to hear their initial words of surprise and greeting, and pleasure, one may readily notice, if one pays close enough attention, a tonal, melodic

layer of communication beneath the explicit denotative meaning of the words – a rippling rise and fall of the voices in a sort of musical duet, rather like two birds singing to each other. Each voice, each side of the duet, mimes a bit of the other's melody, while adding its own inflection and style, and then is echoed by the other in turn – the two singing bodies thus tuning and attuning to one another, rediscovering a common register, *remembering* each other (Abrams 1996).

This is an important dimension of human relationship completely lost in written words. These have proved tyrannical ways of fixing products and deleting the subtlety of human relationships (as debates about the use of emails show). No wonder that in leisure activities a person becomes orate, balancing the product based literateness of work. Without literacy the notion of information as a product would be possible. While we can now pass information from one time and one space to another, we lose as well as gain.

A recent programme on the wash houses of Liverpool described how they were places of process – women met, discussed, helped and shared with one another. They helped the success of the suffrage movement (see Chapter Three).[8] Characteristics of orate cultures are:

- The absence of a definitive form of any story.
- A fluidity in formal structures, which are free flowing rather than linear and analytical.
- Increased subjectivity.
- Transmission by face-face contact not a book.
- Open religion rather than a fixed revelation contained in a book (Ong 1967: 25–9).

Alan MacFarlane, in his letters to his granddaughter Lily, helps her to see herself as process:

> You are not an artificial robot, but you are certainly the product of huge random variations. This process recurs in every interaction you have with every living person, in every moment you spend reading, watching television, in every sentence you speak and every thought you have (Macfarlane 2005: 12).

Music therapists and educationalists have called for a return to orality through improvisation to encourage 'ordinary' people to engage in the musical process. David Aldridge sees its relationship to life because:

8. Weekend Women's Hour, BBC Radio 4, 25 November 2005, 4pm.

the ability for self-regulation is based upon a repertoire of improvisational possibilities. While it is essential to have a standard repertoire of responses for everyday life, it is also necessary to improvise solutions when necessary (Aldridge 1996: 16–17).

Many composers generate ideas orally. What most people lack musically is not the ability to generate original idea, but the ability to elaborate or verify imaginative ideas (Hindemith 1952: 68). Improvisation is a form of playing. Playing is a way of doing without a sense of final product. The arts are places where adults are free to make mistakes, where they are free to explore their own subconscious and also to make mistakes (Winnicott 1971: 15). They are therefore, important arenas of self-development. There is a notion of rebellion, a challenging of the conventions of society in the exploration of the new ideas implicit in the free play of the creative process.

> The person has control of the elements and is free to create and change rules by common or individual consent. In this notion is a rebellious element, a way of challenging the rules of society (Metzger 1997: 57).

The reduction of the stress on product relaxes the need for perfection, which is a dominant trend in the product based value system. Indeed, perfection is a profoundly disempowering phenomenon. Since, I have abandoned the notion of the importance of a final product I have found creating music infinitely easier and I have been able to share 'interim' products more freely and honestly. The reduction in fear level has been remarkable. The current 'perfection' of the CD has disempowered many people. It is, of course, an illusion as even those who produced it cannot produce it in real life as it is a patching together of different performances. Only live recordings can truly reflect the mixture of process and product that is truly human.

Women are beginning to be articulate about their struggles with the demands of the dominant tradition and the problems of balancing the process of child bearing and rearing with the structures of the workplace. Liz Wilcock, a professional violinist, spoke eloquently about how the patterns of the classical world were difficult to blend with the requirements of a family. Her solution to it was to train as a music therapist where there is much more stress on process and a de-perfectionising of the product. The freedom and playfulness of much New Age practice and its democratic underpin can also be seen as a rebalancing of the Western Classical structured music making which in line with capitalism has inevitably has developed elitist product based structures.

To summarize, Western culture is now trapped in a product-based society which is now invading areas like leisure activity where once process was more paramount. People have been polarized into workers and idlers. The rediscovering of the need to play on the creative process, expressed musically through improvisation, particularly the totally free improvisation, is being rediscovered in music therapy and the more democratic processes of the New Age. The perfectionism built into this system has been disempowering for participatory music making.

Theology

Feminist theologians have challenged such a position from a number of perspectives, some of which we have seen above. They have to some extent drawn on the development of process thought (Daly 1973; Grey 1989a). Ruth Mantin writes that she wishes to see spirituality as process and sacrality as performative (Mantin 2002) seeing the process as never completed. Carol Christ (2003) has drawn on the process philosophers, such as Charles Harteshorne, to see God as verb, which I have attempted to capture in the song that starts this section. Her theology – epitomized in the title of her book *She Who Changes* concerns itself with change in the world, creation in constant transformation, rather than fixed eternal laws. She concentrates on life in the body and the finitude of life on earth. In contrast to philosophies rooted in the platonic tradition, which see change as negative because the divine does not change, she sees the need to affirm change – hence God as verb, movement and fluidity.

The valuing of process, in contrast to a society that has been primarily product centred – has already been seen in Chapter Three and earlier in this chapter. The Church has played into the product centred view. People are seen in colonial evangelism as 'souls to be saved'. There have been more courses, for example, to get people to the point of baptism or confirmation than in assisting any process of growth beyond this. Christian doctrine has often in such courses been seen as a product to be consumed as it is (not unlike the substances found on the shelves of a supermarket) rather than wrestled with and contested. Rabbi Lionel Blue draws attention to the Jewish tradition of wrestling with God.

> holy argument is the greatest path to God in Jewish experience (Blue 1987: 6).

Yet, in Christianity this has often been discouraged. My mother was warned in the 1950s that her daughter asked too many questions in her confirmation class. I was given the Catechism to learn and accept; there was no compromise, no argument and the end of debate was carefully contrived to produce that acceptance. As an undergraduate I experienced a similar phenomenon with the Christian Union. Given the Intervarsity Declaration of Faith, I was asked if I could assent to all its statements. After a night of study, thought and prayer I said that I could assent to all but two of them. I was told that it was all or nothing. I never joined the Christian Union. The faith was seen and still is in many fundamentalist churches as assent (for your own good) to a series of doctrinal statements (among which is a prepackaged reading of the canonical texts, particularly the Bible) which must be consumed like a frozen pre-packaged supermarket meal. Any discussion is illusory and designed purely to make the preset taste more acceptable to your palate.

These notions of wholeness as process rather than product start to deconstruct notions of excellence, which have run through classical theology. As we saw in Chapter One, subjugated models of the self see it as always in a process of deintegration and reintegration, spiraling within life's experiences. The feminist theologian, Zappone, describes this as 'tidal movement of ebb and flow' and distances herself from a linear aspiration towards perfection. This will be achieved through the processes of mutuality and relationality (Zappone 1991). The immanent God of the Wisdom traditions is continually making all things new and therefore the manifestations of the divine are impermanent and require constant reworking. As God is reworked in the human condition we see this process taking us through a variety of configurations of the self which now becomes multiple like the rhizomes of Braidotti's imagery (Braidotti 1994). So notions of plurality within the Divine and the human being (and indeed the earth) enable us to recover the subjugated wisdom of the value of process.

Literacy has helped a great deal in the establishment of the product-based culture of the West as we saw in Chapter One. Orate cultures have a far greater chance of relating traditional material to particular contexts than the essentially decontextualized phenomenon of book, notated score or recorded CD. The canonization of sacred texts, be they the Bible or books of liturgy sanctioned by Canon Law, has resulted in decontextualized liturgy and sacred texts that operate more like a museum of past treasures than a vibrant expression of contemporary concerns and spirituality. It is said that one of Pope Gregory's intentions in the development of notation for Gregorian chant was to prevent people incorporating a variety of material into the chant, like local folk material. Once the chant was written down it became codified and canonic and free from outside (multicultural) influences. Canonicity, in terms of music, was established by the triumph of literacy over oracy.[9] In the previous chapter we looked at how in 2002 I wished the choir to sing a student's setting of an inclusive language Magnificat text. We were an upper voice choir for which there is very little material. This young woman had set a text appropriate for her era that was rejected because it did not fit into what can only be called an imaginary museum of liturgical practice set and fixed in the seventeenth century.[10]

In orate traditions such a process cannot happen for the means of preservation is simply not available. There is an ephemerality about oral traditions within literate cultures; there is less desire to retain material from particular situations, which may be inappropriate for different contexts. We see this in contemporary women's approach to liturgy and their music. In several convents I have visited there is no systematic storing of material and certainly in the small liturgy groups meeting and constructing their own resources, as described above, there is often little desire to retain or preserve. If people take away any printed handouts with them it is so they can rework them for a new situation rather than publish

9. Matthew Barley, Introduction to Concert *On the Road* in the John Stripe Theatre, University of Winchester, 26 November 2006.

10. This setting of the liturgical text in the equivalent of the museum's hermetically sealed glass case proved a considerable problem for the Magnificat project which encouraged women composers to set the texts of the Magnificat and Nunc Dimittis. In this particular case we did manage to sing this setting, but as anthem where the text is not controlled by canonical texts of liturgy.

them for eternity. In a recent workshop on liturgy in which groups of women were asked to create a liturgy from aspects of the Easter Story, the group that ran into the greatest problem was the one that started with the printed resources. Far from stimulating their creativity, it appeared to stifle their natural ability to rework from their own memories and experience symbolic actions, words and songs appropriate for the context. People who prefer orality to literacy in our culture (and, in general, women are more skilled in verbal discourse than men) reflect this capacity to 're-member' material in ways appropriate to any given situation in which they find themselves. The concentration is necessarily then more on the content than the form of the expression. There is a greater degree of improvisation and a placing of any product as simply a moment in an ongoing process. This validating of the process can prove remarkably liberating as Western culture in its education (including religious and musical education) has laid a great stress on the perfection of the product. It is this value system itself that often prevents people from sharing their creative work. Given a space of some ten minutes in a liturgy for creative expression around the theme, I now find (since I have shifted my own internal enculturated value system) I can produce something like a song which I am willing to share. This sometimes seems remarkable to others, but it is simply this internal shift in value that makes me see what I have done as simply process and not aspiring anything more than that. It is remarkable that people in these groups are far more able to work in this way with visual media or words than with music. The stress on the excellence of the product in liturgical music has been greater than with the other arts. The restoration of improvisatory elements to liturgy gives far greater scope for happy accidents and the use of humour. The improvisation that we did as members of 'The Holy Fools' – a group of people who clowned in religious contexts – enabled remarkable insights to come about on the spur of the moment. No concentration on pre-planning could ever have produced the spontaneous insights of this occasion.

Joanna Dewey (1989) has pointed to the significance of oracy in the first two centuries of Christianity. Kwok Pui Lan summarizes the issues:

1. The influence of oral traditions on the written text.
2. The power dynamics behind the inclusion of some voices and suppression of others.

3. The relation between the oral and written transmission process.
4. The influence of the medium of transmission on the various modes of biblical interpretation.
5. The importance of understanding oral hermeneutics in feminist biblical interpretation (Kwok 1995: 49).

Jesus was an oral storyteller and Werner H. Kelber points out differences between the oral and the written medium, highlighting the change of audience to one with an education. Jesus moved:

> From one place to another, surrounded by listeners and engaged in debate… His message and his person are inextricably tied to the spoken word, not to the texts (Kelber 1983: 18).

When the stories were committed to the written word the medium changed the nature of the message now trapped:

> In words that floated context free, virtually fixed on a surface, retrievable now by anyone anywhere, as the utterances of the oral kerygma have never been (Ong 1987: 11).

Joanna Dewey stresses the interrelationship between oral and written processes, describing how Mark was intended for a listening audience even when written down, so she describes it as an 'interwoven tapestry'. It is important to see where women's voices are in this process account. Joanna Dewey argues that the stories of women were lost in the process of writing down which was written from an androcentric perspective. She comments on how the women in the stories of the anointing woman (Mk 14. 3–9) and the widow's mite (Mk 12. 41–4) act but do not speak.

The Bible as written text has functioned differently in different periods in history depending on the degree of literacy among the people. When ordinary people had no access to the written text they had no hand in the construction of the meaning. Their access for eighteen centuries of Christianity was largely through preaching and teaching. They did not have access to the whole text but only to those sections that those in power chose to read to them. But meaning is constructed orally and Kwok looks at the ways in which women have interpreted the Bible orally. Methodologies originating in the literate Academy such as the historical-critical method, literary criticism and reader-response criticism:

> Fail to provide tools to analyze the negotiation of meaning in discursive contexts, the retelling of stories to meet the particular needs of an

audience, or the thought processes that lie behind oral transmission (Kwok 1995: 51).

Images from non-Western cultures often help us to recapture the vision of a Jesus who was primarily orate. Following Chung Hyun Kyung, Kim returns to the image of a shaman Christ as potentially liberating for Korean women (Kim 2002: 7). In using this image she returns to an image of Jesus in an oral culture performing oral rituals for healing.

Male liberation theologians have contributed helpfully to this debate. African-American theologians have pointed to the dilemma that was posed by the notion that the Divine could be contained in a book. The Bible with its claims to absolute contained truth entered a culture where the sacred was seen to exist everywhere. The European claims to the boundedness and discontinuous nature of the revelation in the book, to its exclusive authority, the emphasis on the past rather than the intertwining of past and present and the notion of a singular revelation were all foreign to African views of sacrality (Thornton 1992).

Sathianathan Clarke also problematizes the centrality of the book for the Dalit communities in India:

> For the Dalits, and many other such oral and non-literate cultures, textuality itself is alienating and exclusionary…In the Indian context, where the experience of the Dalits has been discounted and disparaged by the knowledge-producing and knowledge-preserving theorists, theologians need to commit themselves to empowering the various forms and modes that house the experience of these marginalized peoples… Two specific areas will need to be pursued in such an endeavour. First the multi-modal nature of god-reflection, exhibited by Dalit communities…Second, the hermeneutics of oral traditions (Clarke 1998: 26–28).

From this position he goes to develop a Christology of the drum in Dalit culture which he describes as 'their unique, creative and constructive text of resistive and emancipatory theography' and as epitomizing orality. He sees the drum as:
- Mediating Divine power – 'the word of wisdom'.
- Conjoining material and spiritual.
- Gathering people.
- Organizing the culture.
- Expressing the strivings of the community.
- Connecting interiority with exteriority.

- Situating people in a participatory present actuality (Clarke 1998: 3–5).

There is, of course, a flow to be found between the oral and literary,[11] the fixed and the variable. These theologians have found a way of revaluing oracy in the face of a tradition of canonic texts.

Case Study One: Process Spirituality

The development of process theology by feminist theologians reflects how more people are adopting a more process based approach to spirituality. Philip Sheldrake (1995) sees the attraction of Celtic spirituality in our times in the notion of wandering and the flexibility of a spirituality of journeying:

> Given the fluidity of contemporary Western culture, a similar flexibility may need to characterize the spirituality of our times (Sheldrake 1995: 69).

This is reflected in the development of new forms of church. One such is called Somewhere Else in the centre of Liverpool. Barbara Glasson describes how she watched the process of life in the city centre before initiating the project and how she had lived with:

> the lost-ness of things. I was struggling to live without many of the familiar signposts of church and I sensed the deepest loneliness. Living out of our own loneliness is a tough agenda, yet to ignore it is like always paddling in the shallow end. Jumping into the context of questions with which we live means we are often on a solitary journey (Glasson 2006: 11).

The project just grew and she describes how:

> I was breaking free from those patterns power in which I assumed I was going to be the one to bring something to the place. Instead I saw the place as a gift that would offer up its own insights and connections...I began to see that "ministry" was not my offering to Liverpool, rather that I was in a place to recognize the ministry that was already going on there (Glasson 2006: 15).

This is similar to the Donovan experience cited in the previous chapter. The group rent a flat above News from Nowhere, a radical

---

11. In contemporary Anglican worship I am always resistant to being offered a printed Bible to follow the readings. For the rest of the service I have often had to follow printed verbal and musical texts fairly carefully. I have a secular job in which I have to receive a great deal of written text for most of the week. On a Sunday I value the chance to receive material orally.

bookshop owned by a women's co-operative. Central to their meeting was the making of bread:

> Having the courage to become a new community takes a number of different ingredients. In our case there were the physical ingredients that make up bread dough: flour, salt, water, honey, oil, yeast. There were also the emotional ingredients of community and loneliness, of engagement with the city and time for reflection, of questions and muddles (Glasson 2005: 35).

A diverse group of people gather at 10.30am on a Tuesday and Thursday to make bread. They talk and share their powerful emotions about life in the city. One of them gives the dough a large thump when he is angry (Glasson 2005: 38–40):

> Because the bread-making process has natural pauses in it there is rhythm to the day which gives time and attention to the community of individuals who gather. One of the things that the people seem to appreciate most about the whole process is that it incorporates space – space to think, space to be listened to, spaces just to be...Mysteriously, although everyone's loaf is different, the bread is always good...The sense of achievement is tangible (Glasson 2006: 40–41).

Here we see process and product brought together in a remarkable way of being church. In individual spirituality people are building their own spiritual frames by gathering ideas together from one tradition or a variety of traditions. In a paper entitled *New Religious Movements: Individualized Belief Systems and the Goddess* (2005), Patricia O'Reilly examines the eclectic belief systems that characterize Paganism, Wicca and Witchcraft in Ireland. She sees how the feminine aspect of the Divine is restored in a process-based spirituality in the broad context of the pluralistic New Age. Its essentially process-based spirituality is seen as a reaction to authoritarianism and structure of an organized religion. Legitimacy for practices lies in tradition. Ecology and subjectivity are other significant features (Boyce-Tillman 2000a: 155–201). Patricia O'Reilly found that interviewees had managed to negotiate a subjective approach to religious structures:

> Wicca, Paganism and Witchcraft can be conceived of as a negotiated religious system within which individuals were able to enjoy all the emotional intensity of organized ritual without having to adhere to one particular doctrine or belief system (O'Reilly 2005).

The negotiation involves a balance of rationality and intuition (see Chapter Six). Terms from quantum physics were often used like 'harmonics', 'frequency', 'spectrum', 'probability'.

Paganism was seen as more open and eclectic spirituality than Wicca which was seen as a semi-structured religion within which people were free to come and go as they pleased. But in this free-flowing spirituality the terms were used fluidly and people often belonged to a number of different groups:

> Paganism according to the respondents is a nature-orientated spirituality within which one can practice Wicca, heathenism, druidism, etc. Witchcraft, while seen as separate, is more closely associated with the definition of magic than it is with paganism. Witchcraft is described as a tool. Magic is universal within paganism but in other traditions such as druidism the type of magic practiced would not be called witchcraft. Witchcraft can also be used separately from Wicca and a witch might not necessarily be a Wiccan. A Wiccan is always a witch, but a witch can practice "the craft" without adhering to Wiccan philosophies (O'Reilly 2005).

Wicca is a polytheistic system of belief often using personifications of nature; it manages to reinstate the feminine principle through the worship of the Goddess, sometimes in some sects to the exclusion of male divinity. Women are prominent in positions of authority.[12] The belief system undermines the traditional practices of the Christian churches by individualizing belief and seeing it as personal endeavour. So they can enjoy the emotional intensity of religious structures without being retrained by an authoritarian belief system. The process is more important than the product.

> As traditional structures of classical modernity break down, new social forms emerge which reject certain aspects of classical modernity on the one hand and accepts other aspects on the other. This appears as a negotiated form of modernity. Wicca can be understood as a negotiated form of structured Religion (O'Reilly 2005).

The polarities of process and product are brought together by a stress on individualized search for truth validated by the traditional forms of ancient wisdom. So in the developing new forms of spirituality, process becomes more important than the fixed creedal statements of traditional denominations.

12. On a recent visit to Lithuania, where none of the Christian denominations ordained women, I saw that one of the main attractions of the increasing pagan movement was that it allowed women spiritual authority.

Case Study Two – Renegotiating Forgiveness

This too represents a renegotiation of a concept that has often been presented by the church as a product to include the notion of process.[13]

> Dear Mister God,
> I know it is difficult being you.
> I have tried and am giving up.[14]

I wrote this letter during a particularly difficult relationship and it highlights, I think, some of the dilemmas posed for me by the Church's traditional teaching on forgiveness. It is God who is eternally all-forgiving and all-loving; but for humans, forgiveness is more of a process than a static feeling. And curiously it was that process of relinquishing and letting go, of allowing God (so common in the literature of contemplatives) that proved to be the beginning of a new phase in my marriage. It allowed me to feel the anger that an aspiring to perfection had prevented. This anger empowered me to say things that should have been said much earlier and to cause the relationship to enter the crisis that it should have entered long before. What could have happened if I had felt it before I shall never know. But certainly it was with this letter that the dynamic of forgiveness could start.

For some time I had found it difficult to say: 'And forgive us our trespasses, as we forgive those who trespass against us'. In Church I had been taught about forgiveness as a nice warm glow inside. It was, they implied, a static feeling that led to a restoration of a relationship. This may be a codification of one stage in what is essentially a dynamic, moving entity, for in my experience, forgiveness is often not a warm glow inside but simply an acceptance of the way things are. As such, a pursuance of the traditional view can be experienced as a papering-over of a crack, and an imposition of 'correct' feelings from without, when truly these should only well up from inside; this may happen when other, perhaps more difficult feelings (from the Church's more traditional position) have been experienced. As with any superficial cover-up operation, in the end the crack will reveal itself again, and behind it, even more

---

13. This paper was first published as *On Forgiveness – Some Thoughts* by Women in Theology, 1992.

14. The use of this term is taken from Fynn (1974).

damage may have occurred in the fabric of the building. The traditional model of forgiveness is of a sinner and a victim. To reverse the oppressor-oppressed model, the scales are traditionally reversed by an act of forgiveness on the part of the victim, who then, in the worst scenarios based on this model, can oppress his/ her former oppressor in a way far more pernicious than the original sin. The model of the forgiver can be twisted into an emotional persecutor of an invidious kind and hold the two parties in a mutually damaging sado-masochistic relationship.

The older version of the Lord's Prayer quoted above gives us more clues on the mutuality of forgiveness, than the more modern replacing of the word 'trespass' with 'sin'. Perhaps this too is because the word 'sin' has become debased. To 'trespass' is to pass through a barrier, to encroach on the territory of someone who did not want you to come that far. If we think of the traditional scene of the barbed wire fence and the notice 'Trespassers will be prosecuted', the boundaries of the territory are clearly defined and the would-be trespasser will probably be aware of the tear of the wire as s/he attempts to cross into a forbidden land. I do not here intend to embark on a political theory on the right ownership of land, but simply to say that if the fence is not in repair and the sign has fallen down, it is more difficult to see the boundaries.

In psychological terms this can be more so. If a person does not keep their sacred territory well-defined — the limits within which they will allow someone else to enter their own selfhood — the invading forces will have an easier task. And each person will have a different size territory and will allow different people in closer. Perhaps our whole life experience is about learning these for ourselves and others, a process involving sensitivity and vulnerability. As such, respect becomes an important aspect of relationship – when to advance, when to retreat. It is perhaps a more significant part of a close relationship than another word of many meanings – love. When an apparently loving relationship founders, it can be that person has caused a breakdown of respect, with the result that someone has trespassed into the sacred territory of another. But to return to the metaphor of the barbed wire and the notice, it could also be that the fences were not in good repair. In such a breakdown in a relationship, it often appears that the person who crosses the boundary is the criminal; but maybe the landowner should have kept the fences in order. In, for example, the traditional marriage breakdown the violent husband may appear to be the one responsible but perhaps the oppressed wife also needs to keep her defences in order. The sooner such oppression is noted and the quicker the woman can be helped to draw her boundaries, (a scenario not encouraged by traditional Church teaching on self-giving love and the nature of womanhood or by the position of women in the media and popular press), the more likely the important quality of respect is likely to grow. If the scenario is allowed to proceed too far, the woman may need a karate course, when in the early stages a few skills like the ability to withdraw to a room alone and a few well chosen words might have sufficed.

And here we come to an aspect of the process of forgiveness that has been overlooked — the barbed wire fence of anger. It is often by controlled anger that we show most clearly that a sacred boundary has been crossed. Just an intensity of speaking may reveal to the potential trespasser that s/he is close to the barbed wire. But the wire may need to vary in height according to the strength and sensitivity of the invading force. The angry interchange in the presence of someone with experience, recommended by psychotherapy, can be the prelude to the redrawing of the boundaries. This is part of the process of the forgiveness, the lessening of the likelihood of further trespassing.

And yet there are, in my experience, occasions when the trespassing has gone on too long, the path into the sacred territory too well worn, for the old boundaries to be re-established. Then the nature of the relationship has to be changed totally. Perhaps this is the reason in British law for the two-year separation before divorce – the chance for both parties to repair their fences, a task that can only be done when they are not living cheek-by-jowl. Only then is there the possibility for any meaningful forgiveness with its essential component of a growth of respect and acceptance of the limits of the personal space of the other.

Here the idea of forgiveness as the restoration of a relationship is often a misrepresentation of what is humanly possible. The word 'restoration' implies a return to a former state, but often what is demanded is a change of relationship, an acknowledgement that it can never be the same again. After that (sometimes a long time after) may come the realization that you would never wish it to be. The cost of the traditional teaching on forgiveness as a sort of warm glow that will enable a relationship to be restored as it was, has meant the trapping of people in relationships that as they were have broken down irretrievably. A theology encompassing a fixed view of marriage or family or kinship relationship has failed to acknowledge the dynamic process of relating, forgiving and accepting in the hands of humans was missing. It is where a divine model of an all-forgiving God has impinged on human limitations.

Yet, from these human relationships maybe we can also learn something of significance to this relationship too. Jesus did not say to the soldiers nailing him to the Cross 'I forgive you' but implored his heavenly Father to do so. Was this because in human terms he felt he could not? Or maybe because he too realized the diminishment he would give to his oppressors by a patronising, 'I forgive you'. In the crucifixion Jesus consented to the role of victim in an oppressor-victim relationship and only after that consent experienced the Resurrection. (My own realization that to stay permanently in the victim role was to deny the significance of the Resurrection was the first stage in my thinking about the marriage as it stood.) Reflection on what had happened in our relationship showed that the path into my territory was too well-worn for us to live alongside each other any longer – that the legacy of unspoken anger and recrimination appeared by then to be too great ever to be expressed; if I cried, I could cry forever, if I raged, there would be no ending to it. And part of that rage was not only for him but also for myself, for allowing it to happen, for allowing him into that centre that is at the heart of all of us, that Sacred Centre where we experience the Divine. There was an acknowledgement that I had had a hand in this invasion.

It was not the Church that could offer us any help in this process – with its theology of the sanctity of marriage vows, carefully enshrined and imposed by the weight of the Marriage Eucharist. The acknowledgement of divorce in religious terms is still a hole-in-the-corner affair. And yet, if you have a weighty liturgy to get you in, surely there must be some sort of ritual to get you out? It was a social worker in the Conciliation Service who offered the two of us the chance to draw a line across the emotional ledger that could have crippled both of us in a cycle of recrimination and bitterness. He offered us a reversal of the marriage ceremony conducted like a presiding minister. 'Hold hands; look into one another's eyes and repeat after me:

Thank you for the good times we have shared together
I am sorry for all the times that I have hurt you
Goodbye as my husband
Hello as the separated parent of our children.

And then the same process by the other partner. There are some who would wish for what they would see as a happy ending. They would want me to write that as we looked at one other we knew that our marriage was restored. But that is not what happened. After it, we sat apart in separate chairs and wept for what might have been, but could never be.

The collection of rituals entitled *Human Rites* that people have created does include one by Vienna Cobb Anderson for divorce. This includes similar elements to the one described above but also includes a theologizing of the process:

> Dearly beloved: We have come together in the presence of God to witness and bless the separation of this man and this woman who have been bonded in the covenant of marriage. The courts have acknowledged their divorce and we, this day, gather to support them as they give their blessing to one another as each seeks a new life.
>
> In creation God made the cycle of life to be birth, life and death; and God has given us the hope of new life through the Resurrection of Jesus Christ, our Savior. The Church recognizes that relationships follow this pattern. While the couple have promised in good faith to love until parted by death, in some marriages the love between a wife and a husband comes to an end sooner. Love dies, and when that happens we recognize that the bonds of marriage, based on love, may be ended.
>
> God calls us to right relationships based on love, compassion, mutuality, and justice. Whenever any of these elements is absent from a marital relationship, then that partnership no longer reflects the intentionality of God (Ward and Wild 1995a: 188).

There is a notion of release as part of the process in this liturgy:

> In the name of God, I _ , release you, _ from your vow to be my husband. I thank you for the love and support you have given me. I ask your forgiveness for my part in the failure of the marriage. I give you this ring, which you gave me as a symbol of our marriage. In returning it, I set you free. I pray you will find peace and joy in your new life (Ward and Wild 1995a: 190).

Such rituals raise the issue of regarding marriage as product rather than process. After a chapter, identifying numerous cases of abuses in marriage, Matilda Joslyn Gage in her critique in 1893 praises Chile for abandoning it:

> This action of the Chilean republic in substituting a civil for a religious ceremony in marriage and declaring the latter to be illegal, is a most important step in civilization of which freedom for woman is such an essential factor. And its results in that country must be felt in woman's every relation of life – promoting self-respect, self-reliance and security in place of the degradation, self-distrust and fear to which its church has so long condemned her (Gage 1893/1998: 227).

So the ending of a relationship, like we have already seen with death, means renegotiating a new relationship. This is where the forgiveness lies. The product and process are intimately bound together.

Summary

The spheres of the public and private have often been divided between those in power and those without power. However, everyone needs to negotiate an appropriate balance. In religion the perceived sinfulness of women has often trapped them in the private sphere. Women have negotiated the public by means of various dress codes like the nun's habit and the veil. There is a concern to make past women's stories better known. There is a great deal of concern about negotiating women's authority within an intensely heteropatriarchal church.

In a product based society the process becomes seriously devalued. Churches deal in marketable belief systems that need uniform acceptance while new forms of church and spirituality bring process and product together. Phenomena like forgiveness, often seen as product, are in fact part of an ongoing process in which products are only staging posts.

Chapter Five

THE RHYTHM OF GROWTH

1. Within our hearts may truth arise
   As moonlight gentle in the night,
   As meteors and shooting stars,
   To challenge wrong and nurture right.

2. Within our hearts may wisdom grow,
   Like rhizomes spreading in the earth,
   Conjoining different faith insights
   To bring new paradigms to birth.

3. Within our hearts may peace prevail,
   And ripple like a bubbling spring,
   To bring earth's deserts into bloom
   So from the margins joy can ring.

4. Within our hearts may justice reign
   And burn with fiery Spirit-flames,
   Creating systems that in strength
   Embody Christ's outrageous claims.

Christ within us, Christ around us,
Christ uniting, Christ dividing,
Christ alone and Christ in gathering,
Christ in public, Christ in hiding,
Christ in body and in spirit,
Christ in freeing, Christ in holding,
Christ relaxing and exciting,
Christ in challenge, Christ enfolding.

5. And so the God of joy and hope,
   Can be revealed in humankind,
   When politics reflect shared wealth
   And nature's growth as intertwined.
   (Boyce-Tillman 2006a: 88–89)

Excitement/Relaxation

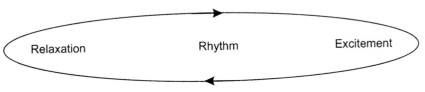

Fig. 10. Rhythm

Society

Western society is frenetically exciting. Margaret Thatcher apparently needed only three hours sleep a night and constructed a UK society where in many jobs that was the only way to succeed at them. The ultimate condemnation of something by the young is not that it is evil or wicked (both of which are now terms of endearment) but that it is 'boring'. These are the characteristics of our society:

- The constant flickering images of the television set or computer game.
- The constantly changing sounds of the walkman or the ubiquitously piped music.
- The need to keep up with the latest fashion which changes rapidly enough to ensure that people will spend a great deal to keep up with the fast moving bandwagon.
- The demands of ceaseless production in the workplace.
- The constant stimulation to violence of computer games.
- The prevalence of stimulating drinks such as coffee, tea and Coca-cola.

All these testify to the marriage of our society with excitement. The news media only report events that are dramatic with the result that violence gets more coverage than the peaceful and the ordinary.[1] We are constantly exposed to apocalyptic style reporting, that makes our own everyday lives seem flat and boring. Little wonder, then, that youngsters buy guns to join this hyped-up scenario. The mundane everyday tasks that keep some rhythm in our lives are

---

1. Following a performance of my one woman show *Juggling: A Question of Identity* which includes a number of roles that women play, a member of the audience remarked how unusual it was to see in a dramatic presentation the ordinary things of life like sewing, dusting and pouring tea being done.

despised in favour of an over-hyped constant stimulation that keeps the adrenalin flowing freely through our veins. Watching the slower rhythms of the natural world that would have been part of agrarian living or the slower pace of oral story telling around a domestic fire are no longer 'cool' because they are 'boring'. Silence is an endangered species. The hyped-up human beings produced by this are, of course, more likely to buy and consume more things, whether that is food of some kind to keep the flagging energy up or domestic gadgetry to reduce boring tasks in favour of more stimulation. All machinery adds to the sonic environment and little attention is paid by those manufacturing it or those using it to the effect of those particular sounds on human consciousness. Operatives operating it wear earmuffs, but what of the unsuspecting public? Pop music has now reached a regular volume level where the ears are being damaged by the decibel level. Played softer, it becomes boring and the human frame, both mind and body, seeks bigger and better thrills to escape the ultimate hell of boredom (which in other societies might be called, rest, peace, or relaxation). As we engage (or rather entrain with this music) our entire body is affected by the speed and volume which keep it in a constant state of arousal. Is it surprising then that on a global scale war is a more attractive enterprise than peace? The control of the rhythm of our waking and sleeping is now in the control of the multinationals who hype up a thrill-hungry society in ways detailed above and then market expensive medication in order to mitigate the effects of the scenario that they have created. The need for rhythm resurfaced in the jubilee campaign. The papers given at the 1996 Bossey consultation examined the notions of rhythm in the Jewish ideas of jubilee (longer term rhythm) and Sabbath (shorter term rhythm):

> For cultures that have come to exploit the environment and that have lost the capacity for communal celebration, there is much to commend such a rhythm, and much in the accumulated law and wisdom of Jews and Christians that points in this direction (Selby 1997: 101).

However, we live in an age of apocalypse when we are easy prey to those fundamentalists who will offer an alternative apocalyptic solution to the possibility of world burn out and extinction. So contemporary society has substituted speed for rest. As the polarity splits relaxation has become boredom while excitement becomes unruliness.

Self

At a personal level the effects are potentially disastrous. The self in a constant state of adrenalin arousal becomes manic and then may well experience the bipolar disorder of unregulated swings from depression-induced sloth to over-excited mania. The people who experience this are merely demonstrating an extreme form of a deep societal sickness. The old arts of relaxing infusions, lullaby-like music and gentle talk with friends as a means of winding down at the end of a hard day are becoming lost arts, but their cultivation would cripple the profits of the drug companies. This binary is closely allied with the product/process work/play dichotomy described in the previous chapter. The busy person is praised over the idle one, so the unemployed seek exciting experiences through drugs and alcohol, while the employed seek it through ambition and overwork. The exposure to loud instruments and fast music (very little popular music is slow) overstimulates both body and mind, and has deleterious effects on both. While some excitement induces happiness this needs to be balanced with relaxation to enable the adrenalin to retreat in the body. So in the self when the idleness of relaxation and the busyness of excitement lose touch with one another relaxation becomes sloth and excitement mania.

Music and Rhythm

Human beings need to establish a rhythm of excitement and relaxation in their lives. Music has long been used for these purposes because it has physiological effects which appear to be transcultural. Loud and fast music induces arousal and slower softer music relaxation. Certain instruments have exciting or calming qualities. Experienced listeners know how to use music to establish this rhythm in their lives and usually have pieces that they will play on the way to work and those they will play on the way home. Classic FM is marketing CDs that are mood coded, to help you in your choice. The working environment of music like others is also too stimulating. Long journeys, too frequent concerts result in the families of professional musicians having the experience of a father (and it usually is a man) only in a state of adrenalin withdrawal. The wife of a successful conductor gave this as a significant reason for the breakdown of her marriage.

There is a rising tide of meditative activities to rebalance society's excitement. Some of these do use music in some way, whether it is the repeated drum beat of the shamanic journey or the sweeping electronic sounds of CDs with titles like 'Tranquil Essence'. We can now purchase the sounds of the natural world in recorded form and they are blended into other pieces, usually with the intention of calming. People go to make recordings by rivers and waterfalls and the idea of a sacred space is now in recorded form rather than being part of everyday reality. This is, of course, instant and does not require us to engage with the 'live' slower paced sounds of the real natural world. It is also dependent on what is commercially produced. Once it was controlled by people singing, whistling and humming. These self-generated musics were subtle ways of managing mood that was not in the control of the multi-nationals and it used the innate human ability to compose. I tried to capture this in a poem:

The Symphony

He sits beside his mother
Cuddling his four years on the planet

The train bleats

And he improvises a symphony
Around its falling minor third

He has yet to learn
That he cannot compose.

But we will soon teach him.

June Boyce-Tillman, November 2004.

The dominant culture of classical music followed a very different path from popular music with a disturbing music that challenged the ear with a variety of difficult sounds, and discords that once would have been resolved now following one after the other like the exciting images of the television screen or the video screen – one unresolved problem after another, leading ultimately to despair. Composers left the needs of the market behind in exploring in more and more intense ways the Angst of the times – a time when in human hands for the first time in their history lay the possibility of cosmic destruction. Whereas some composers handled these with integrity, for others it was a deliberate embracing of a culture of violence.

Subjugated knowers like John Cage, adopted more radical solutions. When he produced his piece 4.33,[2] which consisted of him going to the piano opening the lid and then sitting there for four minutes thirty three seconds, people ridiculed him but as in so many areas, he is actually a prophetic figure looking forward to a time when the concert hall may be the only place where people can go to 'hear' silence, so sonically filled has our environment become. The market went back to the past and filled the concert halls with masterworks that spoke of a greater security, using music like the leisure activities described above as a place for security and comfort. The pieces were familiar and reassuring. Popular culture also went down the market place route, with a constantly changing set of sounds that gave the illusion of change without challenging the boundaries of the culture, rather like the verses of greeting cards. The thing that did change was the increasing volume level as the electronics industry became more skilled at amplification. This was eagerly taken up by a culture longing for more and more thrills to fuel its adrenalin addiction. Drums formed the staple basis of the pop world with acoustic instruments uniformly replaced by amplified and synthesized sounds – a phenomenon carefully explored in the musical *We Will Rock You*. Subjugated knowers explored more esoteric routes, exploring more spiritual concepts and a greater variety of tone colours.

To summarize, human beings need to establish a rhythm of excitement and relaxation in their lives. Music has long been used for these purposes because it has physiological effects, which appear to be transcultural. Experienced listeners know how to use music to establish this rhythm in their lives but this is now done more by the recordings made available by the recording industry rather than self-generated musics.

Theology

The way in which Western theology has concerned itself with grand narratives of salvation, dramatic falls from grace, and elaborate theologies of salvation involving a great deal of violence bears testimony to the human need for excitement. The Wisdom tradition is often much more 'boring'; for it concerns the painstaking, often mundane task of incarnating Christ in the everyday fabric of

2. http://interglacial.com/~sburke/stuff/cage_433.html, contacted 31 July 2007.

ordinary lives in the minutiae of decisions we take all the time often on automatic pilot rather than by conscious choice. The worshipping Church can, however, (depending on the tradition) come out as a 'neither one thing nor another' approach and as repetitive and dull, particularly for the young. Excitement is often provided by loud instruments and in some traditions by repetitions of hymns and songs and a louder and louder pitch and a greater level of excitement – 'One more time everyone, with more fervour for the Lord'. In some traditions there is a great deal of colour in terms of vestments and processions and grandeur that can stir excitement. I remember attending a Papal Mass in St Peter's Rome and being profoundly impressed by the theatricality of it all – the lights dimmed as the service started and the illuminations behind the huge wall statues coming up, the Papal guards in their uniforms, the arrival of the frail Pope Paul to shouts and clapping; in the service a great brazier was kindled. I was reminded of the spectacle of the ancient Roman forum. Very different – I visited the catacombs on the same day where peace and coolness and simplicity reigned in dark ancient tunnels.

The heteropatriarchal church has often presented us with a plethora of sounds and images, often communicated verbally, with little time to absorb them, contemplate or reflect on them or indeed, to make them our own by relating them to our own everyday experience. The receiving of the readings in worship orally enables me to stop listening when I wish, as there is no stream of words pulling my eyes forward. It also opens up the possibility of *lectio divina*, a form of reading practised in religious houses and recommended in the Benedictine Rule, where passages of Scripture would be read aloud during meals and certain passages that seemed relevant to listening religious would be taken by them and dwelled upon in their hearts. It was a way of 'allowing the Word of God to dwell in you richly'. This is in direct contrast to the speed-reading practised by most people today especially in academic circles.

In the rubric of some services there is the instruction, 'And now a time of silence will be kept'. This has often been so short in my experience that it has passed without my noticing. This provision of a continuous web of activity in liturgy with no time for absorption of it at any depth reflects the product-based doctrinal approaches outlined in Chapter Four. It is a take-it-or-leave-it approach with often little notion that the laity have anything that they might contribute to the process other than being swept into the activity themselves as prayer leaders, Eucharistic ministers and so on. In this respect many churches resemble the surrounding culture with its high boredom threshold and its requirement for continually moving images to satisfy the need for continuous stimulation.

And yet privately people are learning meditative techniques for their private use and attending classes in such slower disciplines as yoga. There is a contemplative Wisdom tradition within Christianity, reflected in the silence of some monastic traditions, but from the average church-goer in the average congregation it is often remarkably well hidden. I was brought up in a Christian tradition from the cradle and yet it was not until my twenties, when like many in the 1960s I was attracted to Transcendental Meditation, that I found a spiritual director who showed me the hidden contemplative traditions within my own Faith.

The informal liturgical groups involving women in the UK have often deliberately embraced a different mood from the dominant church culture – closer to the catacombs than St Peter's. There is often a great sense of a need for peace and quiet. We see silence often prominent with times for reflection. There is often a rediscovery of meditative traditions of various kinds. The music used is often slow and functioning as a raft for reflection and healing by drawing the ideas, sounds and images presented into the depth of one's being.

Dominating the musical scene in many churches is the sound of the organ, which although capable of soft gentle sounds and often used in this way is usually characterized by non-organ lovers (many of whom are women) as loud and overbearing. When groups of worshipping women do have access to large liturgical spaces that include organs there is often a general resistance to using them as being the musical representation of a loud triumphalist theology. In general, the instruments used for the informal private groups have to be portable and guitars and flutes have found a ready acceptance. Recently there has been a greater use of the power of the drum, but this has received a mixed reception. Because of its identification with male musicians and its great energizing power, some women have wanted to reclaim it. Others have resisted its militaristic overtones.[3] A further problem is its appropriation from

3. The drums have summoned people to war in many cultures including the West; however, it is actually simply an energizer and energy once raised can be used for destructive or constructive purposes.

other cultures, in particular, the Native American or the African.[4] There is a stronger sense that what is needed is instruments that will relax and sustain like the singing bowl.

Many of the songs used have also been softer and slower and more meditative chants being very popular like those from Taize and Margaret Rizza (2004). As the numbers involved are smaller this may seem inevitable. There are some justice seeking songs that are louder and stronger, encouraging women not to give up (see *Following the Vision* at the opening of Chapter Four). There is, in my opinion, a great need to address this balance in this area of instruments. The reclaiming of energizing instruments and the use of them to empower action for social justice does need to be part of the feminist agenda. Excitement and relaxation need to be brought together and in women's hands.

Case Studies

Case Study One – Renegotiating Risk

The notion of speed seems to be connected with the idea of risk and this is associated with the heroic journey as explored in Chapter Three. This is central to Richter and Francis'(2005) examination of the differences in religiosity between males and females, looking at – not the usual question of why women are more religious than men – but at why men are less religious than women. They draw on the work of Rodney Stark (2002) and their own previous work (Richter and Francis 1998) in which they were concerned with identifying motivation in religious disaffiliation and analyzing of the different reasons for church leaving. This quantitative study based on data from 898 church leavers sees that:

> the masculine perspective on religion is characterized by a greater tendency to live dangerously and to reject faith than is the case among women. Men are more active and more decisive than women in their disengagement from church (Richter and Francis 2005).

Francis (1992), using psychoticism as the dimension of personality fundamental to individual differences in religiosity, sees men as predisposed to be 'fearless risk takers', who seek immediate gratification without regard for consequences.' "Real men take what

4. Conversation with Mary Hunt, Harvard University, 1 May 2003.

they want." "Only wimps go to church."' (Stark 2002: 505). This is linked with the hegemonic masculinity explored in Chapter One. The consequence of this is that men take the risk of betting that God does not exist, in the interest of immediate gratification (Stark 2002: 502).

These findings are interesting in that they would indicate that the Church is at the relaxation end of this polarity and there is too little excitement. As we shall see below, this could indicate a fracture in the polarity; the traditional Church congregation is seeking reassurance rather than risk. Here we may be encountering some of the characteristics of self-policing that we examined in Helen O'Grady's work in Chapter One based on the instilling of dominant values during childhood. For subjugated knowers self-policing is instilled more effectively and earlier. Therefore the desire to seek immediate gratification is inhibited whereas in dominant knowers these are not so instilled.

The Richter and Francis (1998) study also identifies a key reason for church-leaving – 'Too high a cost'. When it demands overcommitment, burnout is experienced and people leave (Richter and Francis 2005). Here we see that the Church itself fails within its internal structures to achieve a right balance between the polarities. Women now already juggling a job and a family are more likely to experience this strain than men, and indeed in a more acute form. There is a raft of women now in their 50s and 60s who still have family commitments and full-time employment. This generation was once the backbone of the Church. They – in the 1950s and 1960s – had only family commitments which were lessening and a new release of energy, which they gave voluntarily to the Church. Now these energies are spent in paid employment, attempting to make up pension shortfalls (acquired by bringing up families); they will look much more to religion for relaxation and nurture than for further excitement and demands on their deplenished energies.

The negotiation of this polarity so that it both balances the need for excitement and risk-taking and the need for some to rest from the strains of increasingly complex lives is managed differently in different denominations; can it be managed so that within a particular service there is a balance of excitement and relaxation? Carter Heyward links this renegotiating with vulnerability:

> We have been taught by virtuous men that to be courageous is to rise
> above relational vulnerability, and that fear is an impediment to

courage. But that is not true. In the process of befriending, courage comes through our immersion in places of mutual vulnerability. Exposed to danger or simply to the unknown, we empower one another to take heart, to keep our courage. This we do by standing together (Heyward 1989b: 139–40).

A prisoner, on being asked what he had learned from his early days in prison, said that he and his cell mate had learned to cry as two men together and both had found that supportive. Is it possible for our society to find other places where excitement and relaxation can be brought together in this way? This can result in genuine compassion. The two prisoners had exchanged their two stories with understanding and togetherness:

> Untransfigured fear which fragments our lives into sad facsimiles of false love and pseudointegrity, need not rule our lives or shape our ethics...Compassion is a gift of our genuine involvement in one another's lives (Heyward 1989b: 141).

What our society so often offers in its pursuit of excitement is this untransfigured fear which can only be transfigured by the meeting of the relaxation of shared courage and vulnerability.

Case Study Two – Renegotiating Death

As part of my training for ordination, I carried out in 2004 a placement with a funeral director in South London. The opening of my diary reads:

> I found the pace very slow at first as I was quite nervous. In the end I loved it and found myself able to pray for the person and their family in the stillness. It was a real antidote to the speed of everyday life.

One of the reasons for the embracing of excitement in our society is its fear of death. Natural death is avoided in numerous ways:

- For hospitals it is a failure.
- Cosmetic surgery is developed to offset the effects of aging, often in women.
- Silence is avoided reflecting a fear of the ultimate bodily silence, which is death.

Our screens are filled with exciting images of unnatural and violent death which are titivated up by the media as entertainment rather than as relating to real human life.

The loss of rituals around grieving and death has meant a loss of the long rhythm of excitement and relaxation that characterizes the human life span. The sadness of my time with the undertaker was to watch how inadequately much of the white community handled the funeral process. The tools that they needed had been removed in white Post-Enlightenment culture. They no longer had:

- A shared spiritual frame.
- A shared bank of songs.
- Permission to cry publicly.
- A sense of the presence of or connection with the ancestors.

The black community, however, often had these tools still intact. I will give some examples from my diary with identities disguised. First of all there was a sense that you can talk to the dead:

> A black family came in. Their mother had asked for £10,000 to be spent on the funeral. The family chose an expensive funeral including an elaborate casket, a horse drawn hearse and six limousines. The cost so far was just over £6,000. As they gathered around the coffin, they entered into refreshingly frank conversation about how they had always tried to carry out their mother's wishes. It was an open natural conversation.

Secondly there was a sense that crying was allowed, even during the service:

> In a Pentecostal memorial service, there was a poem and four tributes to the two-year-old child. One was from his physiotherapist. I got a good picture of a lively chuckling baby and a real sense of the child's presence. By this time both parents were crying. Some kissed him in the casket. Everyone was crying. The Pentecostal Bishop cried as he sang 'What a Friend We Have in Jesus'. The black woman Pentecostal pastor was crying at the graveside but still presiding well over the service. In the graveyard there was much crying and comforting. Hymns were sung in an impromptu fashion including 'This is the Day that the Lord Hath Made' and 'Amazing Grace' and 'Jesus Loves the Little Children'. The coffin was lowered slowly into the grave and people threw flowers in and mementos. This was deeply moving. The men started to fill the grave in. The singing continued and made the whole event feel better. The child's father put so much energy in it and then he cried. Two women supported him. The community carried on singing – 'O When the Saints'. Flowers were placed on the grave including some in the shape of hearts and teddies. Flower bunches were opened and flowers placed as if growing on grave. It was ended with Lord's Prayer (traditional form) with all of us holding hands. Balloons were released into the air. I wrote this poem:

Howling at the Wind

He had carried his son's coffin
He had prayed the prayers
And sung the songs
His jacket sparkled in the setting sun
As he shovelled the earth into the dark hole
Which sheltered the white velvety coffin.
He patted it down carefully
Tucking in his son
For the last time.
He stood back
And howled
The sound – of grief and loss –
The screaming heart of the universe
At unjustified suffering
The cry of the father for his dearly beloved son.

(June Boyce-Tillman, January 2004)

As we see in this story, music played a significant part in holding the community at this time. Music is potentially transformative and holds the strength of the community. It can serve the following functions:

- Maintaining the energy of the participants.
- Enabling them to reminisce about the deceased.
- Creating and holding the sense of community.
- Holding the theology of hope for the participants.

In one memorial service, the strength of the singing and the associated energy rose during the service. The service ended with the viewing of the body; as is the tradition, the family viewed last. The widow came forward with her children on either side. By this time the whole church was singing 'O death where is thy Sting! O grave where is thy victory!' There was a huge amount of energy. I was reminded of my time in the black township Gugulethu in South Africa and a grieving widow coming forward. At this point the whole community started to sing loudly and beat on their hymn books. 'But she is crying' I said to the black woman next to me. 'When you are grieving you need strength, not pity' she replied. I contemplated how by the energy of their singing that black community held the grieving family in their loving support rooted in their faith. In this situation I saw excitement and relaxation beautifully held in balance to create a right rhythm for grieving.

So the dominant culture values and propagates excitement often for commercial purposes. The bringing together of vulnerability and risk in theology and liturgical practice can help to restore a right flow between these polarities.

Challenge/Nurture

1. O Goddess/Jesus/Mary of a thousand breasts
   Come feed us with your milk
   Enwrapping and enfolding us
   In gentle rainbow silk.

2. Abundant grace is flowing out,
   Enough to gift and share;
   Anxiety is swept away
   In all-providing care.

3. The folding mountains draw us in
   To earth's secure embrace,
   Envelop us with gentle joy
   In darkened sulphur caves.

4. For nurture spreads throughout the world
   And greens the fertile earth;
   Embrace us in your loving lap
   And sing us into birth.

This was written in July 2006 immediately after the International Peace Research Association conference in Calgary, Canada. Kevin Clements from Brisbane had talked in his final address about a statue he had seen in Paris of a goddess with twenty-five breasts and used it as an image of what Europe needs – a really nurturing symbol.

Society

The pursuit of excitement and the dominance of the archetypal myth of the heroic journey have led to a profoundly challenging society

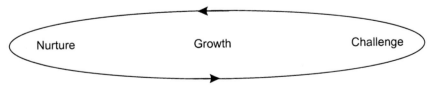

Fig. 9. Growth

devaluing nurture. The greatest financial rewards are given to those able to meet and set the challenges for those who may well fall at the hurdles without some degree of nurture. Our school systems in the UK are a case in point. Children have to meet constant challenges in the shape of standardized tests and individuals and groups – whether teacher, students, schools or education authorities – face penalties of greater or lesser degrees of security as a penalty for failures. Teachers forced into a position of regurgitating the preset knowledge of the National Curriculum have correspondingly less time to nurture individual children according to their needs. In certain areas of British education this was always so, particularly the male dominated public school system.[5] Debates, for example, over entrance exams for Oxford and Cambridge Universities recently are interesting in this respect. As one who was educated at Oxford University, I think it very appropriate to screen out those students who would require any nurturing to achieve their educational goals. To have included them in a system where no nurture was on offer would simply have been unjust and lacking in integrity. It is often women who have highlighted the need for nurture in the system and often their work has been lost or ignored. In 1863, for example, the Peabody sisters Elizabeth Palmer Peabody and Mary Mann published *Moral Culture of Infancy and Kindergarten Guide* in which:

> She stressed the importance of a caring environment in the teaching of young children, and declared that the process of education should be one of eliciting and nurturing certain "faculties" within the child rather than implanting facts by rote recitation (Strong 2004: 44).

The challenge of competition has now eaten into every sector of Western culture. The capitalistic market is based on a philosophy that competition necessarily produces the best solution.

---

5. Nowhere is this clearer than in some of the training programmers for positions of authority within the Church. There are a number of stories of people who feel deeply disempowered after their ordination course, particularly those who hold positions of authority in the secular world. This notion of survival as a good preparation has its roots in the public school system and in preparation for the armed forces upon which the church's selection procedures are based. It would appear strange that an institution that claims to believe in grace, which precedes a sense of sin, cannot see that a system with a better balance between challenge and nurture would enable people to grow. In such a system people would grow by building up their strengths rather than concentrating on their weaknesses.

Unfortunately, separated from nurture, it produces destruction as all sense of connectedness is systematically destroyed (as we saw in Chapter Three). Care separated from competition produces atrophy and the separation of those who need care from those who can withstand competition has left many of the elders of our society atrophying in old people's homes without the challenges posed by association with other generations or the wider society. So when care and competition part company, some areas atrophy while others are destroyed.

Self

Within the self, challenge is associated with an adventuring spirit. I met a Carmelite sister who was living relatively independently outside the convent that had been her environment for 60 years of her life. For her, every day was a great adventure – even unpacking groceries she had chosen herself in the local supermarket. Outside of the nurturing (some might say stifling routines of the convent), the challenge was exciting and a situation of real growth. She knew as a mature woman how to ask for care, when required, but she taught me a great deal about the adventure of everyday life. When, however, this sense of adventure does not know when to ask for care, the result is total collapse. In a discussion one day about what I wanted for my children I was surprised to find others saying that they wanted them to stand on their own feet. I responded that I also hoped that they would know when they needed help and who were safe people to ask for it. When we experience only care we atrophy and can feel stifled and trapped. On the other hand, the growing child challenged continually – whether by abuse or by unchecked intellectual and emotional demands – ultimately will collapse. For when in flow some challenge is stimulating and life enhancing but when they are out of balance and connection it is crippling and destructive. So as caring and adventure lose contact they lead to atrophy in the self or total collapse.

Education as Nurture

Lois Holzman who runs a performance project in New York, describes her own move in her psychotherapeutic practice as one from a linear 'stagist' view based on developmental psychology to a more nurturing one using the work of Vygotsky (1978) based on community building through the arts (Holzman 2002). She describes the All Stars Network programme that attempts to bring together challenge and nurture. Everyone who auditions – 20,000 people aged 5–25 – is accepted. They are then given a variety of skills leading to a final performance. The older participants have a chance to become the teachers at the next course (Fulani 2000).

This is an antidote to the dominant educational regime of challenge including music education. In music, notions of challenge have been part of the Post-Enlightenment classical tradition linked with the notion of the heroic journey. Music teachers have often been so concerned with the challenges of the heroic journey, as expressed in musical notation in particular, that their lessons are often more of a number of hurdles to jump over, than an enriching life experience. In this experience too, both teacher and pupil may well be trapped in the heroic journeying expectations of the parents, who call the tune; and this is despite the fact that there are examples in several cultures of the teaching of singing skills which have empowered disenfranchised sections of society (Jorgensen 1996). In my own workshops the finding of one's note – the one that one finds easiest to sing at any given time – has proved an effective corrective to some of the worst perfectionist excesses of the school music curriculum. Western music therapy has traditionally disassociated itself from the teaching of skills seeing the free improvisatory play, that forms its heart, as using whatever skills the client has.

A philosophy of nurture and challenge (see Theology below) concentrates on birth and flourishing and leads necessarily to a call to pedagogy, both in the Church and beyond to be truly person centred. Schüssler Fiorenza (2001: 31) draws on DuBois to critique the dominant paradigms of competitive, combative modes of inquiry, characterized by adversarial debate and 'acerbic assault' as the basis of argument. She likens this to the practices of policing and interrogation, to 'a dividing, a splitting, a fracturing of the logical body, a process that resembles torture' (DuBois 2001: 13). She calls for a transformation of dominant paradigms to produce:

> A *different*, co-intentional, radical democratic paradigm of biblical learning/reading that allows scholars/authors and students/readers to become collaborators in the creation as well as the communication of the contents and methods of biblical knowledge. In such a political

learning model situated in the *ekklesia of wo/men,* both teachers/authors and students/readers recognize that knowledge is power which can serve domination or liberation. As feminists, however, we construe power, not in malestream terms as control over, but in radical democratic terms, as energy that moves us and invigorates life (Schüssler Fiorenza 2001: 34).

To summarize, notions of challenge have been part of the Post-Enlightenment tradition and this is reflected in the wider society where there is a restless search for novelty. The classical tradition linked with the notion of the heroic journey has embraced this, while the rock traditions have gone for more of an escape. Traditions have arisen with more of a concentration on nurture.

Theology

God forces us to do nothing except *become.* The only task, the only obligation laid upon us is: to become divine men and women, to become perfectly, to refuse to allow parts of ourselves to shrivel and die that have the potential for growth and fulfillment (Iragaray [1987] 1993: 68).

There is a strong sense that the dominant patriarchal traditions have been very challenging for women – whether this is in the relationship of women to the doctrines of original sin, the demonization of women's bodies, the stress on the maleness of God or the glorification of human suffering to name but a few of the challenges. The judgemental God of such pieces as the *Dies Irae* or Cardinal Newman's eschatological *The Dream of Gerontius* reflects the dominant signifier of the phallus, which makes women's position fragile, fragmented and ambiguous (Jantzen 1998: 170). Many feminists would prefer a theology based on Julian's claim that:

All shall be well, all shall be well and all manner of thing shall be well

Gerda Lerner charts the loss of female generativity in European symbolism. She notes that from the third to the second millennium the powers of generativity move from 'the women's vulva to the seed of man' (Lerner 1986: 146). She sees now the replacing of ideas of flourishing and growing with ones of law and order borrowed from the structures of the surrounding society. Female metaphors do occur from time to time. Julian of Norwich asks, 'O Mother Jesus, lead us to her breast' (Betty Wendelborn in Boyce-Tillman and Wootton 1993: 26) and I tried to encapsulate it in a hymn on Julian:

1. 'All shall be well, in love enclosed',
   An anchoress says in her cell.
   Her revelations clearly tell
   Of love that lives in heav'n and hell.

2. All shall be well, in love enclosed.
   A God of judgement stands condemned
   By One who only love can send,
   Whose breath can heal, whose touch can mend.

3. All shall be well, in love enclosed
   By One who holds us in his palm,
   Who made us, shields us with his arm,
   Redeems us, keeps us from all harm.

4. All shall be well, in love enclosed.
   The ring of fire will meet the rose
   In One who all our suffering knows,
   Sweet Mother Jesus, our repose.

(Boyce-Tillman 2006a: 9)

The placing of the image of the mother at the end here has its approach via images of a male God; this has meant that this hymn has not provoked the sort of response that Janet Wootton's hymn, *Dear Mother God* (Boyce-Tillman and Wootton 1993: 1, and see below).

Grace Jantzen also highlights how far the Anglo-American approach to the philosophy of religion is based on violence and death rather than birth and growth. She calls on her readers to 'think otherwise' and critiques the necrophilic models of theology (Arendt 1958: 246), which have generated a culture valuing war and destruction. She suggests a model of theology based on natality rather than mortality, drawing on the work of the philosopher Hannah Arendt (1996):

> The central contention of this book has been that it is urgently necessary for feminists to work towards a new religious symbolic focused on natality and flourishing rather than on death, a symbolic which will lovingly enable natals, women and men, to become subjects, and the earth on which we live to bloom, to be 'faithful to the process of the divine which passes through' us and through the earth itself (Jantzen 1998: 254).

These ideas have started a radical shift in Christology. Jesus can now become a model of human flourishing rather than a male saviour rescuing damsels in distress, by means of a messy and an inevitable death. He becomes an insightful teacher, a person of humour and compassion (Heyward 1989a).

Beatrice Bruteau draws together the themes of Theotokos – God-bearer— with the ecological movement and notions of ecstasy drawing on Rom. 8. 22, 19:

> Birth is bringing what is inside out. Ecstasy is bringing what is inside out. I am saying that the whole natural order, the cosmogenesis, is a cosmogestation. It is growing as an embryo grows, organizing itself, and progressing from stage to stage...This is the ecstasy of the Earth, reaching out of itself, well beyond itself. There is another saying from the Talmud that I like: "Who has Wisdom? The one who sees the unborn?" Our effort is to "see the unborn" in the Theotokos and help bring it to birth (Bruteau 1997: 174–76).

In concentrating on the themes of birth and nourishing, these theologians are returning to the very roots of Christian theology. Rita Nakashima Brock (2003) draws attention to the concentration on the birth and resurrection narratives in the first 1,000 years of Christian iconography. She points to symbols of an empty cross that is often growing and flourishing with symbols from the natural world growing from it, often set in a 'Paradise' garden that looks very like natural gardens in the cultures in which they were conceived. She looks at the absence of the crucified Christ and the numerous pictures of the child Christ in the arms of Mary who becomes, particularly in the Eastern traditions, Theotokos. She describes these times as anastasic – i.e. seeing the gospel primarily in terms of birth and resurrection with baptism as the central sacrament initiating believers into this life of flourishing. She then charts how with the advent of the Crusades, the images of the suffering Christ appear on the cross and a theology of the violence of God towards his Son is developed starting with Anselm. The crucifixion becomes a central feature of iconography and sacrifice the source of salvation, through the development of substitution theories of atonement. She links this with the development of the Church's condoning and legitimizing of violence, starting with the Crusades. It is the legacy of this violent, sacrificial theology that feminist theologians like Jantzen and Bruteau seek to counterbalance.

So this theology of nurture presents a challenge to the dominant culture in that it embodies the centrality of nurture and birth as productive of growth and flourishing; it challenges death-dealing paradigms with the end of producing life and growth. How the final fusion of these with 1,000 years of concentration on death and suffering will be achieved is not yet clear, for it challenges traditional theologies of the Eucharist with its concentration on sacrifice.[6]

Jesus' prophetic ministry often challenged the surrounding culture – for example when he reads the scroll in the synagogue in Lk. 4. 14–30 – by linking a theology of nurture with the prevailing violent theology. This story prefigures the entire course of Jesus' ministry. It contains a number of elements in relation to the surrounding story. In its original setting the story is set in the context of Jewish Messianic expectations. Jesus draws his texts from Isaiah 61 which itself dated from a time of hoped for deliverance from foreign domination. In the story, Jesus' reading forces all eyes to rest on him as he appears to set himself up as a potential leader in the struggle against Roman domination. Jeremias retranslates verse 22:

> They protested with one voice and were furious, because he only spoke about (God's year of) mercy (and omitted the words about messianic vengeance) (Jeremias 1958: 41–46).

Jesus tries to rebalance the surrounding vengeful culture and his audience was angry that he preached 'grace' rather than vengeance. Having already added an additional text from Isaiah, Jesus does not complete the original reading by adding the day of God's vengeance. Indeed, he follows his reading by stories from the Hebrew Scriptures of compassion to Gentiles. His audience's expectations are disappointed and their admiration turns to hostility. The insertion by Jesus, in his reading of Isa. 61. 1–2, of the verse from Isa. 58. 6–7 – let the oppressed go free – gives the passage a social thrust. The poor Jews in Isaiah 58 (elaborated in Nehemiah 5) were having to mortgage vineyards and sell children into slavery with rich Jews. The solution set out is that of the Year of Jubilee:

> Both Is 58 vv5 *et seq* and the Gospel of Luke address the wealthy. Both wish to inspire them to perform extraordinary far-reaching accomplishments, to renounce a large portion of their possessions and waive the recovery of debts, and to give alms generally, in this way alleviating the plight of the poor members of the community. Is 58 vv5–9a spoke to the upper stratum of the community immediately

---

6. Carter Heyward in celebrating the Eucharist in February 2003 substituted the word sacrament for sacrifice in Eucharist prayer. This provoked some discussion in the theological community.

after the Exile; Luke addresses his two-volume work to the upper stratum of the Hellenistic community (Albertz 1983: 203 translated in Bosch 1991: 103).

This clearly has contemporary relevance and has proved very important for the development of contemporary theologies, which have influenced both the nature and the subject matter of our contemporary interfaith celebrations. In this social gospel the established social order is overturned so that the marginalized become the objects of Jesus' compassion. The crossing of traditional boundaries demonstrates Luke's patent concern with peace-making and reconciliation. When Luke was writing, Christianity was not accepted as an approved religion in the Roman Empire and there were clearly pragmatic considerations in a way of non-violence and painting the Romans in a favourable light. Josephine Ford has drawn attention to this aspect of mission (Ford 1984).

The context was very similar to ours in that there was a crisis in identity, as Christianity appeared under attack from both Jews and pagans:

> [Gentile Christians] were asking "Who are we really? How do we relate to the Jewish past?" (Bosch 1991: 85).

Similarly today there is a crisis in understanding the place of Christianity alongside the other great faiths and the rising tide of paganism in the New Age in the present climate of zealous fundamentalism engaging in violence to further their cause. After recent wars in Afghanistan and the Middle East where it would appear that Christianity is locked in conflict with Islam, there is a real sense among various spiritual leaders that the effects of wars between religious zealots have been nothing but destructive. In this context Luke's call for no more vengeance has immense relevance in interfaith relations particularly following the 7 July bombings in the UK. At this time the local churches in Tooting banded together to send their prayers in solidarity with the Imam of the local mosque, which was attacked following the terrorist attacks in central London. Here only compassion can intervene in the cycle of violent revenge. We have an interfaith celebration annually in our church. I end it by saying that our two hours, when children play and sing together represents a model of interfaith dialogue that counterbalances the vengeful weapon-ridden images presented by contemporary media.

This reflects the concern for the outsiders and marginalized within our society. My local church's liaison with the local Sikh gurdwara has brought us in contact with asylum seekers from Afghanistan. The meeting with outsiders and the marginalized as explored in Chapter One – the marginalized Other – has been explored by such theologians as Martin Buber (1970) and developed by post-modern theorists such as Derrida (1972) and Levinas (1969). It is the encounter with the marginalized Other with respect and integrity that leads to personal transformation within the self. This thinking links the themes of repentance and forgiveness with the concern for the marginalized very powerfully.

The gospel of peace and reconciliation is clear in the work of dialogue with other faiths. It has been easy for Christianity to paint the differences between faiths and yet our interfaith group is constantly amazed at the ideas that we have in common. I recall, for example, an amazing conversation with a Sikh on the nature of the generosity of God's grace. This is a similar insight to the way in which Luke balances the mission to both Jews and Gentiles – the Gentiles being traditionally portrayed as subhuman in the Jewish culture of the day (Bosch 1991: 90).

Similarly, the call to interfaith dialogue means a delicate balancing of the needs and identity of the Christian church as well reaching out to those of other persuasions with compassion and understanding. This is incarnational Wisdom theology and challenges dominant perceptions both within and outside Christian circles.

Case Studies

Case Study One: Renegotiating Authority

This is the product of an oral history project examining the move of two of my good friends from Sierra Leone and the UK – an analysis of the narrative of missionary activity that was given to me by Jean and Peter Jones – a Reader in a South London Anglican congregation and his wife. It examines how they, in this migration, moved from a position to being 'nurtured' by their colonial rulers, in a way that they freely accepted and from which they, in their own view, benefited, to challenging the dominant values in England and taking on the role of nurturing their own community. It shows how growth

– in this case in a sense of authority – is achieved as challenge and nurture are negotiated effectively.

They came originally from Freetown, where the Church was identical to the one they encountered when they first came to England. This was because the colony was run until 1808 by the Sierra Leone Company, founded by William Wilberforce and Henry Thornton. It was the first country that deliberately embraced Western civilisation. They founded CMS which established schools and hospitals. There were many links with the UK as Jean says:

> I took the Sunday School Teacher's Certificate in Durham University which involved learning about different type of scriptures, Religious Knowledge and Bible reading. The papers came from Durham to Freetown.

Peter added:

> I was in the choir. The music was exactly the same as we sing. We did the Te Deum, the Psalms and then there were times when we did anthems, almost the same as the anthems at St Paul's [the South London church]. Everything that we practise here now has been done in Freetown, so it was not strange to us at all.

In the Freetown church the priest was black and the bishop was white. That would be the second or the third generation of black priests, because it was in 1804 that the first set of missionaries went to Freetown.

> We were trained with that Victorian discipline. We were brought up, not dragged up, so to speak, in such a way that we respect our elders. My grandmother used to have what you call 'house service'. That would be within the house—something like an intro before we start. (Sings) Oh, Lord open thou our lips. Even without organ. And I'm a child, Show forth thy praise. It's about 5.30 on a Sunday morning. For most of the people who were born in the 30s that is the principle of every Christian home. You must sing your prayer in the morning before you go to Church. No business of having a cup of tea or something.

They regarded all the Westerners in their country as missionaries – missionaries were people who taught them things:

> Missionaries were people who leave their country and come to this country in order to educate and to give them the facility of bringing them up to face whatever the future holds for them. They've built schools, they've built hospitals, they employed people to work in

those places. They can be people who've gone there to teach the African the way that they would like them to do things. In my days, I can remember – my father was a carpenter; and when these Europeans were sent to go and do a job in Freetown, they got the black blokes to teach them what they know, and they can see what they learn from the Africans to see, "O.K., well we'll improve it. We'll bring it up to this standard." Because when a Mr. Moore went to Sierra Leone working for Taylor Woodrow, my dad was the foreman, so they sent him to do the City & Guilds, and having done the City & Guilds, he was working hand in hand with Mr. Moore, you see, so well now I would look on to Mr. Moore as a missionary.

The move to England for them was a logical conclusion to the pursuit of education that the colonial experience had taught them. When he first came to England Peter worked as a labourer on building sites, then in J. Lyons' teashop and then in the factory as an engineer. His wife was doing the book-keeping there. They had no regrets about coming to England, but they found themselves still not in positions of authority. In the South London church they were the only black people and they experienced racism and exclusion. The turning point for them came when a parish priest invited Peter to train as Reader. Suddenly he saw himself as one who had authority in his community. He had turned from the subject of missionary activity to one who could be a missionary in England. They and others like them managed to find their balance between challenge and nurture. Their initial poor reception caused by the challenge they posed to a racist, colonialist society was balanced by their own integrity which remained loving and caring. It was a huge process of education for British society. Then Peter was given authority as a Reader and became a model of the authority that the black man might have. It is a story of courage and of catching a vision, and following that vision through a considerable amount of changes, balancing the roles of challenge and nurturing.

Case Study Two: Renegotiating an Inclusive Church

The traditional structures of the church have not always been good at inclusivity. Various groups of people have been regularly marginalized – the homosexual, the divorced, the mentally ill, the addicts, to name but a few. As Vincent Donovan declares, it is often not Christianity that has been preached but the Church (Donovan 1982: 54), which is a distortion of Christ's message.

Holy Rood House – Centre for Health and Pastoral Care – attempts to incarnate Christ for the excluded through its mission. It is a residential and day visit therapeutic centre. The Trust works within a holistic framework and approach to therapeutic and pastoral care, in close co-operation with medical, educational, religious and charitable bodies. Hospitality is offered within a gentle Christian ethos, with an ecumenical, open and inclusive policy. The place of mutuality and friendship is important, as a safe space is created for many guests who make their way to Holy Rood House from across the UK and sometimes from other countries, at a time of crisis, trauma and vulnerability.

Counselling, psychotherapy, creativity, spiritual accompaniment and meditation, body therapies, such as massage and physiotherapy, stress management with relaxation techniques and a daily rhythm of prayer, are all part of the weekly programme. Guests are self-referred or referred by health professionals, such as psychiatrists, GPs and health visitors, schools, community and youth workers, clergy and religious leaders, probation officers and the police. The Centre for Theology and Health had developed out of the therapeutic work, leading to research and training in associated areas, such as sexual abuse. [7]

Rowan Williams who is a Patron to the House, calls it a new form of Church. The move towards new ways of being church or fresh expressions is taken from the writings of Leonardo Boff, who referred to 'new ways of being church' and argued for the church as an 'event... (which) emerges, is born, and is continually reshaped...The principal characteristic of this way of being Church is community' (Boff 1990: 127–30). This parallels Tillich who declares that the church is 'simply and primarily a group of people who express a new reality by which they have been grasped' (Tillich 1964: 40–41). Stuart Murray echoes this call as he deals with *Post-Christendom: Church Mission in a Strange New World:*

> Deep yearnings for spiritually authentic, culturally attuned and attractive expressions of church are a hopeful feature of contemporary church life. This may mean planting churches that are not clones. It may mean transforming inherited modes of church. In fragmented, individualistic postmodernity, many long for authentic community and friendship. But churches are not always at their best. They can be

7. Based on the Holy Rood publicity leaflet.

superficial, vicious, patronising, dysfunctional and parochial. Mission, community and worship – three crucial components of church – are inspiring and energising emerging churches (Murray 2004: 253–55).

So the Holy Rood community attempts to reach people often considered outside the remit of the parish Church and make the Gospel a reality for them. It is served by a number of people who help to shape its vision. The original vision was that of its directors the Revds Elizabeth and Stanley Baxter who took over the North of England Healing Trust in 1993.[8]

In 2003 Brian Thorne, a consultant to the Trust, from his background in person-centred counselling and spirituality, challenged the churches:

> To the Church in whose arms I have been held and by whose sacraments I have been nourished since childhood, I say:
> - Reveal to humankind the God whose nurture is infinite love.
> - Cease to speak of the God of judgement for the justice of God is part of his infinite love and incomprehensible to humankind.
> - Proclaim to men and women that they are infinitely beloved and show them that they have the capacity to love as God loves.
> - Cease any effort to occupy the moral high ground for there lies the terrain of the hypocrites and the accusers.
> - Embrace and cherish the uniqueness of persons but never forget the mystery of our membership one of another and the interconnectedness of all things.
> - Honour the mystics and make known their passionate intensity so that praying becomes a love affair.
> - Cherish those of other faiths and of none and join with them in the search for that which offers life in abundance.
> - Celebrate the gift of sexuality and let it permeate the offering of unconditional love in all its forms.
> - Be at home in the invisible world so that the whole company of transcendent beings can accompany us in this mortal life.
> - Become a school of love where laughter is heard and intelligence is honoured.[9]

8. This had been at Spennithorne, near Leyurn and then moved to Thirsk, North Yorkshire. In 2003 it became a company limited by guarantee. In 1996 it purchased Thorpe House as a conference and training centre and creative arts resource. In 2005 it received the gift of Hexthorpe Manor in Doncaster where plans are to establish a therapeutic community of young people.

9. From a presentation at Holy Rood House, 1996.

Holy Rood House attempts to carry this out through storytelling and therapeutic engagement, working towards justice in the churches. One of the guests writes:

> 'This is the first place where I have felt safe enough to feel unsafe' Dave whispered as we said goodbye. He'd spent some time at Holy Rood House working with difficult issues in his life, and it is from my experience of working there that I engage in ideas of church as therapeutic community (Baxter 2006: 1).

The church, as a community of storytelling, has not been a safe space for many groups of people whose stories are not told, not heard and not celebrated. Here, a therapeutic community is built upon mutual storytelling, listening and acceptance. When stories are listened to, people become able to identify with one another in areas of grief and loss, celebration and hope. At the heart of Christian faith is the therapeutic journey of the Crucifixion/Resurrection story. This is often interpreted as a set of doctrines creating guilt and fear; at Holy Rood it becomes a journey of hope and liberation and is seen as a therapeutic back-drop for all human experience. The Easter Saturday experience is seen in this context as central to the human journey of waiting, isolation, struggle and process from hopelessness to new hope and new beginnings. It is also an ecological story of justice, forming the heart of a holistic therapeutic approach to being church at this time on this planet. So Holy Rood House becomes a witnessing community through its witness to the vulnerable stories out of which the community is formed.

The community reflects the way Jesus accompanied people on their journeys, and his own need for therapeutic community, the home of Mary, Martha and Lazarus at Bethany where he felt welcomed, fed, rested, conversed with friends and even enjoyed foot massage! Inspiration is drawn from people like the twelfth century mystic Hildegard of Bingen, who referred to God as *Counsellor of Souls* (Boyce-Tillman 2000b: 42). The community builds on the continuity of the churches' healing ministry and recognizes the interconnectedness of all things, helping the community to learn what it means to be wounded healers (Nouwen 1979) for a wounded twenty-first century world.

The community is built on the celebration of the therapeutic authority of *all* people; this expression of church draws on gifts of relational mutuality, while living within the forgiveness and healing of Christ. (Prov. 8. 1–2). God the counsellor who identifies with human processes towards health and well being, the abundant life Jesus spoke of, is in process too, accompanying the journeys as we accompany the be-coming of God through our own wisdom, Christ the wisdom of God, Sophia, present at the crossroads of our lives (Prov. 8. 1–2). She is witnessed through the embodied life of the community, 'as she was in Christ, the Word made flesh, our bodyselves become the ground upon which God moves through, with, and among us' (Heyward 1989b: 33).

Lisa Isherwood argues that divinity is found lying in the heart's fragility; we are vulnerable... as Jesus was, broken-hearted healers. The only way to heal both others and ourselves is in and through our redeeming vulnerability (Isherwood and Stuart 1998: 55). The inter-relation of our own therapeutic process and divine process empowers therapeutic community. The books in every room of Holy Rood House tell the stories of transformation:

> Thank you for being here for me – a place of safety full of God's peace and love.

> I came...I stayed… I am not alone.

> My time here has definitely been an adventure and the start of a new stage of my journey.

The story of Holy Rood House demonstrates how the realized vision of nurturing house concerned with bringing together the fragmented areas of theology, health and the arts challenges the dominant culture of both church and society. It establishes a new form of church – one concerned with nourishing those crippled by the challenges of modern living.

Case Study Three: Renegotiating Hymnody

The history of women hymn writers shows an interesting blend of challenge and nurture. Women are often seen as writing nurturing 'ditties for children'. But this is a skewing of the tradition. I interviewed the Revd Doctor Janet Wootton, who was President of the Congregational Union at the time and Editor of *Worship Live* – a liturgy resource magazine produced by Stainer and Bell. She sees the music of liturgies arranged by women as being very participative and involving music and dance, and therefore, more embodied than other kinds of Church music. She also sees it as freer in rhythm and in form. The woman with whom she collaborates and who often writes music for her words – Marlene Phillips –

challenged her to write her hymns in more free form words, because she said that she felt that was a characteristic of women's approach to writing music. 'Her way of writing challenged me to be more free in my writing.' She sees the starting point for her hymns being either a challenge or an inspiration. *'Here's an idea that is worth people singing about!'* Then comes the struggle. She identifies various areas of challenge in the process:

> It's a struggle with the idea; it's a struggle to be true and to keep integrity with the idea, and it would be so easy sometimes to get a rhyme that would work as far as the scansion and the poetry went, but would not – would let the idea down, and would let the original vision down and, therefore, to – and because it's a hymn, it has to be – the idea has to be made accessible. It has to be, technically, easily singable. It has to be inspiring to the people as they sing it, and to get all those together without losing the integrity – the idea – I find a most enormous struggle, but incredibly rewarding.

She sees the women's hymn writing tradition as neglected.

> I've studied women hymn writers specifically. I see myself in their line and because they were not just – there were a lot of women hymn writers, and those books which … books about hymn writing which had a load of chapters on hymn writers, *and now some women hymn writers*, I think have dishonoured the tradition, because women have played an enormous part in writing hymns, and they haven't just written ditties for children. They've written really good, radical and poetic material.

Women hymn writers have been omitted from collections because:

> The classic quote was that they didn't live interesting lives, and that's staggering!

She sees the development of inclusive language as an important part of developing the tradition:

> The first words that I ever wrote to a hymn were 'Dear Mother God':

This is a good example of a nurturing hymn text but it has proved challenging for some situations. Some people have walked out at the opening line, and failed to hear the very conventional theology of the rest of the text:

1. Dear Mother God, your wings are warm around us,
   We are enfolded in your love and care;
   Safe in the dark, your heartbeat's pulse surrounds us,
   You call on us, for you are always there.

2. You call to us, for we are in your image,
   We wait on you, the nest is cold and bare –
   High overhead your wing beats call us onward,
   Filled with your power, we ride the empty air.

3. Let not our freedom scorn the needs of others –
   We climb the clouds until the strong heart sings –
   May we enfold our sisters and our brothers,
   Till all are strong, till all have eagles' wings.
   (Janet Wootton in Boyce-Tillman and Wootton 1993: 1)

She continues on the distinction between public and private:

> I've written poetry all my life, but only for private consumption, and
> it was quite a big step then to move out into writing for public
> consumption.

She sees herself looking again at the life of Jesus rather than
simply the birth and death narratives.[10]

> Where is all the radical teaching and life of Jesus? The explosion of his
> actual life? So that's another thing. It's to bring that out; the things that
> happened around Jesus. And then the other is to write about the
> challenge of the Gospel, then, to real, honest, human lives, so that – I
> don't want to write particularly about, a lot of – I find a lot of worship
> hymns. I do like worship hymn – the worship song tradition –, and it
> is beginning to change to, but I find that a lot of it is selfish – self-
> centred. *I want to know Jesus. This is what Jesus has done for me…..Jesus has
> washed away my sins, and I have the victory.* Again, if you look down the
> contents list of some of those hymns – some of those resources – the
> section beginning with the word *I* is enormous, and I want to write
> much more about God's challenge to us as a human community –
> what our response should be, and the riches and resources that God
> has for us as people. So I've written a hymn for Homelessness Sunday,
> for example, which challenges the whole community to respond in a
> just way.

She sees herself in a long line of women who did challenge the
status quo like Anna Lætitia Barbauld, or Aitkin as she became,
who wrote a lot of really good, satirical political writing, always
under pseudonyms. She sees worship as anodyne and sanitized
(which links with the sense of risk we identified earlier in this
chapter).She gives as an example a homeless poet she knew whose
poems on homelessness were explosive.

10. The hesitations in the ensuing interview have been taken out.

He said, "I've written some hymns as well," and his hymns were anodyne…. It was all about *Sweet Jesus*, and – and I said to him, "Why don't you write those brilliant, radical ideas into the hymns?" And he couldn't even … he didn't … he just thought it was inappropriate. *It wasn't the sort of thing you wrote in hymns.*

The balance of private devotion and public challenge was one that concerned her:

Anna wrote prose hymns for children, and they've got some very good radical ideas. For example, she writes against the slave trade, so she writes hymns about the poor Negro woman seeing her children go off into slavery, and why should she have to suffer that when other women don't. So that's quite a strong idea to put in the eighteenth century, and she also talks of God as "Mother", but on the other hand she writes hymns saying, about – very moralising hymns….. about people knowing their place in society, and working hard…and getting on with things, and *That was the way to Salvation*. A very Protestant work ethic.

There is a difference between the private poem and the hymn which is a public statement and reflects the dilemmas we explored in Chapter Four over public and private. As well as denominational differences:

with the homeless hymn writer that I'm thinking about, I think he … he isn't from a Protestant background. I think he's from a Catholic background, so the hymn tradition is different…of course there are some brilliant challenging Catholic hymns, Estelle White, and so on. But I think, probably, he's coming from a different kind of tradition, so that the only hymns he knows are the ones that are comforting. With Anna Lætitia Barbauld, I think she really wanted to … she was working in a school, her husband's school, and I think she really … she bought into the moralising work ethic…but in the background she was writing the satirical material against, well against the established Church – against Britain's war effort. Brilliant – a brilliant poem, er prayer, which she suggested could be used well by Britain saying, *We are now about – Almighty God, we are about to go out and slaughter our brothers, and we (you know) we pray for your blessing upon this effort to kill the people that you have made.*

There is a real tension between the devotional song/hymn, such as Charlotte Elliott's *Just as I am*, and other types of hymnody. As the editor of *Worship Live*, she advises hymn writers on their submissions:

Some of the hymns that I get are too challenging and not enough nurturing, or the ideas are too dense – too densely written, and people would – would be interrupted in their singing by having to work out what the words were about – like *Hark the Herald Angels Sing.*

She dislikes the happy ending which appears to be added on:

I do decry the 'happy ending' that says, *All these terrible things are happening, and the world is such a terrible place, but we'll be all right really*....I always send back happy endings to writers and say, you know *This is the thing about integrity that the happy ending fails the integrity of the hymn.* If the hymn is about, about the sorrows of life, and if there's going to be happiness in it – I mean, in other words there's going to be hope, but the hope should be interwoven then, truly in the hymn and not tacked on at the end, as it so often is. And I know, there's a particular hymn of mine – gosh! – *God is our Father, what does it mean when parents abuse and damage their children? When Christ is the Bridegroom, what does it mean when marriages end in false – in sharp disillusion?* And an editor sent that back to me and said, "Can you write a verse that says...", you know, the last line of each verse is *Help us make sense of the dream.* And an editor sent it back and said they couldn't use it in its present form because they wanted a happy ending. They wanted a verse in which – which says *Now we make sense of the dream,* and I tried ever so hard to write that verse, and in the end I couldn't do it because the reality is that parents do abuse and damage their children – not all parents – but it is hard for some people to get the notion of God as Father, or Christ as Bridegroom, and it's challenging. Oddly, it's been sent back twice. Once by the person who wanted the happy ending, and I'm trying to challenge male imagery – the Bridegroom, the Father – and it was sent back by Brian Wren because it started, *God is our Father,* and he said, *couldn't I – haven't I read in some papers about God is Mother?* I thought that was interesting, because it was actually challenging God as the Father.

Although she had a musical education she finds that the challenge of writing music is usually too great, partly because of her fear of rejection:

It would break my heart, I think, if somebody looked at the music and said it was worthless.....music is closer to my soul. ......I can't have music playing in the background. I have to sit down and listen to it. I can't listen to music unmoved. So, therefore, I couldn't go to a concert and listen to music, because I would be embarrassed at my reaction...music is a very, very personal thing, and a very private thing for me.

She is in a tradition of women hymn-writers who wrote words while the writers of the music are male, adding:

> the history of creative – the history of art [music, poetry, painting], generally, has been dominated by men, in terms of what has sold or what has been accepted, or what has been valued, and that makes me extremely angry…because it must mean that thousands of years' worth of women's creativity has been trodden under foot.

Poetry may be the exception starting with Sappho.

> I think…. very definitely, that music writing has – because it's been valued, has been, therefore, only open to men, and that women composers have been de-valued, or women have been told that it's – it's not something that women can do…my generation, or my particular culture, was given – we were educated; very highly educated. But I was told by a man that it was – my mother was told by this man – that it wasn't worth educating me, because I would only go and marry and have babies…the other big thing was a tension between marriage and using this education…for that generation of girls – *if you get married you're going to spoil it all* – when I met Chris, my husband now, I met him while we were at university, and my aunt said, "Oh, that's the end of her career, then. That's the end of … What a shame to throw all that away." And so there was a struggle within my family to prove that I could have a boyfriend, and then a fiancé, and then a husband without throwing away this education which had been expensive within my family. They didn't pay for the education, but school uniforms and things were quite a struggle.

So she chose not to have children. She talked about the loss of the publishers concentrating on women's issues and material and sees a huge backlash from our work in the 1960s and 70s.

> Even the 80s, we always talked about *the backlash would come,* and the backlash has come in the most horrible way, because it's come in apathy – a generation of younger women and men who don't see there's a problem any more.

In this interview with a person who has done so much to nurture women hymn writers the themes of challenge and nurture are negotiated. While she uses and champions the use of nurturing images like Mother God she also sees the need to challenge the glib happy endings often offered by a naïve Christianity and acknowledges that although in the realm of eternity the struggle may already be won, in terms of time the victory is not always apparent and that this experience also needs to be present in

Christian hymnody. Interestingly, just as in Holy Rood House, by using images of nurturing she challenges the dominant culture; but such thinking has certainly produced growth in contemporary women hymn writers who are encouraged through it to write honestly of their experiences through the medium of the hymn.

Case Study Three: Renegotiating Compassion – Compassionate Restraint

We have already seen in Chapter One how the State tends to use violence for the maintenance of its value systems. This is true of both prison and psychiatric services and schools for the differently abled but there are a number of examples of attempts to bring more nurture into these situations and two are cited here. Many websites examine the violence of mental health institutions:

> If the government wanted a mental health service based on compassion it would commission an inquiry into the effects of force in psychiatric treatment, argues clinical psychologist Rufus May.

'Psychiatric assault' includes the use of physical restraint procedures, forced drugging (rapid tranquillisation), seclusion, and pain compliance techniques (where the person is hurt to encourage them to comply with the forced chemical or physical restraint procedure). The process of 'Acuphase' is one of the most common uses of force on the psychiatric ward. It is used to manage challenging behaviour. Forced Acuphase is where a person is pinned down undressed so that his or her buttocks are revealed. The person is then given a psychiatric cocktail (at present this is usually haloperidol and lorazepam) that is administered by hypodermic syringe into the person's buttock. The National Institute for Clinical Excellence (NICE) 'Disturbed Behaviour Clinical Guidance' (2004) draft guidelines suggest that all attempts to avoid forced treatment using de-escalation techniques should be tried prior to the use of force. There are however no structures to enforce this recommendation.[11]

The result of this is that trust is broken and the person is less likely to seek help in future. They also internalize (as self-policing) the anger generated by their experiences and they embrace a lifetime role as a 'sick' patient. Rufus May continues:

> One can feel like a radical writing about a peaceful and fair approach to mental health care. This is mainly because (since the mid-seventies)

11. 7 February 2005, www.psychminded.co.uk (contacted 27 Oct 2006).

there has been a lack of literature looking at it. When I facilitate self help groups in community and hospital settings I do not feel radical. In my experience in in-patient settings more than half of the people who receive treatment for psychosis and or self harm are in touch with and unhappy about how they have been treated and have good ideas about how they would like to have been treated. We need to listen to these testimonies.

Force denies the individual dignity and it damages the spirit... Yet inpatient services designed to care for such states regularly use coercive practice. One of my clients talks about her "secondary mental illness", this is the one created by mental health services and the forced drugging she has endured. She describes it as a shadow in her mind.[12]

He longs for a compassionate approach teaching people to manage their experiences, adding sadly:

Maybe we should rename mental health services 'psychiatric drugging services!' This use of neuroleptic drugs as a maintenance (long-term) treatment occurs despite evidence that alternative approaches work.[13]

He describes the Soteria Project in Scandinavia where medical and humanistic approaches are brought together ending with the challenge:

This is a human rights issue, as democratic citizens we should have the right to a force-free mental health care. Those of us who believe in a compassionate approach to mental health need to come together to struggle for this vision...Over the last ten years I have had the privilege of supporting others to manage their disturbing experiences without the use of force, sometimes without the use of medication.[14]

So here we see people trying to bring a measure of compassion into this challenging environment.

Camila Batmanghelidjh[15] uses a policy of compassionate and robust restraint with the members of her theatre company, Kid's Company. This policy challenges notions of how to treat the ill behaved:

---

12. 7 February 2005, www.psychminded.co.uk (contacted 27 Oct 2006).

13. 7 February 2005, www.psychminded.co.uk (contacted 27 Oct 2006).

14. www.psychminded.co.uk (contacted 27 Oct 2006). Rufus May is a clinical psychologist with Bradford District Care Trust's assertive outreach team, and Honorary Research Fellow with the Centre for Community Citizenship and Mental Health at the University of Bradford. He helps organize a monthly public meeting about different peaceful approaches to mental health called Evolving Minds.

15. Desert Island Discs, BBC Radio 4 interview, 27 October 2006, 9am.

Knoxville Adaptive Education Center (KAEC) has been a lifeline for our son, David, who has Asperger's-type autism and bipolar disorder. At KAEC, public school for grades three through twelve, nearly one hundred "seriously emotionally disturbed" (the designation given by the Individuals with Disabilities Education Act to students with mental illnesses) children are taught discipline in an atmosphere of unlimited kindness. David came to KAEC at ten years old, after a traumatic stay in a mental hospital. He was obsessed with dinosaurs and would often chatter about them with giddy abandon. At other times, he would suddenly bite, kick, or scratch other children, seemingly with no provocation. Yet, after a bipolar rage, he often showed deep remorse or begged to be comforted. Sometimes he said we ought to kill him...We tried every possible "cocktail" of medications, plus a score of behavior modification techniques. My and my husband's eyes met with alarm, hoping for the best as we entered a dim, cavernous lobby. Immediately, something felt right about this place. There are time-out rooms when a child explodes and "compassionate restraint" if a teacher or student is endangered. Support can be summoned in minutes through the walkie-talkie every teacher keeps at hand. Yet most staff members seem to work with ironic good humor at the risk of taking two steps forward even after the most disastrous step back. Teachers who are physically threatened in the morning can be seen walking that same student out to the bus in the afternoon, saying, "Listen, tomorrow is another day." Later, I discovered that in the first few weeks David often needed as many as 15 restraints in a single day.[16]

In these two contexts compassionate restraint provides a synthesis of balance and nurture.

Case Study Four: Renegotiating Anger

Many oppressed groups, women among them, have reclaimed the presence of anger in the Divine to bring the notions of their own challenge being acceptable and can be a source of nurture (as we saw in renegotiating forgiveness in Chapter Four) so that it becomes 'a fire that cooks things rather than a fire of conflagration' (Pinkola Estes 1992: 364).

The transfiguration of anger is a movement *from rage to outrage* (her italics). Rage implies an internalized emotion, a tempest of Rage, or what might be called untransfigured anger, can become calcified bitterness. What rage wants and needs is to move toward positive

16. http://www.kcs.k12tn.net/public_affairs/PIE/features/KAEC-NAMI.htm 27 October 2006.

social purpose, to become a creative force or energy that changes the conditions that created it. It needs to become out-rage.

Outrage is love's wild and unacknowledged sister. She is the one who recognizes feminine injury, stands on the roof, and announces it if she has to, then jumps into the fray to change it. She is the one grappling with her life, reconfiguring it, struggling to find liberating ways of relating. She is the one who never bores God or Goddess (Monk Kidd 1992: 186–87).

Nowhere is this clearer than in Lyn Brakeman's reworking of the story of Jephthah's daughter (Judges 11). Jephthah is a king who makes a vow to God to offer as a sacrifice the first person who comes out of the doors of his house to meet him, if God gives him victory over the Ammonites. It is his daughter (whose name the reader is never told); and for her there is no substitute made available, as in the story of Abraham and Isaac, and all she can do is ask for time to go with her sisters to celebrate her own funeral rites. It is a horrendous story and in her reworking of the story of Jephthah's daughter entitled *The Spirituality of Anger*, shows Jephthah's daughter standing in front of Adonai and going through various stages in her process of grieving. Initially, she understands the weakness of her father but then she finds her anger for her father and her desire for revenge but Adonai stays silent. She remembers her commiseration with her sisters in the mountains and then she turns her anger against Adonai for not protecting her. Adonai stays silent. She remembers the good times with her father and asks Adonai for his opinion of her father. Adonai stays silent. Finally, she dances her 'untamed and ravenous rage'. And now finally Adonai speaks:

Blessed daughter, I see you. I know you. I honor you. I name you Beloved. My vow is this: Your word is now incorporated into my Word, and I will make your raging dance flesh in many women – many, many women. Beloved is your name. Never forget your name, O Woman. Remembering is resistance…and life (Brakeman 2005: 52).

Commenting on contemporary responses to this, Lyn Brakeman ends:

What do we do today to uphold this call to remember our "daughters of Jephthah?" We pray. We band together aggressively rather than huddling together. We work to change cruel traditions and rewrite abusive theologies. We laugh. We rage. We share shreds of story. We coach each other. We empower each other as we support our one-step-at-a-time choices to do what feels powerful. We lament and howl at the moon. We love each other fiercely, body and soul. We claim full right to our sexuality and refuse to define ourselves simply as biological agents of reproduction. We forgive by continuing to gather and to live. And, most of all, we hold our God accountable in violently honest prayer, prayer that is energized by anger. This is the spirituality of resistance then and now (Brakeman 2005: 55).

Monica Furlong sums this up in a poem entitled *Fire in the Stubble:*

Lord, I long for your fire among my stubble.
You have had the grain, such as it poorly was.
The empty field longs for your blistering wrath.
It longs to laugh in the joy of your white-hot rage,
To crackle and fall to ash on the dark-sweet soil,
To be killed and born anew in your furious flames (Furlong 2004: 49).

Can liturgy be used in this process? Anger is not often part of public worship. Denise Dijk describes a liturgy of mourning created by womanist theologians in 1992, remembering 500 years of colonialism and neo-colonialism:

- On one day they fasted and mourned remembering resisters of racism and wrote their names on a mourning band. They walked with chains round their feet and expressed their anger in making a mourning cloth.
- Then they celebrated moving from death to life, singing songs of resistance, burning the cloth and breaking the fast.
- They made a cloth of life celebrating their commitment to a plan of action and dressed in beautiful clothes (Dijk 2001: 76).

This ritual shows literally a re-membering of the past – a putting of it together in a new form that is empowering rather than disempowering. The re-membering of our lost ancestors is an important part of this process and many hymns and songs show that the process of recovering lost stories can lead to empowerment. When Elisabeth Schüssler Fiorenza wrote *Welcome, Biblical Women* she recalled lost women like Sarah, Hagar, Rebecca, Rachel, Leah, Miriam, Jael, Deborah, Judith, Tamar and so on (Neu 2002: 142–43).

Carol Christ (2003) sees some goddess feminists turning to the Hindu image of Kali as a way of finding the nurturing power of anger's presence in the Divine:

> With her tongue sticking out, swords in her hands, and skulls on her
> belt, ready to battle the forces of evil, she encourages Western women
> to express anger about injustice and the restrictions of their lives (Christ
> 2005: 232).

However, she warns of the dangers of such an image being linked
with fundamentalisms. She calls for the retaining of the stuck-out
tongue but the removal of the swords. She also sees her image as a
reclaiming of the dark-skinned goddesses and of the fertile qualities
of the transforming earth (Gimbutas 1989). She recommends rolling
into the image the African water goddess, Oshun, who represents
creativity, sexuality and love (Teish 1985).

Jean Shinoda Bolen dealing with archetype of Kali sees the
psychological task as the holding of the opposites of wrath and
wisdom. Wisdom tempers wrath and reins in the savage lioness or
bloodthirsty Kali. She sees bottled up anger or anger directed
against the self as causing depression:

> Depression, codependency and victimization are not attributes of Kali
> but they are the flip side of this archetype. The ferocity of Kali needs to
> be harnessed rather than suppressed or unleashed in a blind rage.
> Then Kali energizes the insistence that a problem be faced and
> solved....and you become a force to be reckoned with. The mother
> who won't take no for an answer when her child's needs are ignored
> by a school system and perseveres until the system is changed, is one
> example. She is the cancer patient who is an advocate on her own
> behalf. This woman is usually described by her physician as "difficult,"
> because she does not just do as she is told. She is informed, asks hard
> questions, and wants to know why certain tests or treatments are
> proposed and not others (Shinoda Bolen 2001: 91–2).

Her writing is in the context of the development of a
compassionate cronehood for older women:

> Crone archetypes are those potentials for development in individual
> women who come into their crone years and continue to grow
> spiritually and psychologically. Compassion is the essential one.
> Outrage demands justice, but outrage and compassion together become
> justice tempered with mercy (Shinoda Bolen 2001: 120).

Summary

This chapter has started by examining how fast contemporary
society moves. It examined how this may be related to Western

views of death and how funeral rites may provide strategies of resistance to this. It has looked at how the Church's view of risk may have had gender implications for Church membership and how a need for balance might be examined in worship. It has looked at how women hymn writers have brought challenge and nurture together and how Holy Rood House shows how notions of Church can be renegotiated to include notions of challenge and nurture. It has looked at how challenge and nurture have come together in the process of claiming authority. The idea of compassionate restraint is developed alongside a notion of transfigured anger as part of the justice-seeking process.

Chapter Six

UNDERSTANDING WISDOM

1. Let all the stars in heaven
   Sing out to God creator,
   And use whatever sound
   Their various forms can utter.

CHORUS

 And we will praise a God
 That is beyond a name
 Who taking human form
 As Son of Mary came.

2. We cannot tell what womb
   Within th' encircling cosmos
   Is giving birth to God
   To make another Christmas.

CHORUS

3. We cannot tell what shapes
   Can hold our God's revealing,
   But Jesus shared my flesh
   And that for me is healing.

CHORUS

4. We cannot tell what cross
   Today or in the future
   Or many moons ago
   Will bruise God-given nature.

CHORUS

5. Let galaxies rejoice
   And praise divine empowering
   The countless gifts of love
   Of generous God's enshowering.

CHORUS

 (Boyce-Tillman, 2006a: 47)

Rational/intuitive

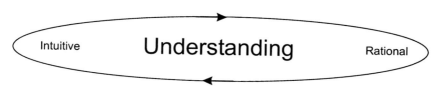

Fig. 12. Understanding

Society

Post-Enlightenment Western culture has valued reason and devalued intuition. The Enlightenment project based on 'I think therefore I am', saw the answer to successful human society as the dominance of reason over human beings' unruly passions and imaginings. The intuitive aspects of the Church were suppressed in favour of theological codifications. Academe was suspicious of anything that smacked of the emotional or spiritual. Methodologies were developed that claimed to be objective, based on the principle that human beings could be dispassionately objective about objects, situations and even other people. Disconnection between the observer and the observed was pursued and a culture of alienation and violence (in such methods as biological dissection) was developed. The emerging discipline of science and the older discipline of mathematics joined hands to develop methodologies that supposedly produced objective truths. These involved generalizing from large groups of objects and people by means of statistical methodologies (which often took little account of the fact that the groups chosen were very similar in ethnicity, gender or social class). This cult of 'objectivity' played a crucial part in tyrannizing groups of all kinds with notions of normality. The story, the oldest form of passing wisdom from one generation to the next, was devalued in favour of the lecture, and in methodological terms stories were reduced to the 'merely anecdotal'. This culture passed from the academy into political judgements which are now supported by processes of number-crunching whether it is the controlled experimentation double blind control trials of the drug companies or the computed statistics of standardized attainment test scores that are used to produce league tables of schools. While there is a danger in seeing a single truth in a single story there is a cold intellectualism in seeing differences reduced to numbers and the natural world and human beings alike reduced to the status of alienated subjects. Emotional responses unchecked by reason lead to violence, but cold principles have also destroyed vast tracts of the earth's surface and peoples. So, when the subjectivity of the story loses touch with the objectivity of the number, then emotionalism will be a twisted form of the intuitive and set itself against cold unfeeling principles.

Self

Within the self the visionary with its stress on imagination is now persecuted by years of educational enculturation and appears in the unhelpful fantasizing and grotesque imagery that characterize both mental illness and the world of film and video alike. Alienated from their own imaginative potential, Westerners hand their imaginative capacities over to the big multinationals. In 2003, I saw a US game that is popular with children. It is an elaborate game with many roles within which the playing cards that feature monsters, dragons and erstwhile deities are asked to function in a series of attacks and defenses. As the child related the rules to me I wondered why he was not using the same material to create his own stories rather than relying on the rules of a large corporation, that somewhere was making a great deal of money out of controlling what was once a free flowing human activity. Alan MacFarlane sees magic alive and well, but in an exploited and controlled form:

> Our modern lives, however apparently "rational" and free of superstition, contain much magical thinking. We curse our politicians, half-hoping the curse will strike them down. We pray for delivery when we are frightened, we engage in a thousand minor protective rituals through our day. One reason, Harry Potter, the hobbits and even Alice in Wonderland strike so many resonances is that because even as adults we are reluctant to relinquish magic. Certainly many great artists seem like magicians.
>
> We may think that we now live in a "disenchanted" world. That we have banished the witches, vampires, goblins.....Magic is alive and well. Its capital is Disneyland (MacFarlane 2005: 92–93).

Emotion is separated from reason too. Many mental illnesses can be laid at the door of the suppression of emotion in the UK. The tears and outpourings of grief that followed the death of Princess

Diana, were only partly related to her. The grief and tears represented a stopper being removed from a national bottle already overfull of unexpressed emotion. There is some indication that one of the causes of senile dementia lies in unexpressed emotion. Certainly, in my own experience, a member of my family was found wandering apparently confused and taken into hospital with suspected, dementia. When I visited him I reminded him that a year previously his only daughter, of whom he had been very fond, had died. We talked about her and he was able to express some of his feelings. Within two days he had returned to his home 'in his right mind'. Unexpressed grief is a serious cause of depression; and despite the collective pursuit of reason, violent angry acts are on the increase. The dislocation of these parts of the person leads to profound disfunctioning, whether it is the lack of perspective of the hysteric or calculating cruelty of the psychopath. If the pilots of the planes that crashed into the twin towers of the World Trade Centre in New York could have felt any empathy with any of their victims they could not have carried out the act. The separation of reason from emotion denies the most central of human emotions – empathy, the ability to walk in the other's shoes. When the visionary part of the self loses touch with the scientific rational part of the self then the person will experience either a lack of perspective or cold cruelty.

Valuing Intuition

In the context of education many educationalists, like William James and John Dewey from the late nineteenth century onwards, have struggled to bring more intuitive elements into the curriculum. This quotation from William James shows how this movement favoured characteristics marginalized by the dominant culture – a call to Wisdom theology:

> Be patient, then, and sympathize with the type of mind that cuts a poor figure in examinations. It may, in the long examination which life sets us, come out in the end in better shape than the glib and ready reproducer, its passions being deeper, its purposes more worthy, its combining power less commonplace and its total mental output consequently more important (James 1900: 10).

The Transcendentalists in nineteenth century USA attempted to rebalance the growing rationalism and scientific methodology of

Western culture. Ralph Waldo Emerson in 1842 prized the value of intuition drawing on the Idealism of Locke and Kant's idea of transcendental forms.[1] Transcendentalism opposed empiricism, which claimed that knowledge was gained only from experience of the material world. They claimed that physical world observations were only appearances of reflections of the spirit. In their thinking reason was applied to the spiritual world. This was their strategy of resistance – drawing on Neo-Platonism – to apply reason in this way individuals would be able to resist customs and social codes relying on an intuition informed by reason which would lead to Absolute Truth.[2] It was a bold attempt to bring intuition and rationality together.

Such thinking is still to be found. Academics in many disciplines are challenging the objectivity that characterizes academic work. We have already seen how Lois Holzman left the traditions of psychology to develop a more improvisatory, intuitive approach which she calls social therapy (Holzman 2002: 8–10). It was the methodology I was using at the same time in my own research with children's developing creativity in the area of music (Tillman 1987). She used methodologies that are very popular in the world of qualitative research which still struggles to find a ready acceptance in the public world, and finally decided to leave academe (Holzman 2002: 14–20).

In her work we see an important move towards accepting performance as a form of research and 'artistic 'products being legitimate research outcomes and ways of accessing truth. Patricia Hill Collins shares her view:

> Oppositional knowledge takes diverse forms; in my view historically oppressed groups do produce social theories. Not only do the forms assumed by these theories – poetry, music, essays and the like-diverge from academic theory, but the purpose of such theory also seems distinctly different. Social theories emerging from and/or on behalf of historically oppressed groups investigate ways to escape from, survive in and/or oppose prevailing social and economic injustice (Hill Collins 1998: xii–xiii).

Here, she draws attention not only to the imbalances in the system but also to the different form the theories might take,

1. http://www.transcendentalists.com/terminology.html. 25 November 2006.
2. http://library.advanced.org/12160/philosophy/trans.htm. 25 November 2006.

moving the debate from the purely rational to include the intuitive forms of artistic expression.

Attacks on scientific methodology have also come from the environmental movement (Lovelock 1979: 16), where there are attacks on the atomistic, deconstructive aspect of scientific methodology (Lovelock 1979: 127). A new empathetic relationship with the natural world is being discovered. I remember a primary school project on water when science as a subject had just been introduced into the primary curriculum. A room full of test tubes and various chemical tests failed to hold the interest of a class of six year-olds. An imaginative teacher decided to abandon the project in that form and have 'Adopt a puddle week'. The puddles in the playground were now named and the study was into the identity of a named friend. The children were now on fire to get to know as much as they could about their 'puddle friend'.

Neil Douglas Klotz sees the balancing of this area as the balancing of light and dark (see Chapter Three):

> The light of *aor* [all varieties of illuminating intelligence] that awakes and makes sense of experience is called *nuhra in* the Aramaic of Jesus. We can compare this light with the darkness of *hoshech* [disordered, chaotic, dense, unknowable darkness] as we would compare two different but complementary forces, like the straight rays of sunlight and the swirling energies of cloud and wind. Psychologically speaking, they are like the start-to-finish, cause-and-effect nature of rational thinking compared with the zig-zag nature of intuitive thinking (Douglas-Klotz 1999: 76).

David Abram's book *The Spell of the Sensuous* calls for a re-evaluation of the nature of language:

> the organic, interconnected structure of any language is an extension of echo of the deeply interconnected matrix of sensorial reality itself. Ultimately, it is not human language that is primary, but rather the sensuous, perceptual life-world, whose wild, participatory logic signifies and elaborates itself in language (Abrams 1996: 84).

All the arts were disadvantaged by the scientific paradigm. In an effort to get itself accepted in the dominant paradigm and hold its place in academe, for example, academic musicologists concentrated on the rational aspects on the art and downplayed all the other aspects. And yet artists' accounts of their process show that intuition and reason are both parts of the creative process as we saw in Chapter Three.

To summarize, Western rationalism has come to be at odds with intuition and its associated expressive and spiritual elements. The world of academe has passed to politics its support of so-called objective methods of evaluation. This has resulted in an imbalance in many areas and excessive alienation in the field of validated Western knowledge.

Theology

Bishop Kallistos Ware in a talk on views of the after-life in Orthodox theology referred to St Augustine's belief that unbaptised babies went to hell. The Bishop described the saint as not a cruel man but a logical one.[3] There is a violence implicit in a paradigm of the self that privileges rationality over intuition. We have seen in Chapter One, how the Enlightenment project was based on this dominance and produced paradigms of objectivity which were *de facto* more 'true' than those based on subjective experience. The upshot of this imbalance has been millions of women executed for witchcraft. Matilda Joslyn Gage in 1893 documents the sorry story of murder, hanging and general persecution. In this process she sets true civilization against the church:

> Thus, now, as in its earlier ages, wherever the light of civilization has not overcome the darkness of the church, we find women still suffer from the ignorance and superstition which, under Christianity teaches that she brought sin into the world (Gage 1893/1998: 165).

Many theologians have striven to place the experiencing subject at the centre of theological discourse rather than the tradition of objectivity rooted in dogmas and doctrines. This has been apparent in several ways. The centrality of lived experience to feminist theology reflects the role of Wisdom in the Hebrew Bible. Although the Wisdom books vary on their approach to actual issues such as marriage and wealth, the Wisdom tradition does appear to represent a discovery within Judaism of a way of examining human experience critically within a theological context (Conn 1980: 24–27).

Kwok Pui Lan calls for a biblical interpretation based on 'dialogical imagination'. She draws this methodology from Asian Christians who are heirs to both the biblical story and to their own story (Kwok 1995: 13).

3. Talk at Sarum College, Salisbury, 4 November 2006, The After Life.

Many feminist methodologies use the interview (particularly of an unstructured or semi-structured kind) as a way of accessing a spirituality rooted in people's lived experience, rather than logic and argument. Academic philosophers and theologians like Grace Jantzen base their work on a philosophy of desire rather than the rationality of creedally based belief systems, drawing on the gap between these creedal statements and the lived experience of women. Her concern is not with an objective truth of the traditional kind but of the effect of the religious symbolic on human subjectivity both at a personal and a global level. This leads her to attack realist theological positions in favour of re-envisioning truth (Jantzen 1998: 192).

In this complexity, the role of the visionary experience is being re-evaluated and rediscovered. There is increasing interest in medieval visionaries like Julian of Norwich, Margery Kemp and Hildegard of Bingen. As one who regularly presents these women dramatically, I find it interesting that following many performances, women, in particular, will seek validation of their own visionary experiences. They will start tentatively with statements like 'I have never shared this with anyone before but...' The telling of the stories of women of the past as a way of validating the experience of contemporary women has helped to redress the oppression of the intuitive response by the tools of the Enlightenment objectivity project. From an encounter with the spiritualities of the so-called New Age[4] comes a rediscovery of a working spirituality of angels redressing their status as dusty relics of a bygone irrational age. So the challenging of the rational leads us inevitably to the mystical. The restoration of the notion of a God who is unknown is a necessary rebalancing of the rationalism of fundamentalism with all its rational answers and its confident security. This is the opening of a liturgy that I wrote that was entitled *The God Who is Beyond All that We can Ask or Imagine:*

V. O God, we long to know
R. O God, we long not to know

V. O God, give us enough security to live
R. And enough insecurity to avoid arrogance

V. O God, help us to be sure where we stand
R. O God, help us to respect the place where others stand

4. For a summary of this phenomenon see Boyce-Tillman (2000a: 153–66).

Many mystical texts were not included in the canonic texts of the New Testament. These texts were often labeled Gnostic. *The Gospel of Mary Magdalene,* is just such a text:

> What is matter? Will it last forever?
> The Teacher answered:
> "All that is born, all that is created,
> All the elements of nature
> Are interwoven and united with each other.
> All that is composed shall be decomposed;
> And everything returns to its roots;
> Matter returns to the origin of matter.
> Those who have ears to hear, let them hear"
> After this, the Blessed One
> Greeted them, saying:
> "Peace be with you-may my Peace
> arise and be fulfilled within you!
> Be vigilant, and allow no-one to mislead you
> By saying:
> 'Here it is!'
> Or 'There it is!'
> For it is within you
> That the Son of Man dwells.
> Go to him,
> For those who seek him find him" (Leloup 2002: 25–27).

This is clearly a Wisdom text – concentrating on the God within. But the tragedy is that without the recovery of its mystical, intuitive elements, Christianity has nothing to offer the young people who are searching other traditions for those elements. This is a view held by Professor Keith Ward, drawing his inspiration from the new cosmology which shows a real re-emerging of the rational and the mystical:

> The theory of a long cosmic evolution, Pope John Paul II said, is no longer a mere speculation. It is a well-established scientific theory...But what will this do to our ancient Christian beliefs. It will certainly put them in a new context...Now that we know that the Earth is a planet circling a small star among 100,000 million galaxies. We are not at the centre of things. The universe has existed for about 14,000 million years, and it will exist for billions of years in the future. It is not about to come to an end...
>
> If we talk about an incarnation of God in Jesus, we are not talking about a culminating event at the end of time. We are talking about an event fairly early in the history of the universe, on one tiny planet,

among a group of primates that have existed as *Homo Sapiens* for between five and ten million years, and has evolved from single-celled organisms that existed on earth as about four billion years ago. This calls for an expansion of Christian vision. It is most unlikely that a human Mary and Jesus will be at the apex of heavenly existence, as they are in most pictures of heaven. They are more likely to be human representatives of a wide diversity of life forms. Our iconography of heaven must change.

The cosmic purpose of God is unlikely to be centred on human beings. It may well be concerned with the flourishing of many forms of sentient life, and humans may just be a passing stage, even in the evolution of life on Earth. The human Jesus will then not be the consummation of creation, though he could be an ideal exemplar of truly human life in relation to God.

The Christian fundamentals can stand firm. God is a creator of unlimited love and compassion. The destiny of humans, as of all intelligent creatures, is to be liberated from self and to share in the divine nature. Jesus is the one who reveals in human history God's purpose of unitive love, and whose life founds a new society, the Church, in which God's Spirit lives and acts. Jesus is the human incarnation of the divine Word and Wisdom, and the one who unites human nature to the divine.

The new scientific cosmology places these fundamentals in a much more expansive and awe-inspiring context. To see things in such a perspective makes some of our present-day concerns seem very parochial (Ward 2005: 10).

As Hildegard was aware, the human condition requires a balance of 'wit and will'. Since the Enlightenment the Church has aligned itself in its theology with the notions of objective truth arrived at by rational thought. The work of feminist theologians has been to redress the necessary balance in a methodology that validates lived experience as a valid source of truth.

Case Studies

Case Study One – Renegotiating Prayer

There is an upsurge in meditative techniques in contemporary society often associated with a rediscovery of the miraculous, the imaginative, and the visionary. The rationalism of such movements as the Sea of Faith again tried to rationalize Christianity, often ridiculing such things as miraculous explanations.

The early theologians of the Anglican Communion saw meditation as a crucial part of the Christian life. Joseph Hall in his *The Devout Soul* and *Holy Raptures* developed his theology of mystical union: 'It pleases God to unite the person of every believer to the person of the Son of God'. His theology is based on a detailed religious practice of prayer and Bible reading, of meditation and sacrament. (McAdoo 1991: 74) . Hildegard, in developing her Wisdom theology, stresses the role of contemplation in the presence of Wisdom within the patriarchs and prophets of the Hebrew tradition:

> Then she [Wisdom] was graced with the dazzling virginity of the Virgin Mary; next, with the solid and ruddy faith of the martyrs; and finally with the brilliant and light-filled love of contemplation, by which God and neighbours ought to be loved through the heat of the Holy Spirit.
> She will go on in this way until the end of the world, and her warning will not cease but will flow out always, as long as the world endures (Bowie and Davies 1990: 81–82).

Later teachers of contemplation have also seen this as a route to deification. Robert Coulson sees contemplation as the place where wit and will are combined:

> The experience of real dwelling in Christ and of being indwelt by Him is so utterly beyond normal human experience that even a beginning seems hopeless....The more distinctly we try to feel ourselves in I AM, and I AM in ourselves, in fact, the less distinct, the more dim and abstract our notion of I AM. Just as the longer we gaze at the sun, the source of mundane life, the less we see because we are blinded...The only effective way of trying to imitate Christ, therefore, is to attempt to dwell in Christ, so that Christ may dwell in us, as in Jesus...As our belief deepens to embrace, not only the mind and he heart, but the will too, whereby the whole striving, active side of our personality becomes fully involved, so we begin to dwell in Him and He is us in the fullest sense of the word. The Incarnation, that is to say, commences in us too (Coulson 1956: 53–62).

Coulson's method is the repetition of the words of Jesus and he adds:

> Concentration is likely to be *extremely* difficult at first. Hence we may have to repeat the sentence aloud at first, until the wandering, distracted mind grows still (Coulson 1956: 64).

Neil Douglas Klotz sees prayer as the establishment of sacred space and sees it as important strategy of resistance to the colonizing tendencies of our times:

In Aramaic, the word pray, *shela,* can mean to incline or bend toward, listen to, or lay a snare for. We lay a snare with our devotion and patiently wait, hoping to catch some inspiration at the right moment. The old Hebrew roots also present the image of a bottomless depth or cavern, or the shadow or shade created by a canopy, roof, or veil...We open up a space for the feeling of the sacred (Douglas-Klotz 1999: 58).

He sees this as a strategy of resistance:

If Europeans saw land that appeared unused or unproductive, they tried to occupy and use it, even if other people already lived there (as was the case in all the colonized societies of the Americas, Africa, Asia, and Australia)...In the modern era, the impulse to make commercial use of wilderness areas rather than leave them as symbols of sacred spaciousness arises from the same inner fixation.

We as Westerners, then, should not underestimate the difficulty we face when we try to cultivate inner space. Western culture has raised us to feel that any private, personal experience of the divine is somehow dangerous. Again the attitude toward inner wilderness – the unexplored regions of our psyches – mirrors our culture's treatment of the outer wilderness. The Western entertainment industry metaphorically fills and colonizes our inner territory of its own choosing...

Significantly, the Gospels report that Yeshua prayed and healed primarily in nature, not inside buildings (Douglas-Klotz 1999: 58).

The Eucharist is also a potential source of mystical engagement. Some theologians. like Jeremy Taylor, saw the celebration of the Eucharist with its sacramental use of bread and wine as the main instrument of the indwelling Christ:

These holy mysteries, being taken, cause that Christ shall be in us and we in Christ (McAdoo 1991: 81).

But even this is often demythologized in contemporary theology. Both prayer and the Eucharist offer possibilities for the meeting of the rational and the intuitive. The method espoused by Coulson, for example, shows the written words of rationality being used as part of an intuitive practice.

Case Study Two – Renegotiating a Spirituality for the Arts[5]

One night four Rabbinim were visited by an angel who awakened them and carried them to the Seventh Vault of the Seventh heaven. There they beheld the sacred Wheel of Ezekiel.

5. This is an adaptation of an article first published in *Modern Believing* (Boyce-Tillman 2006b).

Somewhere in the descent from Pardes, Paradise, to Earth, one Rabbi, having seen such splendour, lost his mind and wandered frothing and foaming until the end of his days. The second Rabbi was extremely cynical: 'Oh I just dreamed Ezekiel's Wheel, that was all. Nothing *really* happened.'

The third Rabbi carried on and on about what he had seen, for he was totally obsessed. He lectured and would not stop with how it was all constructed and what it all meant...And in this way he went astray and betrayed his faith. The fourth Rabbi, who was a poet, took a paper in hand and a reed and sat near the window writing song after song praising the evening dove, his daughter in her cradle, and all the stars in the sky. And he lived his life better than before (Pinkola Estes 1992: 32).

Throughout the history of Western music spirituality and music have been associated – from the ancient goddess traditions (Drinker 1948/1995), through Plato (Godwin 1987: 3–8) and Hildegard (Boyce-Tillman 2000b). In the hands of the philosophers of the Enlightenment the link between music and the spiritual became weakened and the search for the spiritual became an essentially human search located in the unconscious (Harvey 1999). The realm of the imagination became devalued (Robinson 2001: 141–42). This is important for the valuing of the Spiritual domain, as the imaginal is an intermediate realm between the purely sensory and the purely spiritual (Corbin 1998, quoted in Leloup 2002: 14–15).

The spiritual became associated with notions of self-actualization (hooks 1994) and self-fulfilment in Maslow's hierarchy of human needs (Maslow 1967) in which he included the aesthetic – the need for beauty, order, and symmetry. As Western culture edged towards an aggressive individualism, a sense of finding some place in a larger whole – the cosmos – became a priority in the human search. This process of objectifying the cosmos associated with the advance of science had not happened in the same way in Eastern cultures; and it was on these cultures that the New Age (Boyce-Tillman, 2000a: 155–66) and some areas of rock and jazz traditions (Hamel, 1978/1976: 134–35) drew, in order to offer the desired sense of relationality. This included a more holistic view of the mind/body/spirit relationship, with transcendence approached through physical practices such as chanting (Gass and Brehony 1999) or dancing.

I have worked on a phenomenography of music as spiritual experience. It draws on this history to establish the five domains of the music experience (Boyce-Tillman 2004).[6] It is clear that the musical experience is one of encounter and I am using the frame of the 'I/Thou' experience described by Martin Buber (1970) 'But it can also happen, if will and grace are joined, that as I contemplate the tree I am drawn into a relation, and the tree ceases to be an it' (Buber 1970: 57). The philosopher, Levinas, saw the questioning of the Same as the basis of ethics. The encounter with the Other is an encounter with infinity and calls the Self into question. It is precisely in the process of welcoming the Other but not reducing it to the Same as the self that there is the experience of encounter, which he calls transcendence (Levinas 1969: 33).

The domains that I have developed reflect the varied focus of the experiencer during the experience (which here includes a variety of ways of musicking – listening-in-audience, composing/improvising, performing/improvising). They are:

- Expression – anOther self
- Values – anOther culture
- Construction – the world of abstract ideas
- Materials – the environment

All music consists of organizations of concrete Materials drawn both from the human body and the environment. These include musical instruments of various kinds, the infinite variety of tone colours associated with the human voice, the sounds of the natural world and the acoustic space in which the sounds are placed. This area of the musical experience is one that can re-establish the role of the material world in the experience of transcendence. Modernism traditionally denied this (Taylor 1992) for a world of abstraction. Within Western theology, human beings became alienated from the natural world – or indeed superior to it. This

---

6. To take Allegri's choral piece *Miserere* from sixteenth century Italy, in the area of Materials it consists of a choir. In the area of Expression it is peaceful with fluctuations as the plainchant verse come in. In the area of Construction it is an alternating psalm with full harmonic verses and plainchant alternating verses. This is intimately related to its role as a psalm liturgically. In the area of Value it is held as a masterpiece within the Western canon of music and is frequently recorded and achieved a place in classical music charts. It represents an important statement about the Christian's attitude to penitence based on a Jewish psalm, especially as expressed at the beginning of the penitential season of Lent. It has a declared Spiritual intention.

resulted at best in a patronizing stewardship and at worst domination and outright rape. All music making using instruments involves human beings in contact with the natural world. It is one of the most intimate relationships human beings have with the environment other than eating it. In traditional societies a drummer would reverence the tree and the animal that give the material for his/her drum. Sadly, in the West the loss of the connection with the natural world has been reflected in the way we treat and regard instruments. We need to re-establish this reverence in relation to instruments in our Western fragmented culture.

The area I have called Expression is concerned with the evocation of mood, emotion (individual or corporate), images, memories and atmosphere on the part of all those involved in the musical performance. It is the area where emotions are validated within the experience and this was crucial in William James' writing (1903/ 1997). This is where the subjectivity of composer/performer and listener intersect powerfully. The listener may well bring extrinsic meaning to the music – meaning that has been locked onto that particular piece or style or musical tradition because of its association with certain events in their own lives. Popular music, in particular, often conjures up a range of associations, as does hymnody associated, as it often is, with significant rites of passage like baptism, marriage and death. The phrase 'They are playing our tune' reflects the association of certain emotional events with certain pieces. Downplayed by classical theorists (Rahn 1994: 55) this area has been rediscovered in texts such as Green (1988, 1997). The experience of encounter in music may be the music itself or another person within the musical experience as this is an area of empathy, imagination and identity creation.

In the area of Construction, effectiveness often depends on the right management of repetition and contrast within a particular idiom. The way in which contrast is handled within a tradition – how much or how little can be tolerated – is often carefully regulated by the elders of the various traditions – be they the composers or theoreticians of the Western classical tradition (including cathedral organists) or the master drummers of Yoruba traditions. Construction issues are well documented in the pieces that make up the classical canon (Goehr 1992). It is in the area of Construction where many claims for a spirituality associated with order have been made by traditional writers on aesthetics and spirituality linked with James's view of the religious experience associated with harmony (James 1903/1997: 59, James 1993).

The area of Values is related to the context of the musical experience and links the experience with culture and society. The musical experience contains both implicit (within the music) and explicit (within the context) Value systems. However, these two areas of Value interact powerfully. Notions of internal values are a subject of debate in musicological circles (McClary 1991, 2001) but as soon as a text is present – either in the music or associated with it (Blake 1997: 7), Value systems will be declared, like the words of hymns. Music mirrors the structures of the culture that created it and people's ways of being in them (Shepherd and Wicke 1997: 138–39). This is why feminist theologians fail to get a spiritual experience out of much of traditional hymnody with its non-inclusive language.

Whereas these four domains exist as overlapping circles in the experience, Spirituality, I am suggesting, exists in the relationship between these areas. I am defining it as the ability to transport the audience to a different time/space dimension – to move them from everyday reality to 'another world'. The perceived effectiveness of a musical experience – whether of performing, composing or listening – is often situated in this area (Jackson 1998). Indeed some would see music as the last remaining ubiquitous spiritual experience in a secularized Western culture (Boyce-Tillman 2001b). Here, I have subsumed within my own thinking the following ideas:

- Flow, coming in from psychologists of creativity (Csikszentmihalyi and Csikszentmihalyi 1988, Csikszentmihalyi 1993, Custodero 2002, 2005).
- Ecstasy, often associated with idea of 'the holy' coming from the religious/spiritual literature (Otto 1923, Laski 1961).
- Trance coming from anthropological (Rouget 1987), New Age (Collin 1997, Goldman 1992, Stewart 1987) and psychotherapeutic literature (Inglis 1990).
- Mysticism, coming from religious traditions, especially Christianity (Rankin 2005).
- Peak experiences (Maslow 1967).
- Religious experience (Rankin 2005).
- Spiritual experience of children (Hay and Nye 1998, Erricker, Erricker *et al* 1997, Hay 1982, Robinson 1977).
- Liminality (Turner 1969, 1974).

Turner's concept of liminality draws on an analysis of ritual. The notion of transformation is central to religious ritual whether it is a Christian Eucharist or a shamanic healing rite (Driver 1998). It can be personal or communal or both. Van Gennep (1908 quoted in Roose-Evans 1994: 6) saw parallel stages in any ritual. This he entitled: 'severance, transition and return'. Severance he associated with leaving everyday life by means of ritual gestures like holding hands or lighting candles. In the transitional or liminal phase contact was made with the transpersonal; and this might take the form of a change of consciousness. The Return phase signalled a coming back to earth and the beginning of a new life. It is possible to identify these moments in a musical piece, even when not associated with ritual and to relate accounts of transformation through experiencing music with this concept. He develops it to include the notion of encounter, sometimes with the material through the process of healing and sometimes inner to do with mind or spirit.

Clarke's notion of the transliminal way of knowing is drawn from cognitive psychology (Thalbourne *et al* 1997). In her thinking, this way of knowing is to do with our 'porous' relation to other beings and is where spirituality sits. It is in contrast to 'propositional knowing' which gives us the analytically sophisticated individual that our culture has perhaps mistaken for the whole (Clarke 2005: 93). To access the other way of knowing we cross an internal 'limen' or threshold. Langer (1942) suggested a 'non-discursive' form of communication that characterized music and religion which is different from propositional ways of knowing.

McDonagh draws on the concepts of meditation and contemplation in prayer as the descriptors of an experiencer's relationship to an art work. Meditation he characterizes as mental activity, but contemplation is surrender to the work of art:

> Her consciousness has become possessed by a particular 'topic' which is now operating spontaneously from within the subject as it were (McDonagh 2004: 169).

It is interesting to compare how this language reflects a way of knowing that is different from everyday (propositional) knowing (Clarke 2005). It can be described as a *both/and* logic (as opposed to an *either/or* logic) which may appear as a way of *not knowing* for its central feature is paradox. In this way there may be a measure of pain in the spiritual experience as it is held in a paradox with joy, as many people experience in the late Beethoven quartets:

From about age of 36 onwards when listening to certain passages – Beethoven's late quartets – I have had the feeling that he had touched a realm of experience beyond our normal consciousness, full of serenity and joy, the uplands of the Spirit, and through his music, I could reach not so much a sense of God, as of another world (RERC 002285 1971, 59 year-old woman).

The Spiritual domain, then, is defined as a time when in the experience of the experiencer there is a perfect fit between all the domains (Sullivan 1997: 9–10). This can happen gradually as this account shows:

For the first twenty-five minutes I was totally unaware of any subtlety... whilst wondering what, if anything, was supposed to happen during the recital.

What did happen was magic!

After some time, insidiously the music began to reach me. Little by little, my mind all my senses it seemed, were becoming transfixed. Once held by these soft but powerful sounds, I was irresistibly drawn into a new world of musical shapes and colours. It almost felt as if the musicians were playing me rather than their instruments, and soon, I, too, was clapping and gasping with everyone else...I was unaware of time, unaware of anything other than the music. Then it was over. But it was, I am sure, the beginning of a profound admiration that I shall always have for an art form that has been until recently totally alien to me (Dunmore 1983: 20–21).

We see here the Materials of the sound and the 'shapes' of the Construction gradually begin to be integrated into his/her own being so that the experiencer and the experienced become fused. It can be represented like this:

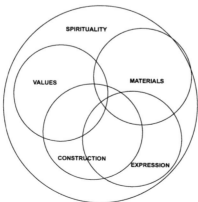

Fig. 13. The complete spiritual experience in music.

To achieve a 'fit' that is likely to produce a spiritual experience in the experiencer, there has to be sufficient congruence between the various domains of the experience (at least two, I suggest) between the experienced and the experiencer. This will be affected by words and experiences surrounding the event.

The converse of this is where this is a disruption in one area or between two areas that means there is no spiritual experience at all. I now find it difficult to listen to Wagner's *Ride of the Valkyries* without thinking of the powerful moment in *Apocalypse Now*, where it is associated with the flight of helicopters in the American war in Vietnam. I am suggesting that it is not possible to put these disruptions in other domains aside and that they will interrupt the likelihood of entering the spiritual domain where notions of culture, meaning, construction and materials need to intersect in a special way for this to occur.

This model shows how the experience of spirituality in music is a merger of the intuitive and the rational – the world of ideas and the world of intuitive imagination interplay dynamically to produce an experience that people define as spiritual. It also combines the material and the non-material – the embodied and the disembodied.

Case Study Three – Renegotiating the Vision

This case study looks at a number of scenarios based on heavily disguised real life situations to illustrate the various issues involved in the negotiating of the intuitive experience in the context of a society suspicious of it. The first one concerns a confirmation class:

> A male Anglican priest close to retirement was taking a confirmation class. He was educated at an older university and belonged to the Sea of Faith movement with its stress on rationality. In a session exploring the Nativity story an intelligent young woman in the class offered her experience of a vision of the Virgin Mary at Lourdes which she had visited with a RC friend. He said that Lourdes was a phenomenon produced by contemporary hysteria and the so-called miracles were simply pseudo-results of placebo effects. The girl thought that the vision might mean that she had a vocation to the priesthood. The priest was unable to handle either the visionary experience or the girl's powerful sense of vocation and she left feeling devalued and stupid. Her vision had been explained away and not interrogated in a way that saw its meaning as having any significance. Eventually, the girl left the Church after her confirmation. Only later in her life did she attempt to unpick what this treatment of a significant experience for her had meant for her sense of self-esteem and self-worth.

The story shows how a number of interlocking issues played out:

- the particular form of rationality played out in the older universities and in movements like The Sea of Faith;
- the meeting of various Christian traditions and the way they validate the intuitive;
- the relation of the valuing of the intuitive to issues of self-esteem and self-worth.

The problem here is that the rational is used to invalidate the experience rather than probe it carefully in the area of what it might mean for the intuitive, in this case the girl.

The second example concerns a women's spirituality group:

A women's spirituality group had developed a pattern of sharing experiences freely and non-judgmentally. A new younger woman with a long history of mental illness started coming and sharing quite powerfully her visionary experiences. The group was unsure of her but were able to accept these experiences although contain her speaking so that she did not dominate the group too much. They also provided her with valuable support in her more difficult times. Over a period of time they were able to help her to discern when her experiences were helpful and when they were not. This took some understanding and only developed over a period of time and involved working through some difficulties within the group.

This example shows how a group of helpful women were able to provide a rational container for their new member's experiences so that they were validated and she was able to work with them effectively. The fact that it was an all women's group made this process, in this case, more possible as her presence enabled other women to share their experiences more freely in a non-judgmental environment.

The next example gives two scenarios involving children, which might to the adults involved, appear similar; but behind the experiences are very different stories. The first one concerns an imaginative child:

A six-year-old girl was in a family where she was regularly taken by her mother to church although her father seldom joined them. She was a highly imaginative child who loved making up stories with toys and often spent long times on her own preparing little plays with her toys. On a visit to her grandmother she was taken to a cathedral. The child was overawed by the wonder of the place. She heard beautiful singing but was too small to see the source of it. At the Sanctus she saw an angel in a light in a pillar. She attempted to tell her father who was caught up in his own thoughts and concerns about his position regarding religion and the fact he had no belief in the Church at all. He was not ready for his daughter's experience and told her not to be so silly and that angels only existed in stories. The child was mystified about how her father who seemed to enjoy her stories should dismiss her powerful experience in this way and decided never to share her experiences with anyone again. She gave up making up her stories with her toys and concentrated on less imaginative activities.

This is a story with which many parents can empathize – when a child's needs come at a time when you are taken up with something else. It would have taken an imaginative leap on the part of the father to see how the cathedral from his daughter's position (as small) and also to see how she would make sense of the experience. The inability to make this empathetic leap has damaging effects in all her creativity. In a stroke she is initiated into the dominant culture of rationality which had dismissed a whole important area of her activity. It is a shame that this area of her experience could not have been kept alive at the same time as she entered the more rational world of the school curriculum.

The next story also concerns the vision of an angel but has a very different origin.

A seven year-old child had been abused by an older relative. During the abuse an angel appeared to her and kept her safe. The abuser had sworn her to secrecy. The girl decided however, that this promise did not extend to the angel vision. She tentatively asked her mother if she believed in angels at the end of a bedtime reading of the Nativity story. The mother was wise enough to enter into a dialogue concerning the origin of the question and was able over a period of time to discuss her daughter's experience of angels. As she gained her daughter's confidence she became more and more aware that her daughter was troubled in some way and was able to seek appropriate help and guidance.

In this story, the validation of the experience was able to open up channels of communication for an event that might otherwise have lain secret for many years. The continuing dialogue around the subject enabled confidence to build and the underlying experience to be subjected to compassionate rational scrutiny.

The next story concerns a charismatic experience and deals with some of the gender issues involved in the intuitive experience:

A first-year male student who had just started a university course had an experience of receiving the gift of tongues. He was so taken up by the power of this experience that he started to tell a number of his housemates. They were divided about this – some regarding him as something of a saint while others as in need of therapy. The older student in charge of the house intervened to stop a difficult situation of division and gave him a lecture on what it meant to be a man.

Here, we see how the hegemonic versions of masculinity in the dominant culture that we saw in Chapter One play out when someone who appears to be in the dominant group investigates a way of knowing primarily associated with a subjugated group, in this case, women. The senior student, in this case, endeavours to keep him within the dominant group by describing the dominant form of masculinity which does not include the intuitive.

The next study concerns a writer used to using the intuitive for his work and the way in which the labels of the dominant culture, propagated by the media, interplay with this:

A fairly well-known male writer, who called himself spiritual but not religious, was used to having intuitive experiences that fed his creativity. A series of intense visions of the Virgin Mary had unblocked his writing and renewed his creativity. He found himself so inspired that he could work for a long time without a great deal of sleep. His wife, however, saw a television programme about bipolar disorder and became anxious about her husband and put great pressure on him to see a psychiatrist. The psychiatrist diagnosed the man as bipolar and put him on medication and all the writer's creativity dried up.

This story illustrates how the ideas propagated by the Press reinforce dominant notions of norms of emotional stability which may be inappropriate for highly creative people. What appears abnormal for many people may be very normal for very creative people. Psychiatry does not deal particularly well with highly imaginative people with its preset tests of normality.

Dominant narratives are often culturally constructed; in some cultural groups intuition is more highly prized than in Western culture. This story tells of the dilemma of cross-cultural interactions:

A 65 year-old woman brought up in Barbados, arrived in England in the 1960s. She had psychic powers and foresaw in a dream the twin towers disaster. In her black sisterhood she was regarded as a woman of considerable authority but she did not usually share her experiences with people outside her cultural circle. The British born members of the congregation regarded her as a little odd and eccentric. However, she shared some of her foresight with a young female priest who she thought might understand her. This was a new area for the young woman who was able to learn from the older woman and also enabled her to make some bridges with the British born members of the congregation. This proved to be very enriching for the spiritual life of the parish.

This story shows how a subjugated culture still retains subjugated value systems by means of supportive groups like the black women's sisterhoods. The ability of the young woman priest to learn from the subjugated culture and bring it together with the dominant white culture proved to be mutually enriching and a valuable piece of cross cultural learning.

The next story concerns a grief experience that coincided with Hallowe'en:

A single mother in her mid-thirties took her children trick or treating at Hallowe'en. Her mother had died a month ago and she was finding it difficult to manage without her. Near the graveyard where her mother had been buried she saw her mother silhouetted against the wall. The mother said that her daughter was not to worry because she was OK. She consulted the priest who had taken her mother's funeral as she had no regular link with the Church. This priest was anti-Hallowe'en and gave her a lecture on the dangers of the pagan festival. The woman went into a state of deep depression and needed a long period of medication.

Here, a priest is unable to see beyond his own view to the place of the visionary experience in the process of grieving. It is not at all unusual for loved ones to see their departed relatives close to the death experience. This one is quite typical and not at all frightening. Had it been validated as part of that experience, it could have been comforting and reassuring. However, unvalidated and dismissed, it became a source of a serious pathology.

The next two stories are taken from Michael Perry's text on the deliverance ministry:

A young mother of twenty-five was experiencing severe poltergeist activity, which included the movement of objects, interference with radio, television and telephone. The family also frequently discovered the house 'ransacked', when they returned home, although plainly there had been no intruder. The woman had a very traumatic childhood, and with the death of her father had reactivated the pain of this period of her life (Perry 1987: 21).

Perry describes how through counselling she is able to deal with the childhood difficulties and her recent bereavement and link these with the poltergeist activity, which then died down and normal life was restored.

The next story concerns how traumatic events leave a memory in a place which can be reactivated by similar events in the lives of the living:

> A young family was awakened one night by what sounded like burglars. The father opened the bedroom door to find groups of people walking along the landing of the house and disappearing through the far wall. He removed his wife and children from the house and called the police. They arrived with a dog. The dog refused to enter the house. A young police officer went in and saw the same phenomena as had been described by the family. The groups of people were dressed in period century costume and looked very sad. They were carrying bundles. On investigation, it transpired that the family had suffered a cot death some three weeks previously (Perry 1987: 34).

The house had been on the site of a plague pit and the place memory had been activated by the family's recent experience. The family was given counselling and the place was blessed.

This case study shows a variety of experiences in the area of the intuitive and that combined with rational scrutiny they can be used for growth but, ignored or ridiculed, they can be a cause of great suffering. A story is told of Gandhi which runs:

> If I receive a good idea in prayer I must test it out from the point of view of other faith perspectives – Jewish, Christian, Muslim, Sikh and so on. If it seems a good idea from these perspectives it probably is a good one. If not, it probably is not.

The practice of medieval spiritual directors was the discernment of spirits, which meant bringing the visionary experience under rational scrutiny. In an age which has dismissed the visionary to the realm of the mad, the fractured polarity reinforces the madness it seeks to cure.

Embodied/Disembodied

1. The wounds are human wounds;
   The tears are human tears;
   Two loving friends beside a cross
   Pour love in spite of fears.

2. In broken human form
   That Christ still lives today,
   And human love can still be poured
   To wipe the pain away.

3. The loving joy of God
   Is poured out in our wine;
   The bread reveals our brokenness,
   Christ's body in the vine.

4. In sharing grief and pain
   And joyful, laughing love,
   We are a priesthood here on earth
   Reflecting God above.

   (Boyce-Tillman 2006a: 69)

Society

Western society constructed as it was around the elements of Christianity had deep in its conceptualizing a notion of body/soul split. The Enlightenment added a third element that could be split off – the mind or intellect. Few other human societies have achieved such an effective split between these elements. The consequences for life in Western cultures have been considerable and these have been inflicted on cultures to which they are absolutely foreign. Manual labour is now split from white and blue-collar labour. One uses the bodies of people as if they have no minds, the other the mind as if it has no body. The ubiquity of computer technology requires most people to use a mind with minimal movements of the body which now has to be exercised separately almost with no mind. Work for the mind and leisure for the body, religion for the

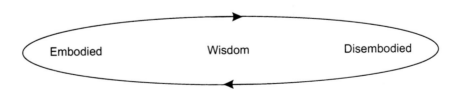

Fig. 14. Embodied Wisdom Disembodied

spirit if your cosmology includes one. The split between belief or understanding and action has filled the corridors of academe for some time. Only a limited number of radical thinkers actually use their bodies for social action. The body is obliterated from the most highly prized of academic assessment – the essay and the exam – sometimes completely by means of ascribing numbers to the candidates, in the interests of objectivity. Politicians dream up political slogans but it is seldom they who put them into action. It is not politicians who fight in the world's battles or keep law and order on the city streets. The managers seldom 'get their hands dirty' on the shop floor. This was explored in the previous century by writers like Thoreau, who in his essay *Civil Disobedience* (1849; originally titled *Resistance to Civil Government*), set out the need for people to give themselves to counterbalance the injustice of government:

> Not a drum was heard, not a funeral note,
>   As his corpse to the rampart we hurried;
> Not a soldier discharged his farewell shot
>   O'er the grave where our hero was buried.

> The mass of men serve the state thus, not as men mainly, but as machines, with their bodies. They are the standing army, and the militia, jailers, constables, posse comitatus, etc. In most cases there is no free exercise whatever of the judgement or of the moral sense; but they put themselves on a level with wood and earth and stones; and wooden men can perhaps be manufactured that will serve the purpose as well. Such command no more respect than men of straw or a lump of dirt. They have the same sort of worth only as horses and dogs. Yet such as these even are commonly esteemed good citizens. Others – as most legislators, politicians, lawyers, ministers, and office-holders – serve the state chiefly with their heads; and, as they rarely make any moral distinctions, they are as likely to serve the devil, without intending it, as God. A very few – as heroes, patriots, martyrs, reformers in the great sense, and men – serve the State with their consciences also, and so necessarily resist it for the most part; and they are commonly treated as enemies by it..... He who gives himself entirely to his fellow men appears to them useless and selfish; but he who gives himself partially to them is pronounced a benefactor and philanthropist.[7]

7. http://sunsite.berkeley.edu/Literature/Thoreau/CivilDisobedience.html. 25 November 2006.

As Western rationalism still prevails, manual work or action as I prefer to call it, is conceived of as having less value and the underprivileged of our society still give their bodies to do essential practical tasks like cleaning, sewing and cooking, often in the power of someone else's mind. People are now prepared to sell their own bodies for all kinds of purposes – whether its parts are for medical purposes, or its sexual functioning in prostitution. Sometimes this is plain exploitation, sometimes it is pornography, and sometimes it is both. All of these can happen, when a person is conceived of as having a body but no mind or soul.

On the other hand, there are disembodied souls in the religious circles preaching of a disembodied life that apparently can be accessed independently of a body, there are disembodied minds in political circles conceiving of principles and ideas with no basis in the lived bodily experience of those for whom they are conceiving them, and in academic circles generating principles which bear no relationship to practice, indeed, which can be used as justifications for doing nothing because of the complexity of the problems involved. Sue Monk Kidd draws on the image of the Tin Man in *The Wizard of Oz* as a metaphor for the role of technology on our society:

> The Tin Man character, at least in the early part of the movie, seemed an apt symbol of patriarchal consciousness....Have you ever wondered how the Tin Man got into such a deplorable, frozen state? The book says the Tin Man was a woodman whose ax became cursed, causing him to cut away his own body, piece by piece, including his heart, until he was no longer covered in warm flesh but encased in an armor of tin.
>
> Through our lopsided valuing, we have come to labor under a "cursed ax", under a patriarchal system that has cut away the body, including the heart, replacing it with technological tin. And like the Tin Man we find ourselves trapped in our own heartlessness (Monk Kidd 1992: 84).

This is the negative form of the positive views expressed by Donna Haraway on the possibilities of cyborgs for empowerment that we saw in Chapter One. So when action becomes separated from belief and understanding we encourage pornographic viewing of the body as devoid of mind and soul and a dogmatic intellectualism that is violent to the bodies of others.

Self

Within the self the life of our society is reflected. Our lives are fragmented into activities, which use either body, mind or spirit. It is perhaps a romantic idealization that says that an agrarian society saw people working in the fields at tasks that required all three in tune with or another. The concern for the body split off from mind or spirit characterizes such illnesses as anorexia and bulimia. These are but acute forms of a basic societal sickness. They have always been a part of women's experience of patriarchy. In the Middle Ages it was the ascetic excesses of the saints who in pursuit of a separated spirit abused their bodies. Today, it is under pressure from the contemporary high priests of advertising or in response to experiences that have led them to regard their bodies as evil or polluted. Young women will have watched hundreds of millions of advertisements setting out ideal bodies by the time they reach puberty. None of them will have presented anything other than an idealized norm that apparently has no connection with mind or spirit. Young men will have been similarly enculturated to expect an obviously bigger and stronger body than a woman. Differences in sexuality will seldom be represented in the broader public sphere or increasingly groups will construct themselves around different images of the body of the one that it is appropriate to love. A narcissistic love of the body *per se* rather than for what it can do or express has been fuelled by an industry anxious to sell it expensive aids for making it more 'attractive.' Even sexual function has now been normalized. Following the discovery of Viagra for men, a corresponding programme has been invented for 'female sexual dysfunction'. This was based on norms established by heterosexual male sexuality. The woman who refuses to have genital relations with her husband as often as he would like, is now dysfunctional, she is pathologised. Once upon a time there would have been a convent for her retreat to where a vow of celibacy might protect her from unwanted advances. With celibacy discredited, largely because of its unnecessary alliance with the priesthood, there is now nowhere for her to retreat to except a guilty haze of pathological dysfunction. More women than the dominant culture would have us believe take temporary vows of celibacy after broken relationships (although they may not be expressed in those terms). One of the reasons I continue to teach the medieval mystic women is that I think it is a place that needs to be on the map – a place which the modern media will not publicize. There is no notion of variety in people's sexual needs and appetites either between different people or at different times within the life of one person.

The place of the concept of soul in our society is interesting. As church going declines a wider search for the spiritual fills the shelves of bookstores and health food shops. Much of it related to bodily conditions; in a way that the church has lost touch with. Fasting was deleted in all but ritual form from Lenten practices only to find its way into detox programmes of the New Age dream. While incense in church was being downplayed because of its sensuality, people now burn it in their homes, while little bells tinkle at the entrance to houses to create good feng shui – bells that once would have signaled high points of a religious ritual. Our age is in search of a soul and there is a large industry seeking to provide it. It remains to be seen whether the gurus of the new spiritualities can effect a merger of body, mind and spirit better than the ecclesiastical authorities of the Christian church. Within Western society a basic human challenge is still to keep body and soul together.

So as our bodies part company with our minds and spirits we become either narcissistic or ascetic.

The Spirituality Project

Spirituality is a favourite term today (Heelas and Woodhead 2005). The concept of 'spirituality' can be traced through Church history in connection with the Holy Spirit (Sheldrake 1998). Robert Fuller, in his book *Spiritual But Not Religious* (2001), traces its roots into the nineteenth century, linking it with such movements in the US as Transcendentalism, Swedenborgianism, Theosophy, Spiritualism and Eastern Religions. It is also linked with a rise in alternative medicines like homeopathy and chiropractice. These links are still to be found in writing on feminist spirituality today. In writing *The Varieties of Religious Experience,* William James (1903) produced a seminal text in such areas as expanded states of consciousness, mysticism and psychic phenomena, such as telepathy. William James' work into theories of consciousness goes on the work of such organizations as the Alister Hardy Trust with its considerable archive of writings in this area.[8] But this has been critiqued by

8. This is now housed at Lampeter University.

writers like Grace Jantzen (1995) who see developments both in the concept of 'spirituality' and of theories of 'consciousness' as a perpetuation of the notion of a mind/split. This thought-experiment to establish the link between the disembodied subject and the concept of the divine illustrates it well:

> Imagine yourself, for example, gradually ceasing to be affected by alcohol and drugs, your thinking being equally coherent however men mess about with your brain....You gradually find yourself aware of what is going on in bodies other than your own...You also come to see things from any point of view...You... find yourself able to move directly anything which you choose...You also find yourself able to utter words which can be heard anywhere...surely anyone can thus conceive of himself [sic] becoming an omnipotent spirit (Swinburne 1977: 104–5).

Notions of spirituality now include other faith traditions as in *World Spirituality: An Encyclopaedic History of Religious Quest* (Dupre 1990), which includes twenty-five examples of 'spirituality spanning a range of eras and faith traditions'. Other faith traditions have not been entirely happy with such a transplantation of a Christian concept to other faith soils. The word is now commonly used and debated (Rose 2001). Shops are filled with books on the hidden self and inner child and they nestle alongside the vitamins and herbal remedies of health food stores. According to Fuller (2001), more people look towards New Age traditions, yoga, ecospirituality, witchcraft, near death experiences, the Tarot, astrology and neo-paganism than towards heaven for their spiritual well-being. Many of these are women aged forty and above and those same people will be found in the feminist liturgy groups outlined above. Kwok Pui Lan links this with notions of the nomadic subject explored in Chapter Three and a locating of the transcendent dimension:

> The Catholics and Protestants would not easily mingle with one another or visit each other's churches in the same neighbourhood. On the contrary nomadic seekers do not have an identifiable place which they can call a spiritual home – they are explorers and sojourners but not dwellers...The institutional forms of religious life –regular worship, membership in a religious organization, and in particular, religious hierarchy – are less vital in their spiritual pursuit, and may even hinder their progress. Instead of accepting religion as it is, the seekers dream of new possibilities and follow their hearts' desire (Kwok 2002b: 4).

These are the characteristics of many in the groups of women meeting for liturgy. The spiritual journey consists in following one's own inner bliss. There is often a concentration on the immanence of God. The groups are often ecumenical and include many who have left the established churches but see these groups as their spiritual home.

So, the Cartesian three-way split originating in Christianity has bitten deep into Western culture. Resulting in a separation between different sorts of people and sorts of tasks. This is not true of popular traditions although notions of soul are often lacking here.

Theology

There are so many strands in this area I will deal with them under a number of headings.

1. The place of the body

Mary Grey sees in the Psyche and Eros myth, a myth of Europe split at the roots:

> in the polarising of body and soul of animals over against humans and humanity over against the earth (Grey 1995/2001: 62).

One of the most remarkable experiences of a placement with a funeral director was my first experience of seeing a human body cut open in real life. Suddenly I was face-to-face with the fact that we are very similar to our animal relations. Our relationship with the animal world lies through our bodies:

> It is surely a question of the dissociation of body and soul, of sexuality and spirituality, of the lack of passage for the spirit, for the god, between the inside and the outside, the outside and the inside, and of their distribution between the sexes in the sexual act. Everything is constructed in such a way that these realities remain separate, even opposed to one another. So that they neither mix, marry, nor form an alliance (Irigaray [1984] 1993: 15).

Post-Christian Europe has often dismissed notions of spirituality as superstitious in line with scientific, objective rationality, but in *Angels: An Endangered Species*, Malcolm Godwin shows how the concept of angel is still retained in such figures as Superman and Batman (Godwin 1993: 203–7).

At the edge of psychology, practitioners like Assagioli (1974) have included notions of transcendence in their overarching philosophy. Maslow's hierarchy of human needs includes notions that have the characteristics of the mystical experience (Maslow 1967: 45–47).

As has been seen in Chapter One, the split of body from mind and spirit can be laid firmly at the door of the Church in such figures as St Augustine drawing on the Greek philosophies of figures like Plato. The excesses of asceticism are to be found in the stories of many medieval mystics and are now counterbalanced by the pornographic concern with the body (now minus mind and spirit) of the secular world.[9] Paul has played a considerable part in the theologizing of the split, but if we look at a passage like 1 Cor. 6. 12–20 we see that, drawing on notions of the temple of Jesus' body (Jn 2. 21) he sets out a theology that is essentially holistic with no division between soul and body at which he hints in other places such as Rom. 3. 24. The passage is set in the context of a Church set in a city that was:

- A centre for trade newly rebuilt.
- A cosmopolitan city that contained freed slaves anxious to rise socially.
- A place where various religions met and cross-fertilized one another rather like the contemporary West Coast of the USA.
- A place exploring a variety of sexual practices.

It is in this context that Paul sees fit to define the nature of immorality in the context of a wider theology of the body. This is closely tied to the setting out of a theology of the bodily resurrection of Jesus. He defines sexual immorality as using the body without reference to God. So he sees the relationship to God as expressed through bodily action. In such an argument he refutes any view that the body and spirit can be split, but sees them (at least for earthly life) as inextricably interconnected; for as Hildegard expresses it:

9. Tatman links contemporary women's attempts at self-mutilation with a desire for wholeness and at-one-ment. She looks at the disconnection of the 'self' from the body as a result of abuse and their need to feel something rather than nothing, which is resolved by self inflicted pain. Although she is anxious to distance herself from notions of a transcendent deity and a separate identifiable self, nonetheless she develops a concept of 'whole enough' in relation to this alienation of the body (Tatman 1998).

> Our souls can only find expression through the actions of our bodies.
> (Boyce-Tillman 2000b: 20).

This passage has often been read as simply a prohibition against sleeping with female prostitutes. In fact, it is the setting out of a Christian theology of the body that goes far beyond a simple moral prohibition.

By the Middle Ages Christian worship had become deeply embodied but Protestantism – an Enlightenment project – helped to widen the body/soul split. As the sensuousness of Roman Catholicism with its visual images, its sweet smelling incense, its array of bodily gestures and variety of musics was systematically dismantled, the experience of God came to be located purely in the mind and spirit and worship became denuded of symbols that involved the rest of the body. As a family, we chose to take our sons to a 'higher' Anglican church when they were young simply because the liturgy was more clearly enacted and gave scope for engaging in dialogue about the nature of the underpinning theology. The reliance of words as the main purveyors of truth in the Protestant traditions confirmed a theology of a God accessed primarily through the mind, or even the brain, which was now construed as being closely related to the Spirit. Lisa Isherwood and Elizabeth Stuart explain the centrality of embodiment to medieval Church very clearly:

> Christianity of the medieval period provides us with a rich tradition of embodiment. This was the time when the cult of relics proliferated. However, it was not only the bodies of the dead saints that were felt to hold miraculous powers but the bodies of the living. Holy people spat or blew into the mouths of others to cure or convey grace (Isherwood and Stuart 1998: 146–52).

But the female body could not represent Christ; and while female mystics saw Christ's body feeding them and dying and bleeding for them (Bynum 1991: 222), Aquinas reversed this in seeing the body simply as a home for the soul. The difficulty that some feminist theologians may have with the standard definition of a sacrament is that it appears to place more meaning on what is not seen than on what is, so lending itself to dualism (Isherwood and Stuart 1998: 146–52).

Neil Douglas-Klotz reworks the account of the Last Supper in Mt. 26. 27–29 in a more embodied way in the light of Aramaic concepts. He claims that the word for blood includes concepts of 'juice, wine, sap and essence' and is related to the word Adam – the first human. The word for fruit can also mean a human offspring. He links blood with forgiveness and sees it as an entry into greater inclusivity:

> Blood releases us, heartbeat-by-heartbeat, breath-by-breath, from the physical impressions of the past. The potential to forgive ourselves and others is just as close, immediate, and ever present as is our blood.
>
> From this view of his Aramaic words, we could see Jesus here initiating a new ritual, which, in addition to the Passover ritual of remembering the Jewish freedom from bondage in Egypt, recalled the mythic origin of listeners as primal humans, before the divisions of "chosen" and "non-chosen" people even existed. (Douglas-Klotz 1999: 166–67).

In reworking notions of the body as an identification with his dead body, he sees him as drawing on Holy Wisdom who:

> Produces food for our consumption that is ultimately made up of the dead bodies of other beings, including human ones after they return to the earth. In this sense, we can see that Yeshua [Jesus] both foretells his impending death as well as implies the ultimate equality of all bodies in the eyes of Wisdom (Douglas-Klotz 1999: 167–68).

The dilemma of Christianity's relationship with the body is nowhere more clearly seen than in the area of sexuality. The mind/body split has often meant a distancing of the Church from notions of sexuality. In a chapter provocatively entitled *Sin is a Sexually Communicable Disease*, Karen Jo Torjesen writes:

> Christianity inherited a troubled relationship to sexuality from the cultural world in which it first took shape. The values of male honor and female shame and the opposition of the public man and the private woman had a profound influence on the way that Christian theologians came to view the sexual self. Through their assimilation into Christian institutions such asceticism, monasticism and clerical celibacy, sin and human nature, the values of the Greco-Roman world shaped Western attitudes toward women and sexuality for nearly two millennia (Torjesen 1990: 203).

The issue of right celibacy is now a problem for the Church. Two contemporary phenomena work against a right view of celibacy. One is the cases of sexual abuse by Roman Catholic priests and the other is the images of sexual relationships presented by the media, which imply that not to be in a heterosexual relationship is not 'normal'. My academic fellowship in the US brought me into contact with US women religious. They explained how their vow of celibacy had freed them for prophetic action. They had engaged in acts of civil disobedience around the US policy in El Salvador and the use of nuclear submarines. They saw their vow as freeing them from the responsibilities of family life for risky social action. Mark Jordan sees celibacy as a way of legitimizing differing forms of masculinity as we saw in Chapter One:

> The 'feminine' excess is forgiven or expected because they [priests] are officially 'unsexed'. As modern eunuchs they are permitted to take on the strategies of women (Jordan 2000: 199).

The problems of sexuality are further highlighted by the construction of notions of divinity in the Virgin Mary linked with her distancing herself from human sexuality through her unbroken hymen (see Case Study Two below). Here, Christianity is a much weaker position than other spiritualities with more overt sexual characteristics in their divinities, such as Hinduism and ancient Greek traditions. The call to revisit these notions has often come from queer theologians. But their call is not only for the inclusion of gays, lesbians, bisexuals and transsexuals within the Church and a challenging of the tyranny of heterosexism, but a complete re-envisioning of Christianity's approach to sexuality (Goss 2002 and Althaus Reid 2001 are but two of the texts in this area.) There is an increasing production of liturgical material and a widening of its acceptance from the initial storm that greeted the ground-breaking anthology, *Daring to Speak Love's Name* (Stuart 1992). The reinstatement of sexuality within the concept of the Divine has enabled an element of loving passion – the erotic – to be seen as central to Divine energy (Gilson 1995, Brock 1991). This draws on images of Sophia in the Hebrew Scriptures as Lover. This is clear in the line of Ecclesiasticus: 'Whoever loves her, loves life' (Ecclesiasticus 4. 12).

In the development of their body theology, Lisa Isherwood and Elisabeth Stuart included the development of a theology of the disabled God (1998). They link this with Nancy Eisland's liberatory theology of disability. From the lived experience of those who are disabled, Eisland develops a new incarnational theology. She describes an epiphany of a disabled God, revealed through the 'impaired' body of a survivor Christ (Eisland 1994).

2. Immanence

The establishment of the sacred in the midst of lived experience has been a significant step in re-embodying the metaphysical traditions of the Church. It has resulted, in some cases, in a revising of notions of Divine presence, and in some cases a near abandonment of notions of divine transcendence. There have been attempts to balance the triumphalism of a patriarchal male God with a concentration on immanence and embodiment. Some would abandon notions of transcendence completely, while others rework it in a variety of imaginative ways. This is seen in a re-examination of the church's attitude to sexuality, ecology, dance and the relationship between belief and social action. This establishment of a theology of immanence has, however, certain potential problems. Simone de Beauvoir raised this initially in *The Second Sex* (1948/ 1972) in which she saw the need to remove women from their association with immanence. Her attitude has been questioned by feminist theorists such as Butler (1990) and Braidotti (1994), because of her construction of the female subject. In the 1990s, Jantzen draws on Irigaray's concept of a 'sensible transcendence...a transcendence which is wholly immanent, not in opposition to the flesh but as the projected horizon for our (embodied) becoming' (Quoted in Jantzen 1998: 271).

Jantzen wrestles with this issue in her critique of Arthur North Whitehead. She problematizes his distinction between the 'primordial nature' (God's containment of infinite possibility) and 'consequent nature' (involvement in the continually renewing processes of the cosmos) of God. However, Jantzen retains a notion of transcendence to prevent the 'reduction' of an embodied God into mere physiology (Jantzen 1984: 127) while Carter Heyward argues for a notion of relationality rather than metaphysical distance, by using the 'trans' of transcendence as a movement 'across' rather than 'out of ' (Heyward 1984). Beatrice Bruteau's solution is one of 'cosmic incarnational mysticism' which recalls some of the thinking explored in Chapter Three:

> The ecstasy of the Theotokos is transcendent of nature, but it is also continuous with nature, is itself perfectly natural. I would prefer to enlarge the concept of "nature" until it includes all these transcendent acts of human consciousness, but without denying their transcendence or attempting to reduce them to notions of matter. Transcendence, emergence, and integration of the components are the very pattern of

cosmic movement…The incarnational model relieves us of the classical "problem of evil" by not using its assumptions. Those assumptions are that God is both outside the creation and yet capable of acting as an independent agent inside creation, changing some aspects of the creation without changing others. The incarnational model says that God is incarnate as the creation, thus acts as the whole of the creation in terms of lawful operations of that creation, and thus cannot (any more than any other agency) change some problems without upsetting others (Bruteau 1997: 176–77).

The return of these women to a mystical view of God marks a stripping away of the male discourse that has overlaid the ample evidence in the Scriptures and later traditions that the mystery of God is beyond all comprehension (Johnson 1993: 33). Many theologians would see the sacred as only in the process and relinquish ideas of a stable metaphysical reality resulting in the move to verbs as on expression of the Divine rather than nouns, as we saw in Chapter Four.

3. *Belief, Worship and Action*

The result of Paul's high theology of the body in 1 Cor. 6 is that right prayer and right action is inextricably joined together. Right action is right prayer. This is clear in verse 13:

> The body is for the Lord and the Lord for the body.

This prepares the way for the inextricable link between mysticism and prophetic action as set out by Dorothy Soelle in her book *The Silent Cry: Mysticism and Resistance* (2001) and Myra Poole in *Prayer, Praise and Protest* (2001); see Case Study Three below.

All the Wisdom traditions have stressed the quality of the consequence of Divine immanence being proper action:

> Truthfulness, fidelity, kindness, honesty, independence, self-control, doing justice – these are all means of walking in the way of Wisdom… it is a search for justice and order in the world that can be discerned by experience. Wisdom teaching does not keep faith and knowledge apart; it does not divide the world into religious and secular, but provides a model for living a "mysticism of everyday things" (Schüssler-Fiorenza 2001: 28).

The development of an embodied spirituality of social action has resulted in a powerful activist element among feminist theologians. Rosemary Radford Ruether in her ground breaking book *Sexism and God-Talk* (1983) laid out the socio/political implications of classical theology. She saw the classical location of the Divine outside of the realm of physical and licensing all forms of domination. She develops a concept of 'hierarchy of being' rooted in this paradigm of a God separated from the physical worlds (Ruether 1983). She pursues the logic of this position to its final conclusion of denying the possibility of immortality. There are, indeed many feminist theologians who, although sharing the desire for an immanent God, would wish to retain some notion of eternal life within their theological paradigm. In terms of social action, however, it does liberate people from the more paralyzing effects of looking to an afterlife for any improvement in their conditions as a sort of opium. Ruether's position makes sacred the world of political action and social disruption in the cause of justice. Rosi Braidotti pursues this line calling metaphysics a 'political ontology' which devalues the material in favour of distanced Divine separated from the vicissitudes of lived experience (Braidotti 1994: 108).

The activism of feminist theologians is seen in their involvement in movements such as the ordination of women, reproductive rights, against global capitalism, against sexual violence, for environmental justice, to name but a few. Mary Grey's involvement in the Wells for India Project is but one example of this. In her overview of the implications of the feminist theologians' re-imaging of God (Grey 2001) she sets out a theology of Sophia (Wisdom). In her attempt to move beyond the classical dualisms, she sees the need for a God immanent in the material world and deeply involved in struggles for communal and individual justice. God is present within the ambiguity of unexplained suffering itself. This calls us to 'epiphaneous action' (Grey 2001).

4. Human Vulnerability

The concentration on the vulnerability of God as we saw in Chapter Five sees God as linked with vulnerable humanity and is beloved by feminist liturgists. The identification of women's suffering with a vulnerable Christ Sophia on the Cross has led to a development of iconography including a female figure at its heart like the Christa. Initially, such images as the Christa were regarded as deeply shocking, but they are becoming increasingly available through such media at the Internet and are finding acceptance with people who feel marginalized and alienated. These stress the quality of divine immanence. All the Wisdom traditions have stressed this:

> The goal of Wisdom teaching is to impose a kind of order on the myriad experiences that determine a person and thus enable one to cope with life. Wisdom teaching is an orientation to proper action, to knowing when to do what. It means engaging in value judgements that urge a certain course of action (Schüssler Fiorenza 2001: 28).

The traditional model of incarnation is that God relinquishes power and takes the form of a vulnerable human being and becomes bound by gravity and poverty. The Asian theologian C. S. Song sees the value of this gravity-boundedness, warning that when it is gravity-free it becomes a repulsive, alienating force. 'God is drawn to the world through a gravity-bound love' (Morley 1992: 41). This question of balance and acceptance is something that we, as humans, wrestle with:

> We have to enter into a very fine balance of life, the fine frequency of the Spirit, to find the simplicity and subtlety to respond to Christ's dynamism. To enter into that depth, to open up that depth means becoming vulnerable and remaining vulnerable, not only in prayer but in very part of life…That particular balance between vulnerability and resilience is part of the unique intellectual, psychological and spiritual amalgam that a human being is, each one starts from a different kind of imbalance but all are called to the same balance and centrality, the same rootedness in Christ who was wounded but was resilient in the transcendence of forgiveness (Freeman 1986: 106-7).

The centrality of incarnation to Christianity led Archbishop William Temple to say that 'Christianity is the most materialistic of all religions.' This is reflected in our use of water for Baptism and our theology of the bread and wine at the Eucharist. Within some parts of Christianity like the Quakers and the Eastern Orthodox Churches, the whole earth is sacrament in which God is eternally immanent. The story of Jesus shows him using the material sacramentally in the use of spittle for healing and using touch to deal with troubled spirits:

> Even the wood of the cross, it seems to some, has healing power. In all this Jesus is a good Jew, who does not split off body and spirit, nor for that matter person and community (Frost 2002).

So within Christianity incarnational theology is necessarily green theology.

So the problems of keeping body and soul together are a manifestation of the doctrinal problems around the divinity and humanity of Jesus. Traditionally the indwelling of Christ in the believer is achieved by the practice of contemplation and/or the Eucharist. Western culture has tended to split soul, body and mind, although this was not part of Jewish tradition. Within the idea of incarnation is the sacredness of the earth and the natural world. In stressing the immanence of God in the material world, some contemporary theologians have discussed the problem of notions of a transcendent God. Finally, the consequence of incarnational theology is that right belief and right action are inextricably linked.

Case Studies

Case Study One: Renegotiating the Divinity of Jesus

The issues around embodiment are bound up with debates about the identity of Jesus – his humanity and his divinity. It effectively has two sides, certainty and uncertainty – the unmanifest and the manifest balanced – body and soul. In Mark's Gospel there was a clear desire to present Jesus' identity as Son of God and/or Son of Man. It represents some of the earliest Christological thinking. So the first eight chapters present Jesus as a divine man with healing powers; this is then corrected in the last eight chapters with the teaching of the suffering of the Son of Man. Mark's Gospel redefines Christ the miracle worker and does not make the explicit claims about his humanity and divinity as are found in John's Gospel (Burridge 1994: 50–51). In Mark, Jesus does not preach himself. His claims are oblique using the title Son of Man but his action is authoritative and he challenges men and women to accept or reject him. As Jesus accepts the suffering, Jesus is revealed as Christ to those who can see. (Hooker 1991: 15–20) The view of his suffering presented here is one of the consequences of embodied prophetic action:

> The kind of Christ I am is one who serves – and ends up suffering, not because I'm really into suffering but because that sometimes happens when you challenge the status quo. When you serve people who don't have power, sometimes people who have power react badly against you. So suffering is a consequence of that kind of service (Struthers Malbon 2002: 55).

Brian Thorne, reflecting as a therapist upon the humanity/divinity question, sees Jesus' divinity reflected in his full humanity:

It is as I reflect on the Passion of Jesus, however, that the well-nigh inevitability of such a process becomes clearer. Jesus, as we have seen, was as secure in his identity as any human being has ever been. He was welcomed into the world, loved devotedly, respected by his elders and fully integrated into the society and culture of his day. It was precisely this wholeness of being that led him into suffering and death for it made him, in the words of the German poet, Rainer Maria Rilke, no longer at home in the interpreted world. As he came more and more to live out his vision and to follow the vocation demanded by his Father's business, so the world in which he found himself was increasingly unable to support his presence. The full humanness of Jesus in all its glory was finally an intolerable affront to those weighed down with guilt, anxiety, ambition, fear and the lust for power. What is more, the humanity of Jesus, which in its completeness revealed his divinity, was at the same time the manifestation of utter vulnerability. The life of Jesus Christ, the incarnate God, reveals that to be fully human means to embody a vulnerability, which may well court and invite a wounding unto death (Thorne 2006: 64).

Jeffrey John sums up the dilemmas of Christology in the early Church:

It is generally thought unlikely that he [Jesus] foretold his own resurrection and the identification of his risen body with a church. The most common scholarly view is that these sayings have been read back into the story by the evangelist, writing after, or near to, the destruction of the temple by the Romans in 70 AD, who naturally understood the destruction as God's punishment on Israel for rejecting their Messiah, and saw the Church as being now the new or true Israel, to whom the promises made to the old Israel had now passed (John 2001: 195).

In the early Church, Jesus' identity was a subject of considerable debate. Only by tradition after the Council of Chalcedon in 451 and the fifth Ecumenical Council in 553 did it codify; but the controversy continued into the seventh century:

Chalcedon expressed that in the union in Christ the characteristic properties of both the divine and human natures concur into one person and one hypostasis. St. Maximus is going to employ the Christological notion of a hypostatic union – that is, a personal union – not only for the development of Christological understanding itself, but also to understand the divine-human relationship at large in the process of deification, as well as to understand the ultimate union that is to be attained between the Godhead on the one hand and universal creation on the other (Govaerts 2005).

This echoes some of the themes in Chapter Three and in seeing contemplation as a means to the union it echoes themes explored earlier in this chapter. The seventh century St. Maximus however, saw that both body and soul belong inseparably together and attempted to reduce the duality of Origen by perceiving the created multiplicity as very positive and as willed by God.

Debates about Jesus today are also informed by his place as a prophet in Islam and in Hinduism as an avatar. The distinctiveness of the incarnation in Jesus for Christians is drawn primarily from Paul with some support from St John's Gospel (Moule 1977: 135–37).

The wrestling with and shifting perspectives of the dilemma of Jesus' humanity and divinity reflects the human dilemma of keeping body and soul together. 'I know my soul hath power to know all things, Yet she is blind and ignorant of all' writes Sir John Davies (1569–1626).[10] Symeon the New Theologian (949–1022) says that:

> You have made me a god, a mortal by nature, a god by your grace, by the power of your Spirit, bringing together as god a unity of opposites (McGrath 1994: 353).

I tried to encapsulate some of these debates in a hymn written as a result of Carter Heyward's Christology class:

1. Christ, Sophia, Jesus,
   Which are names for you?
   Christ, Sophia, Jesus,
   Make all things new.

2. Christ, Sophia, Jesus,
   Which name is mine,
   As I taste your presence
   In bread and wine?

3. Christ, Sophia, Jesus,
   Earth is your name;
   Rooted deep within you
   All blooms again.

4. Christ, Sophia, Jesus,
   You stand outside,
   Peering through the locked gates,
   Access denied.

10. http://www.bartleby.com/101/181.html. 24 November 2006.

5. Christ, Sophia, Jesus,
   I would name you too,
   Name you in a life that
   Makes all things new.

6. Christ, Sophia, Jesus,
   All bear your name,
   Mystic Christic body,
   Love's erotic flame.

(Boyce-Tillman 2006a: 17)

Case Study Two: Renegotiating Mary

And Jesus' mother, Mary, plays a crucial part in the working out of this debate. The Roman Catholic theologian, Hans Ur van Balthasar sees for her three roles:

- Mary the Virgin (Pre-redemptor) – the necessity for her willing consent so that God and humanity co-operate mutually, her ability to bring her Son up as a good Jew, the notion that her 'flesh welcomes him perfectly'.
- Mary the Mother (Co-redemptor) – her consent to the crucifixion and her distance and presence at it as witness.
- Mary the Bride (Trans-redemptor) – as giving birth to the Church (Nichols 2000).

While playing a significant role as a feminine in the Divine in Catholicism, her fate is very different in Protestantism:

> There are no remnants of the goddess in Protestant Christianity except the structure of divinity as three in one: only now, the trinity is Father, Son, and a (male) Holy Spirit...The Holy Spirit appeared in the form of a dove in the New Testament which is an ancient goddess symbol, associated with Aphrodite in classical Greek mythology and a feminine archetype...In contrast, in Roman Catholicism, the Virgin Mary has been elevated in significance to where one could say that there is a Christian quaternity of Mary and the Trinity. It could be even said (especially by others outside the Roman Catholic Church) that the goddess is returning into the culture through Mary (Shinoda Bolen 2001: 117–18).

The figure of the Virgin Mary has in many ways been through similar dilemmas to that faced in the identity of Jesus. The year 1954, four years after the doctrine of the Assumption had been defined, was declared a Marian year by Pope Pius XII. Eamon

Duffy,[11] in his Aquinas Lecture, describes how his hometown on the East Coast of Ireland responded:

> The women were invited to donate jewellery, the men money, towards the creation of a solid gold crown for the statue of the Blessed Virgin in our parish church. It was a poor community, most of the men, like my father, working as labourers in the local railway works, or in one or other of the town's shoe-factories. No one had much money to spare, there was a great deal of unemployment, and constant haemorrhage of the young to England in search of jobs. Yet the response to the appeal for the Virgin's crown was remarkable, many of the women even donating their wedding-rings. The statue, an insipid life-sized plaster replica of Our Lady of Lourdes, white-robed, blue sashed, small busted, neither a recognizably maternal nor even a very convincingly human image, was duly decorated with a crown which would have paid several times over for any one of the houses in which most of the donors lived (Duffy 2006).

Duffy describes how it was a particular 'vision of goodness, femininity emptied of danger and the shadow of the apple in Eden.' Yet this has been critiqued by many, notably Marina Warner (1985). She, like many others, has seen the cult as damaging to women because she represented an unattainable perfection for human women in the linking of virginity with motherhood. Elizabeth Johnson in *Truly our Sister,* extends this to show that it was Mary's divinity without apparent humanity that made her oppressive to many women, telling such stories as a women's prayer group in South Africa which decided to omit from the litany of Loreto the phrase 'Mother inviolate, Mother undefiled' (Johnson 2006).

Negative views of Mary, in my experience, are widely held by Roman Catholic women but not shared by Protestant women who come to her with a freshness impossible for those of a RC background, as Jean Shinoda Bolen points out in the opening quotation in this section. Other writers see the cult as a manifestation of the repressed motherhood of Western culture (Carroll 1992a, 1992b). He takes a Freudian line in analysing Marian shrines such as centres like Our Lady of Guadalupe (with 12,000,000 pilgrims a year) or Lourdes (4,000,000 pilgrims a year) as signs of the deeply repressed motherhood in Europe born of patriarchy. He sees it born in subjugated cultures as a reaction to the poverty (the han of Chapter One) and far from empowering people as a sort of opium

11. www.bfpubs.demon.co.uk/duffy.htm, contacted 30 November 2006.

to keep them trapped in a self-punitive position – indeed as part of the self-policing we saw in Chapter One. Because of the archetypal quality of Marian devotion he sees it as always outside the control of priestly hierarchies or theologians. He sees it as the product of such negative social phenomena as poverty, low self-esteem and social alienation.

In 431 CE, the council designated Mary Theotokos, which was an important moment in the placing of Mary theologically. As we have already seen, it was intended to say something about the divinity/humanity of Jesus – indeed to secure the humanity as well as the divinity of Jesus as a central doctrine of the Church. However, it brought Mary into prominence and led to her being placed initially at the head of the saints and eventually into a virtually separate category from all the others and potentially equal with her Son. It is Eastern Orthodoxy that has kept alive, calling her both Theotokos and pan-hagia, All Holy. The use of the title Blessed Virgin in the Western churches has perhaps led to some of the dilemmas that she now poses for women today. Indeed, in the iconography associated with places like Guadeloupe and Lourdes she is no longer a mother with a child but a young girl standing in her own right. Duffy (2006) points out that in Marian hymnody of the Victorian period, Mary (somewhat unhelpfully) becomes the personification of all goodness – light – in a dark and sinful world.

> O purest of creatures, sweet Mother, sweet maid,
> The one spotless womb wherein Jesus was laid!
> Dark night has come down on us, Mother, and we
> Look out for thy shining, sweet Star of the Sea (Quoted in Duffy 2006).

And it is not only society that is sinful but the individual believer for whom she must plead. These dualistic hymns set Mary up (not unlike the Protestant church has done with Jesus) in a realm of unreachable perfection as a distant divine being pleading with an ever accusing God. As such, she becomes a representation and a cause of deep alienation for human beings. Women are alienated from their bodies by her virginity and from their souls by her perfection. The duality between the world and the divine is deliberately reinforced to make the image of the Virgin, at best, unhelpful and at worst pernicious. It is a comforting image for those oppressed by secular military forces such as the Italian Risorgimento, defacing churches or by those other denominations which appeared to oppress them, as in Ireland. Between the denominations of Christianity, more battles are fought over Mary than Jesus.

Duffy sees beyond these problems to the use of Marian devotion and, in particular, visions to provide a counterbalance to Enlightenment rationality (which we explored at the opening of this chapter):

> These were hymns for people with no votes, or who disapproved of the states in which votes might be cast. Till the nineteenth-century the official church had often frowned on popular Marian devotion, the world of visions and apparitions, holy wells and spontaneous pilgrimage, as theologically suspect and prone to abuse. In the nineteenth century, however, for the first time the papacy threw its full weight behind all that: the apparitions at Lourdes and Knock and Marpingen and Fatima became a rallying-point for the Church against the world, simple faith against secular sophistication, the virginal softness of Mary against the hard aggression of modernity. The result was that Marian shrines and Marian devotion often took on a disturbingly anti-democratic dimension. And so the softness of the feminine could be harnessed in favour of hardness and strife: the Virgin of Fatima became a Cold Warrior, her message a fear-laden denunciation of Communism, laced with rumours of a terrifying end to history, and calls for a Rosary Crusade (Duffy 2006).

Seamus Heaney saw Irish Marian folk-religion as an antidote to the masculine, phallic, active nature of Irish Protestantism:

> He was fascinated by the liquid, yielding character of the Irish language and of the Gaelic place-names of his home territory, which seemed to him to match the religion of his home and his tribe: Ireland, like its Catholicism, seemed to him yieldingly feminine, Britishness and Protestantism, aggressively male. The soft black earth of Heaney's native bogland became for him a symbol of the ancient feminine religion of Europe, in Ireland translated into the supplicatory Catholicism of a subject race…The feminine, submissive character of Catholicism, its female piety, its mournful emphasis on the Mother of Sorrows, had helped, Heaney thought, to shape a collusive, submissive mentality for the Northern Irish nationalist community (Duffy 2006).

One helpful hymn that seems to bring together Mary's humanity and divinity for me is the Stabat Mater. This medieval Franciscan hymn does relate to experiences of powerlessness in the face of the suffering of a child. The grief-stricken Mary stands at the foot of the Cross. What I find interesting here is that Duffy (2006) interprets this as a poem of devotion to the Cross, whereas I have always seen it as a fellow mother with similar feelings to mine and to any parent watching a child suffer. However, eventually he sees how Mary lost her place as a bringer together of humanity, and became an isolated divine supernatural figure in the hands of the Church after the Council of Trent, which was 'an abrasively masculine entity', while ecclesiology became 'a bureaucratic and managerial exercise, authoritarian and impatient of nuance or ambiguity.' The Church then loses its imaginative texts about Mary:

> The Marian tradition itself narrowed, captured too exclusively by forms of folk belief insufficiently anchored in the scriptural and patristic tradition, vacuously pietistic, and increasingly cut off even from the simple human biological reality of Mary's child-bearing, from which all Mariology takes its rise. In this context, for example, I think it would be revealing to make a study of the rise and fall in Catholic tradition of devotion to and interest in Mary's milk and her breast-feeding of Christ, for, as belief in the Immaculate Conception grew, theologians became increasingly uneasy about the attribution to Mary of bodily processes like lactation or menstruation, aspects of human sexuality which they associated with the consequences of the Fall (Duffy 2006).

He cites Vatican II as an attempt at a drastic reorientation of the whole basis of Mariology re-relating it to ecclesiology. But it failed:

> The reasons for that failure are too complex and too uncertain for me to explore at the tail end of a lecture already too long, but they include a deep cultural unease with the virtue of chastity and the concept of Virginity, and a suspicion that somehow the image of Mary has been responsible for holding women down and trapping them within misogynistic stereotypes (Duffy 2006).

His final conclusions reflect the previous debate on rationality and intuition and he sees Mary as simply as a cerebral and abstract example of human obedience which is to be imitated, much drier and therefore, less useful than medieval Mariology. He calls for a re-embodiment – a concentration on her birthing capacity and the embodiment of this process, concluding sadly like the feminist theologians in Chapter Five that:

> Mary's womb, like her milk, has become invisible (Duffy 2006).

Case Study Three: Renegotiating Sexuality

This is a highly complex area that has been alluded to by a number of theological texts already. The legalizing of single sex partnership has shown how pressure from subjugated ways of knowing can affect the dominant orthodoxy:

> I was illegal for more than half my life...The fear. The ever growing fear of discovery, which really lurked beneath the surface all along...The worst part of it was love. Meeting someone you wanted to live with for the rest of your life, and not being able to, or doing so, trying to juggle two lives, and living a lie (Miller 2005).

This section of a gay man telling his story has shown how sexuality has been renegotiated in the UK in the late twentieth century. Here, the Church is left with a confusing situation in relation to the changing dominant values of the surrounding culture. David Lyon in *Jesus in Disneyland: Religion in Postmodern Times* (2000) showed how contemporary society has become obsessed with issues around the body and the rise of more embodied issues sometimes in twisted form because of the loss of the flow between the embodied and the disembodied. So sexuality is often associated with issues like:

- smoking and alcohol consumption,
- genetic engineering,
- abortion and a range of controversies associated with reproduction,
- the family and committed partnerships,
- sexuality.

He sees as indicative of the way in which postmodernity has developed the way in which these are at the front of the agenda for many conservative campaigning groups in North America and Western Europe.

Stephen Hunt (2005) examines how the Alpha initiative handles sexuality highlighting the views of Nicky Gumbel, author of the Alpha initiative, who sees the change in the dominant view of the primacy of heterosexual marriage in the surrounding culture as an alarming revolution. In *Searching Issues* there is to be found the following statements:

> Many people find themselves trapped in promiscuity which destroys their self esteem, exposes them to sexually transmitted disease and often ruins their ability to form a lasting relationship' (Gumbel 2000: 38).

Hunt shows how Gumbel largely expounds standard evangelical teaching, but how the support is through psychology (giving it, therefore the greater possibility of credibility in the dominant culture). He claims that the one-partner (heterosexual) relationship is for life and for the best since 'God does not want us to get hurt' (Gumbel 2000: 42). The *Alpha* literature conjoins a number of issues around the body, presenting a bastion of conservatism in the face of considerable changes in the dominant secular orthodoxy:

- marital breakdown,
- single mothers,
- abortion.

Gumbel sees a relationship between the decline in Christianity and the change in the dominant value system:

> The vast majority of the population of the United Kingdom does not attend church, and of those who do, many only go at Christmas or Easter. Following in the wake of the decline in Christian belief, there has been a decline in the moral climate. The fabric of our society is unraveling. Everyday in Britain at least 480 couples are divorced. 170 babies are born to teenage mothers and 470 babies aborted. In addition, at least one new crime is committed every six minutes. Although there are 30,000 clergy of all types, there are more than 80,000 registered witches and fortune tellers (Gumbel 1994).

Stephen Hunt highlights the rigidity of the views (Hunt 2003):

> Many ("guests") are still a long way off (a real experience of God) when they begin Alpha. Some are convinced atheists, some are New Agers, some are adherents to other religions or cults. Many are living lifestyles which are far from Christian. Some are alcoholics, others are compulsive gamblers, many are living with partners to whom they are homosexual in lifestyle (Gumbel 2000: 26).

Such simplification into rigid moral codes of complex issues can be seen as an attempt to shore up a dominant value system that is rapidly becoming subjugated – at a time when the embodied and the disembodied start to associate effectively so that the gay and lesbian communities can reclaim their souls and their integrity.[12]

Within the churches, however, the orthodoxy is painfully and slowly (much too slowly for some) shifting, for the previous orthodoxy meant a pernicious confusion of private and public (see Chapter Four) where single sex partnerships were lived out in secret; therefore when issues of breakdown in relationships occurred, with

---

12. It is interesting to reflect how phrases like 'confirmed bachelor' have enabled gay men to survive within the dominant orthodoxy that would force them to live a lie.

all the associated hurt, these could not be dealt with openly as in theory they were not allowed to exist:

> Whether or not they identify themselves as "gay" or "lesbian", they have sadly often found the Church is not a place of grace for them, but rather, in Michael Vasey's words, "a place of danger." As long as this is the case the gospel is not being obeyed and the Church needs to keep asking itself where it is in error (Goddard 2004: 31).

The confusion within the Church demonstrates quite clearly what happens when a dominant value system is effectively challenged and changed in the wider culture. Debates about whether gay and lesbian partnerships can, or should, function like heteropatriarchal marriage will rage on for some time:

> The Church needs to encourage a lifelong commitment between homosexual partners in much the same way it does between heterosexual partners (Fletcher quoted in John 2000: 48).

Jeffrey John sees how hurts will need to be forgiven as a right relationship with the new value system is established:

> Almost as long as it has existed, the Church has been directly responsible for evils and injustices committed against homosexuals...Yet there is not a glimmer of repentance, rather the opposite – an arrogant and unintelligent reaffirmation of bigotry...It will not be quickly forgotten (John 2000: 49).

This is interesting for it sees the need for forgiveness in the renegotiating of right relationship (see Chapter Four). Goddard highlights the dilemmas of a multiplicity of views co-existing:

> Unless care is taken, there will be a *de facto* division into congregations upholding traditional teaching but with a few gay people within them, and congregations attracting gay people but embracing 'revisionist' views. Finding ways of genuinely welcoming those with whom we differ is, therefore, a priority and essential for real dialogue and progress. In particular, "traditionalists" must consider how to "welcome and accept sexually active homosexual people" rather than building barriers to their presence (Goddard 2004: 30).

Case Study Four: Renegotiating Mysticism and Social Action

Defining mysticism has challenged academics and theologians across the ages and definitions have changed and varied:

> A mystic is a person who is deeply aware of the powerful presence of the divine Spirit: someone who seeks, above all, the knowledge and

love of God and who experiences to extraordinary degree the profoundly personal encounter with the energy of divine life. Mystics often perceive the presence of God throughout the world of nature and in all that is alive, leading to a transfiguration of the ordinary all around them. However, the touch of God is most strongly felt within their own hearts (King 2004: 3).

Ursula King goes on to see that the mystical experience is not a celestial sweet given purely for self-fulfillment, but is associated with social action. This is a counterbalance to some of the constructions of spirituality we saw at the end of the theology section as privatized, individualized experience given for personal gratification:

> For some, this is a social gospel or one of liberation; for others it is an inward, mystic call. Yet for many Christian mystics of the past it was a combination of an inner and an outer quest, a journey that led deeply into the divine centre of their own souls, but then moved outward again to the concerns of God's created world and those of suffering humanity (King 2004: 4).

Many medieval women visionaries stress their humility and unlearnedness. The visionary text of Elisabeth of Schoenau, a Benedictine nun at the convent near St Goarshausen on the Rhine begins:

> I am a mere poor woman; a vessel of clay. What I say comes not from me but from the clear light: man is a vessel which God fashioned for himself, and filled with his inspiration, so that, in him, he could bring his works to perfection (Bowie and Davies 1990: 130).

What is interesting is that the reason these women mystics give for this lowly view of their personal circumstances is that they are only women. Although the male mystics also point away from themselves towards God, they do not claim to do this on the grounds of their gender. Women, excluded from positions of authority such as priesthood and bishoprics and positions in academic institutions, used their visions to draw that authority directly from God. This is still true of groups of people excluded from the dominant culture who tend to lose their self esteem and sense of advocacy (Boyce-Tillman 2000a). To the groups of subjugated knowers identified in Chapter One, visions can be a great source of power to push the norms of the dominant culture:

Women mystics are women who push out the boundaries for other women, beyond the norms of their society, as far as they can within the 'patriarchal' restrictions of their time. They are among the most actualized women of history (Poole 2001: 51).

We see this call in the final chapter of Teresa of Avila's great mystical work *The Interior Castle*:

The fruit of the spiritual marriage must be good works. The interior calm fortifies these persons so that they may endure much less calm in the exterior events of their lives, that they may have strength to serve (Kavanaugh 1979: 29).

Dorothy Soelle in her seminal text *The Silent Cry*, draws on St Teresa's teaching to underpin contemporary protests:

The language of mysticism includes in itself a silence that learns to listen and risks being submerged in the dark night of the soul. In Teresa's life work for reform, this silence is contextualised within the social resistance that worked for the liberation of women from restriction, tutelage and mindlessness. In clinging undeterred to her praxis, Teresa showed how a different language could present a different freedom...When young people maintain 'vigils of peace' in the shopping malls of our cities, in the very places where the golden calf is venerated, they make God visible simply by standing in those places...In these new forms of piety, which openly acknowledge and own their lack of power and do not hide inside churches, there is a mystical kernel. It is a silence that follows after information, analysis and knowledge (Soelle 2001: 76).

Once the mysticism becomes embodied, the mystic poses a considerable threat to the established order; and the stories of women mystics usually include struggle and persecution. Their authority is no longer drawn from without but from within. Their authority comes from an immanent God.

For Margery Kempe (ca 1373–1440), for example, the vision was a remarkable source for personal affirmation and enabled her to live a life that challenged the cultural norms of her time in terms of women's freedom which included a vow of celibacy within marriage. They were the central core of her resistance strategy. Margery has often been dismissed as a hysteric, but in her story – dictated towards the end of her life – we have a useful document in which the visionary experiences are located in the context of her life. It shows the visionary experience as a source of inner comfort and strength in the life of a woman who refused to conform to the dominant norms of her society.

The story of Hildegard of Bingen (1098–1179) shows the vision as the source of protest and a call to justice. Central to Hildegard's position in her time, in which she was known as 'The Sybil of the Rhine', were her visionary experiences. Having received the visions from an early age, she was advised to keep silent about them; but in a mid-life crisis she was encouraged to make them public.

Although there was a tradition of visionary experiences at the time, including her contemporary Richard of St Victoire, Hildegard's descriptions of her own differ markedly from the traditional distinctions that classified them as imaginative, intellectual and spiritual. Gradually, the male visionaries used more of the methods of scholarship and this led to a definition of mysticism which tended to marginalize the more imaginative visions associated with women. Genuine mysticism became defined using criteria laid down by the patriarchal authorities.

The conflation of the Old and New Testaments with contemporary issues that characterize her explanations of the visions was born in the practice of *lectio divina* – the meditative study of the Scriptures. This would have been an important spiritual practice in the Benedictine rule. Within this tradition, there was an inbuilt distrust of the dialectical thought being developed at the time in Paris.

Hildegard's claim to be 'unlearned' made it absolutely certain that the revelations that she received were directly from God. In it lay her claim to be an authentic authoritative prophetic voice. Slowly she got this view confirmed by external authorities (Boyce-Tillman 2000b).

In *The Book of Divine Works* – her most developed piece of theology – her visions are concerned with restoring justice. The consequence of this is passages like the following, mercilessly attacking the failings of the clergy:

> How long will we suffer and endure these ravening wolves, who ought to be physicians and are not?
>
> And how can it be right that the shaven-headed with their robes and chasubles should have more soldiers and more weapons than we do? Surely too, it is inappropriate for a cleric to be a soldier or a soldier a cleric? So let us take away from them what is not fairly but unjustly theirs…

For the Almighty Father has rightly divided all things...God indeed has not decreed that the tunic and cloak should be given to one son while the other remains naked, but has ordered that the cloak should be given to one, the tunic to the other. And so let the laity have the cloak, because of the bulk of their worldly concerns and on account of their offspring who are always growing and multiplying. But let the tunic be given to the religious population, so that they lack neither food nor clothing, but do not possess more than they need (Bowie and Davies 1990: 104–5).

The story of Julie Billiart, (1751–1816) founder of the Sisters of Notre Dame de Namur, shows the vision as a source for women's empowerment. She was a crippled and artisan peasant woman (a term for all except priests and nobility) who worked to realize her visionary experiences with her friend Francoise Blin de Bourdon, a noblewoman. It was directly from a vision at Compiegne in 1792 that she claimed the authority to establish schools for the poor, to develop the concept of personal and congregational poverty for her order. This led her into difficulties with the church authorities:

Julie's message of compassion, resistance and liberation was only possible because of her refusal to be made a victim, rooted in her profound friendship with God...The resurrection is not simply the survival of the soul but the transformation of the world as we know it. (Fiorenza 1994: 121) Liberation means not just self-liberation but an ethic of protest and it reached its zenith in her anger at the poverty that raged around her. But her anger was channelled into the life-giving powers of the resurrection (Poole 2001: 163).

For Mother Ann Lee (1736–1784) the vision was a source for a venture in social transformation. Nardi Reeder Campion in her influential book *Mother Ann Lee, Morning Star of the Shakers* states:

To escape British tyranny, Mother Ann took her small band of disciples on a perilous fifty-nine-day voyage across the ocean to an unknown land called America. In the wilderness of upstate New York, She and her followers carved out the first Shaker settlement. During the American Revolution, Mother Ann, a dedicated pacifist, stood unequivocally for nonresistance, quoting Jesus; "Love your enemies, bless them that curse you, do good to them that hate you, and pray for them which despitefully use you, and persecute you." Again she was sent to prison.

Later she trekked by carriage and sleigh through New England, enduring unbelievable hardships and persecution in order to attract new members to the Society of Believers. This Society, ruled by *both* women and men, was based on a conviction that God had to be *both* male and female. To generations of followers, she became the female Christ. Clearly Mother Ann Lee was a morning star, not just for the Shakers, but for the independence of women in the New World (Campion 1990: xvi–xvii).

So, in this case study, we have seen the role of the vision in the lives of four women mystics:

- Personal affirmation (Margery Kempe).
- Protest (Hildegard of Bingen).
- Women's empowerment (Julie Billiart).
- Social and theological reform (Mother Ann Lee).

At the end of Dorothy Soelle's book in a conversation with her husband she develops her relationship between mysticism and resistance:

> And this has led us by a circuitous route to your second concept: resistance. Mysticism is the experience of the oneness and the wholeness of life. Therefore, mysticism's perception of life, its vision, is also the unrelenting perception of life, of how fragmented life is. Suffering on account of that fragmentation and finding it unbearable is part of mysticism. Finding God fragmented into rich and poor, top and bottom, sick and well, weak and mighty: that's the mystic's suffering, the resistance of Saint Francis or Elisabeth of Thuringia or of Martin Luther King grew out of the perception of beauty. And the long lasting and lost dangerous resistance is the one that was born of beauty (Soelle 2001: 302).

From this she develops a useful table that summarizes the relationship set out here:

Here the notion of withdrawing from embodied reality leads to the experience of amazement. This vision of the extraordinary beauty of the Divine leads to a sense of being set apart and of letting go of

BEING AMAZED	LETTING GO	HEALING/RESISTING
Via positive	*Via negative*	*Via transformativa*
Radical amazement	Being apart	Changing the world
Bliss	Letting go of possession, violence and ego	Compassion and justice
Praising God	Missing God	Living in God
The rose	The 'dark night'	The rainbow

Soelle (2001: 93).

the received wisdom of the surrounding society. This release leads a radical drive towards the transformation of this society.

Summary

This chapter has examined the dilemmas posed by the split between the rational and the intuitive and the mind/body/spirit. The part played by Christianity in the perpetuating of these has been exposed. Various strategies of resistance have been explored in the case studies including the role of contemplation, the place of the arts in contemporary spirituality and the place of mystics in our culture. The second part has looked at the dilemma posed by the notion of deification and the debate the human/divine identity of Jesus. It has seen this as rooted in the human experience of keeping body and soul together.

Chapter Seven

DANCING IN WISDOM'S WAYS

Between

Between the God and Goddess
And the mosque and the synagogue

The bullet holes in the tumbled statues
The grass blades on the landfill,

The shaman and the cleric
The hysteric and choleric

The slaying and the praying
And the coping and the hoping

In the fractured rapture
In the hole in the soul

At the crack
The lack

Might
Bite

The Contradiction of 'both'
Meets
The Paradox of 'and'

Christbirth.

(Boyce-Tillman, November 2004)

This book has been about paradox and flow. It has established in its structure a flow between various traditions, highlighting paradox and uncertainty in an interdisciplinary approach to the subject of Wisdom. Western theology has often been more about certainty and single truths. Yet paradox has always been part of the subjugated Wisdom traditions.

Dorothy Sayers addresses these dilemmas when she sees Mary pondering the identity of her son in scene 11 of *The Man Born to Be King*:

CASPAR: O lady, clear as the sun, fair as the moon, the nations of the earth, salute your son, the Man born to be King. Hail, Jesus, King of the Jews!

MELCHIOR: Hail Jesus, King of the World!

BALTHAZAR: Hail, Jesus, King of Heaven!

CASPAR, MELCHIOR and BALTHAZAR together: All Hail!

MARY: God bless you, wise old man; and you, tall warrior; and you, dark traveller from desert lands. You come in a strange way, and with a strange message. But that God sent you I am sure, for you and His angels speak with one voice. "King of the Jews" – why, yes, they told me my son should be the Messiah of Israel, "King of the World" – that is a very great title; yet when he was born, they proclaimed tidings of joy to all nations. "King of Heaven" – I don't quite understand that; and yet indeed they said that he should be called the Son of God. You are great and learned men, and I am a very simple woman. What can I say to you, till the time comes when my son can answer for himself?

CASPAR: Alas, the more we know, the less we understand life. Doubts make us afraid to act, and much learning dries the heart. And the riddle that torments the world is this: Shall Wisdom and Love live together at last, when the promised Kingdom comes?

MELCHIOR: We are rulers, and we see that what men need most is good government, with freedom and order. But order puts fetters on freedom, and freedom rebels against order, so that love and power are always at war together. And the riddle that torments the world is this: Shall Power and Love dwell together at last, when the promised Kingdom comes?

BALTHAZAR: I speak for a sorrowful people – for the ignorant and the poor. We rise up to labour and lie down to sleep, and night is only a pause between one burden and another.

Fear is our daily companion – the fear of want, the fear of war, the fear of cruel death, and of still more cruel life. But all this we could bear if we knew that we did not suffer in vain; that God was beside us in the struggle, sharing the miseries of His own world. For the riddle that torments the world is this: Shall Sorrow and Love be reconciled at last, when the promised Kingdom comes?

MARY: These are very difficult questions – but with me, you see, it is like this. When the Angel's message came to me, the Lord put a song into my heart. I suddenly saw that wealth and cleverness were nothing to God – no one is too unimportant to be His friend. That was the thought that came to me, because of the thing that happened to me. I am quite humbly born, yet the Power of God came upon me; very foolish and unlearned, yet the Word of God was spoken to me; and I was in deep distress, when my Baby was born and filled my life with love. So I know very well that Wisdom and Power and Sorrow can live together with Love; and for me, the Child in my arms is the answer to all the riddles.

CASPAR: You have spoken a wise word, Mary. Blessed are you among women, and blessed is Jesus your son. Caspar, King of Chaldaea, salutes the King of the Jews with a gift of frankincense.

MELCHIOR: O Mary, you have spoken a word of power. Blessed are you among women, and blessed is Jesus your son. Melchior, King of Pamphylia, salutes the King of the World with a gift of gold.

BALTHAZAR: You have spoken a loving word, Mary, Mother of God. Blessed are you among women, and blessed is Jesus your son. Balthazar, King of Ethiopia, salutes the King of Heaven with a gift of myrrh and spices (Loades 1993: 102–3).

The Prophetic Tradition

The call set out in this book is in line with the Hebrew prophetic tradition. The prophetic call has always been to rebalance society when it has swung too far in one direction causing it to get out of balance and some feminist theologians have been keen to emphasize their relationship with traditions. Schüssler Fiorenza sees the need for rebalancing the traditions of biblical scholarship and recontextualizing them, declaring the standpoint of their authors.

> A critical feminist liberation theology therefore does not obstruct but enhances the self-understandings of critical biblical scholarship when it insists that all theological and biblical scholarship begin with an analysis of its own historical-political situation and with an expression of its own "hermeneutical option" rather than with the deceptive posture or representing detached, neutral, scientific and unbiased scholarship (Schüssler Fiorenza 1984: 143).

In this book we have many authorial voices. We have heard calls from many groups who have suffered the experience of han that we saw in Chapter One; the context of each group will dictate the words they utter. By hearing and responding, society is rebalanced.

Prophetic texts can be read at a societal and an individual level, for we are, as Chapter One has shown, intimately bound up with our society – we internalize its values, often to our own detriment. Nevertheless, the notion of a rhythm of de-integration and reintegration in the interest of balance and change that underpins this interpretation can, as we have seen above, be applied equally to the self as to a society as the mores of that society are quickly developed in subjugated knowers into policies and self-policing:

> The prophets, in a collage of specific utterances around a rich diversity of images and metaphors, bear a common witness to the claim that Yahweh will order all of public history according to Yahweh's will for justice, righteousness, and equity, without special privilege for Israel. Thus the prophets characteristically resist the exceptionalism of election faith (Brueggemann 1997: 640).

If we rework this, it says that the world will generally attempt to rebalance itself according to these laws. The notion of God then becomes a claim that at heart of the cosmos is a powerful rebalancing principle that is a 'given' and cannot be manipulated – that in the end the subjugated knowers will be heard. That process can involve war and rebellion or negation and understanding on the part of both dominant and subjugated knowers. This is the central core of this book – that this principle which Christians and Jews call God – is inescapable and can be achieved only by negotiation between dominant and subjugated ways of knowing and the people who know in these ways. If that is not on offer, then it will result in violence. We have seen that process happening in the wider Western society in the area of sexuality. We have seen it happening in some areas of the Church in women's priestly ministry.

The call of the Hebrew prophets varied according to the needs of the time; sometimes like Deutero-Isaiah they were comforting and supportive, exalting the values of nurture. At other times, in Malachi for e.g., they are condemnatory of a society that had lost its roots in the Mosaic law – one that had become self-satisfied and smug. It is then a call back to the communitarianism of the Mosaic Law – a right form of community, non-oppressive in its operation:

> I take the core of this prophetic accent to be that all members of the community, rich and poor, urban and rural, wise and foolish, powerful

and marginated, are bound to each other in a common historical and social enterprise. Every member, by virtue of membership in the community, has entitlement that cannot be abrogated. Thus "widow, orphan, alien" are ciphers for those most vulnerable and powerless and marginated in a patriarchal society, who are without legal recourse or economic beverage. They are entitled and must be given their share.

The negative counterpart to this affirmation is that there are no escape hatches or exceptional treatments for the wise, the rich, the powerful, or the well-connected. Their destiny is linked to the destiny of the whole community. Thus the Mosaic ethic, as practiced by the prophetic mediation, is a broadly based covenantal communitarianism, in which justice and righteousness assure that individual good is a subset of communal well-being.

In every season of prophetic utterance, but especially the prophets situated in the decline of the monarchy in the eight and seventh centuries, this claim that community membership has on each of its members, especially on the rich and powerful, is made a non-negotiable condition of a viable future...The argument being made, however, is that this future, conditioned by justice, is not an arbitrary imposition of an angry God, but is a conditionality found in the very fabric of creation. It is indeed how life works, no matter how much the strong and the powerful engage in the illusion of their own exceptionality (Brueggemann 1997: 645).

As we have seen, the unrestrained liberal autonomy of hetero-patriarchy has paid no attention to the plight of the poor, the women (Belenky *et al* 1986), the natural world (Grey 1989, 1993), those of other ethnicities (Douglas and Kwok 2001) the abused, including those abused by Church structures (Churches Together 2002), alternative sexualities (Ellison 1986) and a variety of others who become subjugated by the unrestrained capitalist enterprise.

The call of the prophets is to see that human beings have responsibilities as well as rights and this is particularly true of those in positions of authority in government. Their role becomes that of an egalitarian distribution of wealth, land and privilege. Everywhere that it stands for its own privilege, monopoly and self-indulgence, it stands in opposition to the central core of communitarianism – of connection between rich and poor, wise and foolish, bound and free.

The prophetic texts redeem anger (as we saw in Chapter Four) by seeing it at the heart of God, occurring when sections of the world community are allowed to be marginalized, ostracized and hidden. This anger can be seen as a version of the 'han' generated by subjugating various ways of knowing aggressively. The values of the Yahweh of the prophets are inextricably bound up with a right relationship to the whole creation. The hetero-patriarchal authorities will only reach their God-given potential and fulfil their right function by aligning themselves with these values. And so we arrive at an image of the world as it was intended to be (often referred to as the Kingdom of God but reworked by Schüssler Fiorenza as the kindom). When the polarities are connected in flow, we shall see a cosmic flourishing, a rebirthing of new forms of justice, peace, security and well-being, sometimes called shalom. God is committed to this process of rebirthing through connection with those groups traditionally defined as marginalized, deviant others.

These themes can be worked out today in a prediction that the pursuance of the heteropatriarchal values will necessarily bring about a judgement – call that judgement God or simply a re-balancing principle. Although today it is often the Market that functions in a way once ascribed to Yahweh as we saw in Chapter One. The contemporary prophetic call is to the values of communitarianism, justice and so on, which are not part of the Market Economy. Some ecologists have interpreted some of these natural disasters, like the floods of 2002 in the UK, as part of that theophany in the context of an abuse of the natural world. James Lovelock (1988) explores this in some detail, along with a number of other ecologists and ecotheologians. Bryld and Lykke examine the phenomenon from a feminist perspective (2000). But the promise is in the end of a restoration of relationship, for God loves the whole creation and seeks to get all its component parts into right relationship (Grey 1992). There is hope in prophetic utterances offering the ultimate possibility of redemption at a variety of levels – human beings, the wider community of nations and the creation.

But unlike some texts this books queers Wisdom theology by saying that it is not an either/or but a both/and theology – it is a negotiation with the dominant values, the bringing of the subjugated into relationship with the dominant. Just as The Enlightenment saw a swing in one direction and freed people from the distorted forms of community that had kept them bound in punitive and religious communities, so now the individualism that it provoked needs a rebalancing with a form of community that is in flow with the individualism.

I see the need for a return to the values of balance at the heart of the universe set out in this chapter as what, in Israel, was described as Yahweh, not as a male patriarchal God but as a set of value systems that see salvation in the appreciation of the plight of the suffering – in a God seen in the experience of the marginalized. So the suffering servant now acquires many different body shapes including those of women. 'Women not men, are suffering servants and Christ figures. Their stories govern the use of leitmotifs, Scripture thus interpreting scripture undercuts triumphalism and raises disturbing questions for faith' (Trible 1984: 3). Salvation for ourselves and our society and the natural world is in our understanding of suffering – in a God seen in the experience of the marginalized. It is in contra-distinction to an androcentric, individualized spirituality, a move from phallocentric violence, from fascist dictatorship whether in the self or in society, from unsupported challenge, from disembodied principles that are used to bind people's bodies in various servitudes. Just as the prophets of the Hebrew scriptures did not see a complete end to the worship of the Baals, the values of patriarchal capitalism are not to be totally eliminated but need tempering with other value systems. It is a spirituality of justice and right relationship. The prophetic literature calls us to a radical rethink of the financial, political, psychological and spiritual structures of our society.

> You have set sail on another ocean
> Without star or compass
> Going where the argument leads
> Shattering the certainties
> Of centuries (Janet Kalven quoted in the frontispiece to Schüssler
> Fiorenza 1984).

So the prophetic tradition has always called for a rebalancing and has called for strategies of resistance.

The prophetic role is as problematic today as it was in biblical times. The role of the prophet is to counterbalance the excesses of any society and is always contextual. In a different society with different value system like those of indigenous peoples, the message would be different for the prevailing value system would be different. The prophetic message is essentially contextually dependent. The call of prophecy is always to contemplate and interrogate the norms and conventions of society, to enable growth and change, in order to prevent any claim that a particular set of conventions can claim the totality of truth. This can only be embraced by a notion of God who can contain apparent contradictions and paradoxes. This God is, in the end, unknowable and can only be worshipped. The act of worship is the ultimate bastion against human cultural arrogance. Worship, at its best, is the ultimate acknowledgment of the limitations of our knowledge. Worship reminds us to bear in mind that: We May be wrong.

A Prophetic Message for Today

I have attempted to rework Hosea Chapter 11 as a message for today:

> When the earth was young, I loved it, and called it out of captivity. However, the more I called the human race, the more they went from me and separated themselves from the earth as a whole; they kept on sacrificing the vulnerable and the natural world to the patriarchal gods of competition, production, materialism and offering the smoke of their dreams of unlimited freedom and Western-style political systems to the idols of capitalism in the cathedrals of their shopping malls and banking halls.

> Yet it was I who taught the human race to walk, I took them up in my arms; but they did not know that it was I who healed and cared for them. I led them with the reins of human kindness, with the leading strings of love. I was to them like those who lift infants to their breasts. I bent down to them and fed them.

> Yet because they forgot their high calling as children of God, they shall return to a time of captivity, and they shall be ruled by forces beyond their control, because they have refused to return to me. Disquiet rages in their structures both institutional and material, it consumes the oracle-priests of their day – the financiers, politicians and media moguls – and devours them because of their scheming. My people are bent on turning away from me. They call for help, but I am unable to raise them from the consequences of their actions.

> But how can I give you up, O human race? How can I hand you over, O leaders of the Western world? How can I make you like the citizens of Hiroshima? How can I treat you like the victims of the Holocaust? My heart is overwhelmed within me; my compassion grows warm and tender like a fever in my innermost being. I will not give rein to my fierce anger; I will not again destroy the world; for I am God and not only human; I am the Holy One who am inextricably bound up with my creation, and I will not come to you in wrath.

Humankind *will* turn towards the values of a God whom they will find dwelling lovingly within creation; they will go after a God who roars like a lion; when God roars, God's children shall come trembling from the values of Western culture. They will come fluttering like birds from their enslavement to unlimited self-aggrandisement and like doves from the pursuit of destructive value systems; they will see that these need balancing with mercy, compassion and wisdom; and I will return them to their true place in the glorious interrelationship upon which this planet depends.

The Dance of Wisdom

So the dance becomes the ultimate metaphor – not only the circle of the popular circle dance traditions but the right hand and left hand stars of the English folk traditions where pairs of people link hands across one another and pull just hard enough to keep the group balanced. Then there is the basket of the square dance tradition, where hands are joined behind backs and the circle turns because the weight is shared and the inequalities are balanced out by careful sensitivity. This is the dance of the creative synthesis suggested in this book:

> "Dancing in the hours of Wisdom" or "Waltzing in Wisdom Ways" [means] stepping and twirling – creating an interpretive, communal dance and breaking out of the rhythm of the rhythm of culturally ascribed steps. I visualize a diverse group of women dancing in a circular formation inside the pillars of an open-air house – their dance circle open, ready to accept the reader inside. The dance could be edifying to the mind, body and spirit of the reader (Ellison 2000 quoted in Schüssler Fiorenza: 18).

Here are some of the figures:

- An acknowledgement of circular cyclic forms in the formation of inclusive communities involving human beings with one another, the natural world, and the spiritual however this is conceived, reflecting the immanence of Wisdom in her creation alongside the more separated linear transcendental view of patriarchal traditions.
- An embracing of diversity and novelty as positive and creative, alongside the stress of unity and conservation as a marker of excellence, reflecting the diverse forms that Wisdom can take as well as the single source from which s/he/it emanates.

- An acknowledgment of the interface between public and private and the need for openness to both spaces for all, exploding canonical systems that limit freedom of access and reflecting the hiddenness and the revealed nature of Wisdom.
- A delighting in the making of the ephemeral and the oral for their own sake alongside the valuing of the beautiful product reflecting Wisdom's playfulness, contextuality as well as orderedness.
- A validating of the strong and powerful sounds of triumphalism with their sense of optimism alongside the gentler sounds of vulnerability with their emotional charge, reflecting the power and weakness of the Wisdom of emotion.
- A sense of the need for the challenge of justice-making activity as well as a peace making one, reflecting the prophetic as well as the nurturing roles of wisdom.
- A valuing of the intuitive visionary experience alongside the processes of reason as a source of authority, reflecting the immediacy and the restraint of Wisdom.
- The mutual agreement of mind, body and spirit reflecting the mystery of humanity and divinity entwined at the heart of Wisdom.

In her *Antiphon to Wisdom* Hildegard sees the figure of Wisdom as having three wings. One wing reaches the heaven – the vision – one the earth – lived reality – and the third flies everywhere. Wisdom theology has often been set up as an alternative to the dominant triumphalist theology but this book has queered that tradition by seeing the need for relationship with the dominant values without collusion and compromise. Many examples have been given of people who have attempted to do this. This relationship is the third wing of the Hildegard figure – continually flowing between the two others to keep both in a true and helpful form for all:

> O the power of Wisdom:
> You, in circling, encircle all things,
> You are embracing everything in a way that brings life into being;
> For you have three wings.
> One of them reaches highest heaven
> And another is sweating in earth
> And the third is flying everywhere.
> Therefore it is right to give you praise,
> O Sophia wisdom (Boyce-Tillman 1994).

BIBLIOGRAPHY

Abrams, David, *The Spell of the Sensuous* (New York: Pantheon Books, 1996).
Adorno, Theodor W., *Philosophy of Modern Music* (New York: Continuum, 1973 [1948]).
Agrotou, Anthi, 'Spontaneous Ritualised Play in Music Therapy: A Technical and Theoretical Analysis', in Margaret Heal and Tony Wigram, *Music Therapy in Health and Education* (London: Jessica Kingsley, 1993), pp. 175–91.
Aldridge, David, *Music Therapy Research and Practice in Medicine – From Out of the Silence* (London: Jessica Kingsley, 1996).
Alfred, *Peace, Power and Righteousness: An Indigenous Manifesto*, George Erasmus, *Third Annual LaFontaine-Baldwin Lecture* (2002 [cited 16 March 2002]), http://cbc.ca/nws/indeph/lafintaine_lectures/. Is
Althaus-Reid, Marcella, *Indecent Theology: Perversions in Sex, Gender and Politics* (London: Routledge, 2000).
Anderson, Pamela Sue, *A Feminist Philosophy of Religion: The Rationality and Myths of Religious Belief* (Oxford: Blackwell, 1998).
Arendt, Hannah, *The Human Condition* (Chicago: University of Chicago Press, 1958).
Arinze, Cardinal Francis, The Christian Commitment to Inter-religious Dialogue, *L'Osservatorio Romano,* 17/7/89 par. 3, 9, in Marcus Braybrooke, *Faith and Interfaith in a Global Age* (Oxford: Co-nexus Press, 1998).
Assagioli, R., *The Act of Will* (Baltimore: Penguin Books, 1973).
Aune, Kristin, 'Being a "Real" Heterosexual Man: British Evangelicals and Hegemonic Masculinity', paper presented to the British Sociological Association Study of Religion Group, 11–13 April 2005, University of Lancaster.
Azzam, Maha, 'Gender and the Politics of Religion in the Middle East', in Mai Yamani (ed.), *Feminism and Islam.*
Bacon, Francis, *The Advancement of Learning* (ed. G.W. Kitchin; London: J.M. Dent and Sons, 1973).
Baker Miller, Jean, *Toward a New Psychology of Women* (London: Penguin, 1988).
Barth, K., *Church Dogmatics III/4* (Edinburgh: T.&T. Clark, 1961).
Barthes, Roland, *Mythologies* (London: Vintage, 1972).
_____*The Fashion System* (London: Cape, 1985).
Baxter, Elizabeth, Draft article for SCM Magazine, March 2006.

Bayton, Mavis, *FrockRock: Women Performing Popular Music* (New York: Oxford University Press, 1998).

Bauman, Zygmunt, *Identity: Conversations in Benedetto Vecchi* (Cambridge: Polity, 2004).

Belenky, M. Field *et al.*, *Women's Ways of Knowing* (New York: Basic Books, 1986).

Berger, Margret, *Hildegard of Bingen: On Natural Philosophy and Medicine* (London: Boydell and Brewer, 1999).

Berger, Teresa, *Women's Ways of Worship: Gender Analysis and Liturgical History* (Collegeville, Minnesota: The Liturgical Press, 1999).

_____*Dissident Daughters: Feminist Liturgies in Global Contexts* (Louisville and London: Westminster John Knox Press, 2001).

Berman, M., *All That is Solid Melts into Air* (London: Penguin, 1988).

Blake, Andrew, *The Land without Music: Music Culture and Society in Twentieth Century Britain* (Manchester: Manchester University Press, 1997).

Blue, Lionel, *Day Trips to Eternity* (London: Darton, Longman & Todd, 1987).

Boff, Leonardo, *Church Charism & Power:Liberation Theology and the Institutional Church* (New York: Crossroad, 1990).

Bonisolialquati, Anna, 'Representations of the Masculine in Indian Epic and Kavya Poetry', paper presented to the British Sociological Association Study of Religion Group, 11–13 April 2005, University of Lancaster.

Boorse, C., 'What a Theory of Mental Health Should Be', *Journal for the Theory of Social Behaviour 6 (1976)*, pp. 61–84.

Bosch, David J., *Transforming Mission: Paradigm Shifts in Theology of Mission* (Maryknoll, N.Y.: Orbis Books, 1991).

Bowie, Fiona, 'Trespassing Sacred Domains: A Feminist Anthropological Approach to Theology and Religious Studies', *Journal of Feminist Studies in Religion*, 14.1 (1998), pp. 40–62.

Bowie, Fiona and Oliver Davies, *Hildegard of Bingen: An Anthology* (London: SPCK, 1990).

Boyce-Tillman, June, *Singing the Mystery – An Evening with Hildegard of Bingen*, one woman performance, performed at the Thomas More Centre, London, 1992a.

_____*On Forgiveness – Some Thoughts* (London: Women in Theology, 1992b).

_____*Singing the Mystery: Twenty-eight Liturgical Pieces of Hildegard of Bingen* (London: Hildegard Press and Association for Inclusive Language, 1994).

_____*Constructing Musical Healing: The Wounds that Sing* (London: Jessica Kingsley, 2000a).

_____*The Creative Spirit: Harmonious Living with Hildegard of Bingen* (Norwich: Canterbury Press, 2000b).

_____*The Healing of the Earth* (London: The Hildegard Press, 2001a).

_____'Sounding the Sacred: Music as Sacred Site' in Karen Ralls-MacLeod and Graham Harvey (eds.), *Indigenous Religious Musics* (Farnborough: Scolar, 2001b), pp. 136–66.

_____*Lunacy or the Pursuit of the Goddess* (unpublished performance, 2002).

_____Unconventional Wisdom – Theologising the Margins, *British Journal of Feminist Theology*, 13.3 (2005), pp. 317–41.

_____'Ways of Knowing: Science and Mysticism Today' in C. Clarke (ed.), *Ways of Knowing* (Exeter, UK: Imprint Academic, 2005), pp. 8–33.

_____*A Rainbow to Heaven: Hymns, Songs and Chants*, (London: Stainer and Bell, 2006a).

_____'Music as Spiritual Experience', *Modern Believing: Church and Society*, 47:3 (2006b), pp. 20–31.

Boyce-Tillman, J. and Janet Wootton (eds.), *Reflecting Praise* (London: Stainer and Bell and Women in Theology, 1993).

Braidotti, Rosi, *Nomadic Subjects* (New York: Columbia University Press, 1994).

_____The Body as Metaphor: Seduced and Abandoned: The Body in the Virtual World (1995), videotape quoted in Mantin 2002.

Brakeman, Lyn, *Spiritual Lemons: Biblical Women, Irreverent Laughter and Righteous Rage* (Philadelphia; Augsburg Books, 2005).

Branham, Joan R., *Bloody Women and Bloody Spaces*, *Harvard Divinity Bulletin* (2003), see http://.hds.harvards.edu/dpa/news/bulletin/articles/branham.html

Brock, Rita Nakashima, *Journeys by Heart: A Christology of Erotic Power* (New York: Crossroad/Herder & Herder, 1991).

_____Kellogg Lectures, May 2003, Episcopal Divinity School, Cambridge, Massachusetts.

Brown, Callum, G., *The Death of Christian Britain* (London: Routledge, 2001).

Brueggemann, Walter, *The Theology of the Old Testament: Testimony, Dispute, Advocacy* (Minneapolis: Fortress Press, 1997).

Bruteau, Beatrice, *God's Ecstacy: The Creation of a Self-creating World,* (New York: Crossroad Publishing, 1997).

Bryld, Mette & Nina Lykke, *Cosmodolphins: Feminist Cultural Studies of Technology, Animals and the Sacred* (London & New York: Zed Books, 2000).

Buber, Martin, *I and Thou* (trans. Walter Kaufmann; New York: Charles Scribner's Sons, 1970).

Bunyard, Derek, 'Sticky Fingers, or How to Love a Post-modern Child', *Contemporary Issues in Early Childhood*, 6. 5 (2005), pp. 292–300.

Burridge, Richard A., *Four Gospels, One Jesus: A Symbolic Reading* (London: SPCK, 1994).

Butler, Judith, *Gender Trouble: Feminism and Subversion of Identity* (London: Routledge, 1990).

Bynum, Caroline Walker, *Holy Feast and Holy Fast: The Religious Significance of Food to Medieval Religious Women* (Berkeley: University of California Press, 1987).

Campion, Nardi Reeder, *Mother Ann Lee, Morning Star of the Shakers* (Hanover and London: University Press of New England, 1990 [1976]).

Cannon, Katie Geneva, *Black Womanist Ethics* (Atlanta: Scholars Press, 1988).

_____*Katie's Canon* (New York: Continuum, 1995).

Carroll, Michael P., *The Cult of the Virgin Mary: Psychological Origins* (Princeton: Princeton University Press, 1992a).

_____*Madonnas that Maim: Popular Catholicism in Italy since the Fifteenth Century* (Baltimore and London: The John Hopkins University Press, 1992b).

Chopp, Rebecca S., 'Foreword' in Nancy L. Eisland, *The Disabled God: Toward a Liberatory Theology of Disability* (Nashville: Abingdon Press, 1994), pp. 9–12.

_____'From Patriarchy to Freedom: A Conversation Between American Feminist Theology and French Feminism' in Graham Ward (ed.), *The Postmodern God: A Theological Reader* (Oxford and Massachusetts: Blackwell, 1997a), pp. 235–48.

_____'Theorizing Feminist Theology' in Rebecca S. Chopp and Sheila Greeve Daveney (eds.), *Horizons in Feminist Theology: Identity, Tradition and Norm* (Minneapolis, MN: Fortress Press, 1997b), pp. 210– 24.

Christ, Carol P., *Diving Deep and Surfacing: Women Writers in Spiritual Quest* (Boston: Beacon Press, 1980).

_____*Odyssey with the Goddess: A Spiritual Quest in Crete* (London and New York: Continuum, 1995).

_____*Rebirth of the Goddess: Finding Meaning in Feminist Spirituality* (Reading, MA: Addison Wesley, 1997).

_____*She Who Changes; Re-imagining the Divine in the World* (New York and Basingstoke: Palgrave/Macmillan, 2003).

Churches Together in Britain and Ireland, *Time for Action: Sexual Abuse, the Churches and a New Dawn for Survivors* (London: Church House Publishing, 2002).

Clark, Mary, *In Search of Human Nature* (New York: Routledge, 2002).

Clarke, Chris, *Living in Connection: Theory and Practice of the New World-view* (Warminster: Creation Spirituality Books, 2002).

Clarke, Chris (ed.), *Ways of Knowing: Science and Mysticism Today* (Exeter, UK: Imprint Academic, 2005), pp. 8–33.

Clarke, Isabel, 'There Is a Crack in Everything – That's How the Light Gets In' in Chris Clarke (ed.), *Ways of Knowing* (Exeter: Imprint Academic, 2005), pp. 90–102.

Clarke, Sathianathan, *Dalits and Christianity; Subaltern Religion and Liberation Theology in India* (Delhi: Oxford University Press, 1998).

Cole, Susan, Marian Ronan, and Hal Taussig, *Wisdom's Feast: Sophia in Study and Celebration* (Kansas City: Sheed and Ward, 1996).

Collin, Matthew, *Altered State: The Story of Ecstasy Culture and Acid House* (London: Serpent's Tail, 1997).

Conn, Joanna Wolski, 'Women's Spirituality: Restructions and Reconstruction', *Cross Currents 30* (1980), pp. 24–27.

Connell, Robert, *Gender and Power: Society, the Person and Sexual Politics* (London: Polity Press, 1987).

_____*Masculinities* (London: Polity Press, 1995).

_____*The Men and The Boys* (Santa Cruz: University of California Press, 2002).

Coulson R.G., *Into God: An Exercise in Contemplation* (Oxford: The Bocardo Press, 1956).

Cross, Lawrence, The Redemption of Sophia: A Sophiological Survey from Hermas to Bulgakov in Julie S. Barton and Constant Mews, *Hildegard of Bingen and Gendered Theology in Judaeo-Christian Tradition* (Monash University: Centre for Studies in Religion and Theology, 1995), pp. 19–28.

Csikszentmihalyi M. and Csikszentmihalyi I.S., *Optimal Experience: Psychological Studies of Flow in Consciousness* (Cambridge: Cambridge University Press, 1988).

Csikszentmihalyi, Mihaly, *The Evolving Self* (New York: Harper and Row, 1993).

Custodero, Lori, Seeking Challenge, Finding Skill: Flow Experience in Music Education, *Arts Education and Policy Review*, 103. 3 (2002), pp. 3–9.

Custodero, Lori A., 'Observable Indicators of Flow Experience: A Developmental Perspective of Musical Engagement in Young Children from Infancy to School Age', *Music Education Research*, 7.2 (2005), 185–209.

Daly, Mary, *The Church and the Second Sex* (New York: Harper Row, 1984).

———*Beyond God the Father; Towards a Philosophy of Women's Liberation* (Boston: Beacon Press, 1973).

Davis, F., *Fashion, Culture and Identity* (Chicago: Chicago University Press, 1992).

Dawkins, R., *The Selfish Gene* (London: Paladin, 1978).

De Beauvoir, Simone, *The Second Sex* (Harmondsworth: Penguin, 1972 [1948].

Deane-Drummond, Celia, 'How Might a Virtue Ethic Frame Debates in Human Genetics?', in Celia Deane-Drummond, *Brave New World? Theology, Ethics and the Human Genome* (London and New York: T. & T. Clark, 2003), pp. 225–52.

Derrida, Jacques, *Margins of Philosophy* (Chicago: University of Chicago Press, 1972).

Dewey, Joanna, *The Gospel of Mark as an Oral-Aural Event: Implications for Interpretation* (New Haven: Yale University Press, 1989).

Diamond, Beverley and Pirkko Moisala, 'Introduction: Music and Gender-Negotiating Shifting Worlds' in Pirkko Moisala, and Beverley Diamond, *Music and Gender* (Urbana and Chicago: University of Illinois Press, 2000), pp. 1–24.

Diamond, Beverley, *The Interpretation of Gender Issues in Musical Life Stories of Prince Edward Islanders* in Pirkko Moisala and Beverley Diamond, *Music and Gender*, pp. 99–139.

Dijk, Denise J. J., 'Praying with Our Eyes Open: Women, Language and Liturgy' (unpublished paper, 1997).

———'Celebrating Women's Power', in Teresa Berger, *Dissident Daughters: Feminist Liturgies in a Global Context* (Louisville and London: Westminster John Knox Press, 2001), pp. 69–85.

Donovan, Vincent J., *Christianity Rediscovered: An Epistle from the Maasai* (London: SCM Press, 1982 [1978]).

Douglas, Ian and Kwok, Pui Lan (eds.), *Beyond Colonial Anglicanism: The Anglican Communion in the Twenty-First Century* (New York: Church Publishing Incorporated, 2001).

Douglas-Klotz, Neil, *The Hidden Gospel: Decoding the Spiritual Message of the Aramaic Jesus* (Wheaton, Illinois and Madras, India: Quest Books, 1999).

Drinker S., *Music and Women: The Story of Women in Their Relation to Music* (New York: City University of New York, The Feminist Press, 1995 [1948]).

Driver, Tom F., *Liberating Rites: Understanding the Transformative Power of Ritual* (Boulder, Colorado: Westview, 1998).

DuBois, Page, *Torture and Truth* (New York: Routledge, 2001).

Duffy, Eamon, *Madonnas that Maim? Christian Maturity and the Cult of the Virgin* http://www.bfpubs.demon.co.uk/duffy.htm, contacted November 30th 2006.

Dulles, Avery, *Models of Church* (Dublin: Gill and McMillan, 1988).

Dunmore, Ian, 'Sitar Magic' in *Nadaposana One* (London: Editions Poetry, 1983).

Dupre, Louis, *World Spirituality: An Encyclopaedic History of the Religious Quest Vol. 18* (London: SCM Press, 1990).

Duraisingh, Christopher, 'Toward a Postcolonial Revisioning of the Church's Faith, Witness and Communion,' in Douglas and Kwok (eds.), *Beyond Colonial Anglicanism* (New York: Church Publishing Incorporated, 2001), pp. 241-70.

Eccles, Janet, 'Why are Women Leaving the Church – And Then What are They Doing?'; paper presented to the British Sociological Association Study of Religion Group, 11-13 April, 2005, University of Lancaster.

Eisland, Nancy L., *The Disabled God: Toward a Liberatory Theology of Disability* (Nashville: Abingdon Press, 1994).

Ellison, Marvin M., *Erotic Justice: A Liberating Ethics of Sexuality* (Louisville: Westminster John Knox Press, 1996).

Ellsberg, Robert, *Blessed Among All Women: Women, Saints, Prophets and Witnesses for Our Time* (London: Darton, Longman & Todd, 2006).

Engelsman, Joan Chamberlain, *The Feminine Dimension of the Divine* (Philadelphia: Westminster Press, 1979).

Entwistle, J., *The Fashioned Body* (Cambridge: Polity Press, 2000).

Erricker, C., Erricker J., Ota, C., Sullivan D. and Fletcher, M., *The Education of the Whole Child* (London: Cassell, 1997).

Floyd Malcolm, 'The Trouble with Old Men: Songs of the Maasai' in *Change and the Performing Arts,* Proceedings of a Research Day of the School of Community and Performing Arts, King Alfred's, Winchester, 1998.

_____*Composing the Music of Africa: Composition, Interpretation and Realisation* (Aldershot: Ashgate, 1999).

Ford, J., Massyngbaerde, *My Enemy is My Guest: Jesus and Violence in Luke* (New York: Orbis Books, 1984).

Fordham, M., *Jungian Psychotherapy* (London: Maresfield, 1986).

Foucault Michel, *Madness and Civilisation: A History of Insanity in the Age of Reason* (trans. Richard Howard; London: Tavistock Publications 1967 [1961].

_____*The Archaeology of Knowledge* (London: Tavistock Publications, 1972 [1969].

_____*The Birth of a Clinic* (trans. Alan Sheridan; London: Penguin, 1973 [1963]).

_____*Discipline and Punish: The Birth of the Prison* (Harmondsworth: Penguin, 1975).

_____'The Subject and Power' in *Michel Foucault: Beyond Structuralism and Hermeneutics,* (eds. Hubert Dreyfus and Paul Rainbow; Chicago: University of Chicago Press, 1983).

_____*The Use of Pleasure: The History of Sexuality II* (trans. Robert Hurley; New York: Pantheon, 1985 [1984]).

_____*The History of Sexuality: An Introduction, I* (Harmondsworth, Penguin, 1990).

_____'The Ethic of Care for the Self as a Practice for Freedom', in J. Bernauer and D. Rasmussen (eds.), *The Final Foucault*, (Cambridge, MA, MIT Press, 1991), pp. 1–20.

Foucault Michel and Colin Gordon (eds.), *Power Knowledge: Selected Interviews and Other Writings 1972–77* (Hemel Hempstead: Harvester Wheatsheaf, 1980).

Foulkes, Pamela, 'Lady Sophia' in Julie S. Barton, and Constant Mews, *Hildegard of Bingen and Gendered Theology in Judaeo-Christian Tradition* (Australia: Monash University, Centre for Studies in Religion and Theology, 1995), pp. 9–18.

Frahm-Arp, Maria, Negotiating the Identity: Between Romary Creams and Oreos, paper presented to The British Sociological Association Study of Religion Group, 11–13 April, 2005, University of Lancaster.

Francis, L.J., 'Is Psychoticism Really a Dimension of Personality Fundamental to Religiosity?' *Personality and Individual Differences*, 13 (1992), pp. 645–52.

Frank, Gelya, 'On Embodiment: A Case Study of Congenital Limb Deficiency in American Culture', *Culture, Medicine and Psychiatry 10* (1986), pp. 189–208.

Fraser N., *Unruly Practices: Power, Discourse, and Gender in Contemporary Social Theory* (Minneapolis: University of Minnesota Press, 1989).

Freeman, Laurence, *Light Within: The Inner Path of Meditation* (London: Darton, Longman & Todd, 1986).

Frost, Brian, *'A Plea for Green Discipleship'* in idem *Nine Explorations and Poems* (Reigate: New World Publications, 2004).

Fulani, L., 'Race, Identity and Epistemology' in L. Holzman and J. Morss, *Postmodern Psychologies, Societal Practice and Political Life* (New York: Routledge, 2000), pp. 151–64.

Fuller, Robert, *Spiritual but Not Religious: Understanding Unchurched America* (Oxford: Oxford University Press, 2001).

Furlong, Monica, *The C of E: The State It's In* (London: Hodder, 2000).

_____*Prayers and Poems*, (London: SPCK, 2004).

Fynn, *Mister God, This is Anna* (London: Collins, 1974).

Gage, Matilda Joslyn, *Woman, Church and State: A Historical Account of the Status of Woman Through the Christian Ages with Reminiscences of the Matriarchate*, (ed. Sally Roesch Wagner; Aberdeen, SD: Sky Carrier Press, 1998 [1893]).

Gass, Robert and Kathleen Brehony, *Chanting: Discovering Spirit in Sound* (New York: Broadway Books, 1999).

Geertz, Clifford, *The Interpretation of Cultures* (New York: Basic Books, 1973).

Giddens, Anthony, 'Tradition', Third Reith Lecture BBC, 1999.

Gilligan, Carol, 'A Moonlight Visibility', in David Scribner (ed.), *Hawthorne Revisited* (Lenox, MA: Lenox Library Association, 2004), pp. 83–95.

Gilson, Anne Bathurst E., *Eros Breaking Free: Interpreting Sexual Theo-ethics* (Cleveland, OH: The Pilgrim Press, 1995).

Gimbutas, Marija, *The Language of the Goddess* (New York: Thames and Hudson, 1989).

Glasson, Barbara, *Mixed-up Blessing: A new Re-encounter with Being Church* (Peterborough, UK: Inspire, 2006).

Godwin Malcolm, *Angels: An Endangered Species* (London: Newleaf, 1993).

Godwin, Joscelyn, *Music, Magic and Mysticism: A Sourcebook* (London: Arkana, 1987).

Goddard, Andrew, *Homosexuality and the Church of England* (Cambridge: Grove Books, 2004).

Goehr, Lydia, *The Imaginary Museum of Musical Works: An Essay in the Philosophy of Music* (Oxford: Clarendon Press, 1992).

Goldenberg, Naomi, *Resurrecting the Body: Feminism, Religion and Psychoanalysis* (New York: Crossroad, 1990).

Goldman, Jonathan, *Healing Sounds – The Power of Harmonics* (Shaftesbury, Dorset: Element Books, 1992).

Gooch, Stan, *Total Man: Towards an Evolutionary Theory of Personality* (London: Allen Lane, Penguin Press, 1972).

Goodall, Howard, *Music and Mystery* in Stephen Darlington and Alan Kreider, *Composing Music for Worship* (Norwich: Canterbury Press, 2003), pp. 29–30.

Goss, Robert E., *Queering Christ: Beyond Jesus Acted Up* (Chicago: The Pilgrim Press, 2002).

Govaerts, Robert, Transformation Towards Jesus Christ According to St. Maximus the Confessor, Research Presentation, Lampeter University, Wales, 17 September 2005.

Greeley, A., 'Religion in Britain, Ireland and the USA', in R. Jowell, L. Brook, G. Prior and B. Taylor (eds.), *British Social Attitudes: the Ninth Report*, pp. 51–70 (Aldershot: Dartmouth Publishers, 1992).

Green, Lucy, *Music on Deaf Ears: Musical Meaning, Ideology and Education* (Manchester and New York: Manchester University Press, 1988).

_____*Music, Gender, Education* (Cambridge: Cambridge University Press, 1997).

Grey, Mary, 'Weaving New Connections: The Promise of Process Thought for Christian Theology', Inaugural lecture at University of Nijmegen, Holland, 1989a.

_____*Redeeming the Dream, London: Feminism, Redemption and the Christian Tradition* (London: SPCK, 1989b).

_____*Creation, Liberation and Praxis in Hildegarde of Bingen*, Hildegard Monograph 1 (Andover, UK: The Hildegard Network, 1992).

_____*The Wisdom of Fools: Seeking Revelation for Today* (London: SPCK, 1993).

_____'Till We Have Faces' in Gloria Atkinson-Carter (ed.), *In Being: The Winton Lectures 1979–2000* (Winchester: King Alfred's, 2001), pp. 61–68.

Greenwood, Robin, *Transforming Priesthood: A New Theology of Mission and Ministry* (London: SPCK, 1994).

Grosz, Elizabeth, *Jacques Lacan: A Feminist Introduction* (London and New York: Routledge, 1990).

Gumbel, N., *Telling Others: The Alpha Initiative* (Eastbourne: Kingsway, 1994).

_____*Searching Issues* (Eastbourne: Kingsway, 2000).

Halsall, Anna, Jayne Osgood, and Marie-Pierre Moreau, 'The "Hellish" Task of Negotiating Multiple Identities: The Case of a Christian/Mother/Wife/ Teacher.' Paper given at The British Sociological Association, Sociology of Religion Study Group Annual Conference: Religion and Gender 11–13 April 2005, Lancaster University.

Hamel, Peter, *Through Music to the Self – How to Appreciate and Experience Music Anew* (trans. Peter Lemusurier; Tisbury: Compton Press, 1978 [first published in German in Vienna 1976]).

Haraway, Donna, *Simians, Cyborgs and Women: The Re-invention of Nature* (New York: Routledge, 1991).

_____'*Ecce homo*, Ain't (Ar'n't) I a woman, and Inappropriate/d Others: The Human in a Post-humanist Landscape', in Joan Scott, and Judith Butler (eds.), *Feminists Theorize the Political* (New York: Routledge, 1992a), pp. 87–101.

_____'The Promises of Monsters: A Regenerative Politics for Inappropriate/ d Others', in Lawrence Grossberg, Cary Nelson, Paula A. Treichler (eds.), *Cultural Studies* (New York; Routledge, 1992b), pp. 295–337.

Harding, S., *Whose Science? Whose Knowledge? Thinking from Women's Lives* (Ithaca: Cornell University Press, 1991).

Hardy, Alister, *The Divine Flame: An Essay Towards a Natural History of Religion* (London: Collins, 1966).

Harvey, Susan Ashbrook, 'Women's Service in Ancient Syriac Christianity', in *Mother, Nun, Deaconess: Images of Women According to Eastern Canon Law, Kanon XVI*, Yearbook of the Society for the Law of the Eastern Churches (Egling: Edition Roman Kovar, 2000), pp. 226–41.

_____*Spoken Words, Voiced Silence: Biblical Women in Syriac Tradition, Journal of Early Christian Studies* 9:1 (2001), pp. 105–31.

Harvey, Jonathan, *Music and Inspiration* (London: Faber and Faber, 1999).

Hart, Mother Columba and Jane Bishop, *Hildegard of Bingen: Scivias* (New York, Paulist Press, 1990).

Hauerwas, S., 'Community and Diversity: The Tyranny of Normality' in Stanley Hauerwas, *Suffering Presence: Theological Reflections on Medicine, the Mentally Handicapped and the Church* (Edinburgh: T. & T. Clark, 1988), pp. 211–17.

Hay, David, *Exploring Inner Space* (Harmondsworth: Penguin, 1982).

Hay, David and Rebecca Nye, *Spirit of the Child* (London: HarperCollins, 1998).

Heelas, P. and L. Woodhead, *The Spiritual Revolution: Why Religion is Giving Way to Spirituality* (Oxford: Blackwell Publishing, 2005).

Herndon, Marcia, Epilogue to Pirkko Moisala and Beverley Diamond, *Music and Gender* (Urbana and Chicago: University of Illinois Press, 2000), pp. 347–60.

Heyward, Carter, *Our Passion for Justice: Images of Power, Sexuality and Liberation* (Cleveland, OH: The Pilgrim Press, 1984).

_____*Speaking of Christ: A Lesbian Feminist Voice* (New York: Pilgrim Press, 1989a).

_____*Touching our Strength: The Erotic as Power and the Love of God* (San Francisco: HarperSanFrancisco, 1989b).

_____*A Priest Forever: Formation of a Woman and a Priest* (Cleveland, OH: The Pilgrim Press, 2nd edn., 1999).

Hill Collins, Patricia, *Fighting Words: Black Women and the Search for Justice* (Minneapolis: University of Minnesota Press, 1998).

Hills, Peter and Michael Argyle, 'Musical and Religious Experiences and Their Relationships to Happiness', *Personality and Individual Differences 25* (1998), pp. 91–102.

Hindemith, Paul, *A Composer's World* (New York: Doubleday & Company, 1952).

Hobson, B. (ed.), *Making Men into Fathers: Men, Masculinities and the Social Politics of Fatherhood* (Cambridge: Cambridge University Press, 2002).

Holloway Richard, *Godless Morality* (Edinburgh: Canongate, 1999).

Holzman, Lois, 'Practising a Psychology that Builds Community', East Side Institute for Short Term Psychotherapy, New York, USA. Delivered as the Keynote Address, APA Division 27/ Society for Community Research and Action Conference, Boston, March 2002. www.eastsideinstitute.org

hooks, bell, *Killing Rage, Ending Racism* (London: Penguin, 1996).

Hozeski, Bruce W. (trans.), *Hildegard of Bingen's Book of the Rewards of Life* (Oxford: Oxford University Press, 1994).

Hull, John M., *In the Beginning There Was a Darkness: A Blind Person's Conversations with the Bible* (London: SCM Press, 2001).

Humm, Maggie, *The Dictionary of Feminist Theory* (Cleveland, OH: Ohio State University Press, 1995).

Hunt, Stephen, 'The Alpha Course: UK Evangelism in an East European Setting, Challenges of Religious Plurality for Eastern and Central Europe', Paper presented to the fifth International Study of Religion in Central and Eastern Europe Association, Ivan Franko Lviv National University, Lviv: The Ukraine, 12 December 2003.

_____'"Basic Christianity": Gender Issues in the *Alpha* Initiative', paper presented to The British Sociological Association Study of Religion Group, University of Lancaster, 11–13 April 2005.

Imtoual, Alia, 'There Are Always Eyes on You Because You're Wearing a Hijab': Muslim Women's Experiences of Religious Racism (Islamophobia) in Australia. Paper presented to The British Sociological Association Study of Religion Group, University of Lancaster, 11 –13 April, 2005.

Inglis, Brian, *Trance: A Natural History of Altered States of Mind* (London: Paladin, Grafton Books, 1990).

Irigaray, Luce, *An Ethics of Sexual Difference*, (trans. Carolyn Burke and Gillian C. Gill; London: Athlone University Press, 1993 [1984]).

_____*Sexes and Genealogies* (trans. Gillian C. Gill; New York: Columbia University Press, 1993 [1987]).

_____*Speculum of the Other Woman* (trans. Gillian C. Gill; Ithaca NY: Cornell University Press, 1985, [1974]).

Isasi-Diaz, Ada Maria, *Mujarista Theology* (Maryknoll, NY: Orbis Books, 1996).

Isherwood, Lisa, *The Power of Erotic Celibacy: Queering Heteropatriarchy* (London and New York: T. & T. Clark, 2006).

Isherwood Lisa and Elizabeth Stuart, *Introducing Body Theology* (Sheffield: Sheffield Academic Press, 1998).

James, Jamie, *The Music of the Spheres: Music, Science and the Natural Order of the Universe* (London: Abacus, 1993).

James, William, *Talks to Teachers on Psychology* (New York: Rhinehart and Winston, 1900).

Robinson, Ken, *Out of Our Minds: Learning to Be Creative* (Oxford: Capstone Publishing, 2001).

James, William, *The Varieties of Religious Experience* (New York: Simon and Schuster, 1997 [1903]).

Jantzen, Grace M., *God's World, God's Body* (London: Darton, Longman & Todd, 1984).

_____*Power, Gender and Christian Mysticism* (Cambridge: Cambridge University Press, 1995).

_____*Reflections on the Looking Glass: Religion, Culture and Gender in the Academy* (Manchester: Centre for Religion, Culture and Gender, The University of Manchester, 1996).

_____*Becoming Divine: Toward a Feminist Philosophy of Religion* (Manchester: Manchester University Press, 1998).

Jarviluoma, Helmi, 'Local Constructions of Gender in a Finnish Pelimanni Musicians' Group' in Pirkko Moisala, and Beverley Diamond, *Music and Gender* (Urbana and Chicago: University of Illinois Press, 2000), pp. 51–79.

Jeremias, Jorg, *Theophanie: Die Geschichte einer alttestamentlichen Gattung* WMANT 10 (Neukirchen-Vluyn: Neukirchener Verlag, 1985).

John, Jeffrey, *'Permanent, Faithful, Stable'* (London: Darton, Longman &Todd, 2000 [1993]).

_____*The Meaning in the Miracles* (Norwich: Canterbury Press, 2001).

Johnson Reagon, Bernice, *Compositions: One* (Washington DC: Songtalk Publishing Company, 1986).

Johnson, Elizabeth A., *She Who Is: The Mystery of God in Feminist Discourse* (New York: Crossroads, 1993).

_____*Truly Our Sister: A Theology of Mary in the Communion of Saints* (New York and London: Continuum, 2006).

Jordan, Mark, *The Silence of Sodom – Homosexuality in Modern Catholicism* (Chicago: Chicago University Press, 2000).

Jorgensen, Estelle, The Artist and the Pedagogy of Hope, *International Journal for Music Education*, 27 (1996), pp. 36–50.

Joseph, M.P., *Third World Debt – First World Responsibility* (Edinburgh: Centre for Theology and Public Issues, 1991).

Kavanaugh, Kieran and Otilio Rodriguez (eds.), *Teresa of Avila: The Interior Castle* (London: SPCK, 1979).

Kay,W.K. and L.J. Francis, *Drift From the Churches: Attitude Toward Christianity during Childhood and Adolescence* (Cardiff: University of Wales Press, 1996).

Kelber, Werner H., *The Hermeneutics of Speaking and Writing in the Synoptic Tradition, Mark, Paul, and Q* (Minneapolis: Fortress Press,1983).

Kirwan, Michael, *Discovering Girard* (London: Darton, Longman & Todd, 2004).

Kemp, Anthony E., *The Musical Temperament* (Oxford: Oxford University Press, 1996).

Kempe, Margery B., *The Book of Margery Kempe*, (ed. Barry Windeatt; London: Penguin Classics, 1985).

Kim, Grace Ji-sun, *The Grace of Sophia* (Cleveland, OH: The Pilgrim Press, 2002).

King, Ursula, *Women and Spirituality: Voices of Protest and Promise* (Basingstoke: Macmillan, 2nd edn, 1993).

_____*Christian Mystics: Their Lives and Legacy Throughout the Ages* (London and New York: Routledge, 2004 [2001]).

Knott, Kim and Myfanwy Franks, 'Gender and Religious Space in Two Secular Organizations'. Paper presented to The British Sociological Association Study of Religion Group, 11–13 April 2005, University of Lancaster.

Knox, Crawford, The Healing Powers of God, paper presented at The Seventh Ecumenical Conference on Christian Parapsychology, 10–12 September 2006, Exeter University.

Koestler, A., *The Act of Creation* (London: Hutchinson, 1964).

Kraemer, Ross S., *Maenads, Martyrs, Matrons, Monastics: A Sourcebook of Women's Religions in the Graeco-Roman World* (New York: Oxford University Press, 1988).

Kristeva, Julia, 'Women's Time' in *The Kristeva Reader* (ed. Toril Moi; New York: Columbia University Press, 1986 [1979]), pp. 187–213.

Kyung Chung, Hyun, 'Han-pu-ri: Doing Theology from Korean Women's Perspective' in Virginia Fabella, and Sun-Ai Lee (eds.), *We Dare to Dream* (Maryknoll, NY: Orbis Books, 1990a).

_____*Struggle to be the Sun Again* (Maryknoll, NY: Probis Books, 1990b).

Kwok, Pui Lan, *Discovering the Bible in the Non-biblical World* (Maryknoll NY: Orbis Books, 1995).

_____*Spiritual and Also Religious? The Brown Papers, Vol. IV No.3*, January/February (2002a).

_____'Feminist Theology as Intercultural Discourse' in Susan Frank Parsons (ed.), *The Cambridge Companion to Feminist Theology* (Cambridge: Cambridge University Press, 2002b), pp. 23–39.

Lacan, Jacques, *Ecrits: A Selection* (trans. Alan Sheridan; London: Routledge & Kegan, 1977 [1966]).

Lacan, Jacques (Juliet Mitchell, and Jacqueline Rose, eds.) *Feminine Sexuality: Jacques Lacan and the Ecole Freudienne* (Basingstoke: Macmillan; New York: Pantheon Press, 1982).

Langer, Suzanne, *Philosophy in a New Key* (Cambridge, MA: Harvard University Press, 1942).

_____*Feeling and Form: A Theory of Art* (London: Routledge and Kegan Paul, 1982).

Laski, Marghanita, *Ecstasy: A Study of Some Secular and Religious Experiences* (London: Cresset Press, 1961).

Law, J., *Power, Action, Belief: A New Sociology of Knowledge?* (London: Routledge and Kegan Paul, 1986).

_____ 'Notes on the Theory of the Actor-Network: Ordering, Strategy and Heterogeneity', in *Systems Practice* 5 (1992), 379–93.

Lazreg, Marnia, *The Eloquence of Silence: Algerian Women in Question* (New York & London: Routledge, 1994).

Lederach, John Paul, *Building Peace: Sustainable Reconciliation in Divided Societies* (Washington DC: United States Institute of Peace Press, 1997).

Lee, Sang Hyun, 'Called to Be Pilgrims: Towards an Asian-American Theology from the Korean Immigrant Perspective' in Lee, Sang Hyun (ed.), *Korean American Ministry: A Resource Book* (New York: Consulting Committee on Korean American Ministry, Presbyterian Church, 1987).

Leloup, Jean-Yves, *The Gospel of Mary Magdalene* (trans. Joseph Rowe; Rochester, Vermont: Inner Traditions, 2002).

Lerner, Gerda, *The Creation of Patriarchy* (New York: Oxford University Press, 1986).

Levi-Strauss, Claude, *The Raw and the Cooked: Introduction to a Science of Mythology* (trans. John and Doreen Weightman; London: Jonathan Cape, 1970).

Levinas, Emmanuel, *Totality and Infinity: An Essay on Exteriority* (trans. Alphonso Lingis; Pittsburgh: Duquesne University Press, 1969).

Loades, Ann, *Dorothy Sayers: Spiritual Writings* (London: SPCK, 1993), pp. 102–3.

Loewe, Brigitta, *Storytelling – An act of Liberation* (Unpublished DMin thesis, Episcopal Divinity School, Cambridge, Massachusetts, 2003).

Lorde, Audre, *Sister Outsider: Essays and Speeches* (New York: Crossing Press, 1984a).

_____ 'An Interview: Audre Lorde and Adrienne Rich' and 'Poetry is Not a Luxury' in *Sister Outsider* (Freedom, CA: Crossing Press, 1984b).

Lovelock, James, *Gaia: A New Look at Life on Earth* (Oxford: Oxford University Press, 1979).

Lugones, Maria, 'Playfulness, "World"-Travelling, and Loving Perception' in G. Anzaldua (ed.), *Making Face, Making Soul-Haciendo Caras: Creative and Critical Perspectives in Feminists of Color* (San Francisco: Aunt Lute Foundation Books, 1990), pp. 390–402.

Lyon, D., *Jesus in Disneyland* (Cambridge: Polity Press, 2000).

McAdoo, H.R., *Anglican Heritage: Theology and Spirituality* (Norwich: Canterbury Press, 1991).

McClary, Susan, *Feminine Endings* (Minnesota: University of Minnesota Press, 1991).

_____ *Conventional Wisdom* (Berkeley, CA: University of California Press, 2001).

McDonagh, Enda, *Vulnerable to the Holy in Faith, Morality and Art* (Dublin: The Columba Press, 2004).

McFague, Sallie, *Models of God: Theology for an Ecological, Nuclear Age* (London: SCM Press, 1987).

McGrath, Alister, *Christian Theology: An Introduction* (Oxford: Blackwell, 1994).

McLean C., 'The Politics of Men's Pain' in C. McLean, M. Carey, and C. White (eds.), *Men's Ways of Being* (Boulder, CO: Westview Press, 1996).

McNay, Lois, *Foucault and Feminism: Power, Gender and the Self* (Cambridge: Polity Press, 1992a).

———*Foucault: A Critical Introduction* (Cambridge: Polity Press, 1992b).

McNiff, Shaun, *Art as Medicine: Creating a Therapy of the Imagination* (Boston, London: Shambhala, 1992).

MacFarlane, Alan, *Letters to Lily on How the World Works* (London: Profile Books, 2005).

Mantin, Ruth, *Thealogies in Process: The Role of Goddess-Talk in Feminist Spirituality* (Unpublished PhD Thesis, Southampton University, 2002).

Marjanen, Antti, *The Woman Jesus Loved: Mary Magdalene in the Nag Hammadi Library and Related Documents* (Leiden: E.J. Brill, 1996).

Maslow, Abraham. H., 'The Creative Attitude' in R.L. Mooney and T. Razik (eds.), *Explorations in Creativity* (New York: Harper and Row, 1967), pp. 40–55.

Mazamisa, L.W., *Beatific Comradeship: An Exegetical-Hermeneutical Study on Luke 10:25–37* (Kampen: Kok, 1987).

Mellor D., 'The Experiences of Vietnamese in Australia: The Racist Tradition Continues', *Journal of Ethnic and Migration Studies*, 30. 4 (2004), pp. 631–58.

Messer, Neil G. 'Human Cloning and Genetic Manipulation: Some Theological and Ethical issues', *Studies in Christian Ethics*, 12.2, (1999), pp. 1–16.

Messer, Neil (2003) *Theological Issues in Bioethics: An Introduction With Readings* London: Darton Longman & Todd Ltd, 2003.

Metzger, Deena, 'Writing: The Gateway to the Inner World' in Michael Toms (ed.), *The Well of Creativity* (Carlsbad: Hay House, 1997).

Midgley, Mary, *Myths We Live By* (London: Routledge 2003).

Miller, Robin, 'The Old Man's Tale – A Gay Man's Testimony' (Unpublished story, 2005).

Mitchell, J., *Women: The Longest Revolution* (London: Virago, 1984).

Mollenkott, Virginia Ramey, *Omnigender – A Trans-Religious Approach* (Cleveland, OH: The Pilgrim Press, 2001).

Monk Kidd, Sue, *The Dance of the Dissident Daughter* (San Francisco: HarperSanFrancisco, 1992).

Morton, Nelle, *The Journey is Home* (Boston: Beacon Press, 1985).

Moisala, Pirkko and Beverley Diamond, *Music and Gender* (Urbana and Chicago: University of Illinois Press, 2000).

Moule, C.D.F., *The Origin of Christology* (Cambridge: Cambridge University Press, 1977).

Murray, Stuart, *Post-Christendom: Church and Mission in a Strange New World* (Milton Keynes: Paternoster Press, 2004).

Myers, Margaret, 'Searching for Data about Ladies Orchestras' in Pirkko Moisala and Beverley Diamond, 2000, pp. 189–218.

Myers, I.B., *Gifts Differing: Understanding Personality Type* (Palo Alto, CA: Consulting Psychologists Press, 1993 [1980]).

Myers, I.B. and McCaulley, M.H., *Manual: A Guide to the Development and Use of the Myers-Briggs Type Indicator* (Palo Alto, California: Consulting Psychologists press, 2nd edn, 1985).

Neu, Diann L., *Return Blessings, Ecofeminist Liturgies Renewing the Earth* (Cleveland, OH: The Pilgrim Press, 2002).

Newman, Barbara, *Sister of Wisdom; St Hildegard's Theology of the Feminine* (Farnborough: Scolar, 1987).

Nichols, Aidan OP, 'Von Balthasar and the Co-redemption', paper presented at the International Conference on Marian co-redemption, Ratcliffe College, Leicester. Available at http://www.Christendom-awake.org/pages/balthasar/coremp 29/12/05

Nietzsche, F. 'On Truth and Lies in a Nonmoral Sense', in *Philosophy and Truth; Selections from Nietzsche's Notebooks of the Early 1870s* (trans. and ed. Daniel Breazeale; Hassocks: Harvester, 1979 [1873]), pp. 79–97.

Nouwen, Henri J., *The Wounded Healer* (London: Darton Longman & Todd, 1979).

Olyan, S., *Asherah and the Cult of Yahweh in Israel* (Atlanta GA: Scholars Press, 1988).

O'Grady, Helen, *Woman's Relationship with Herself: Gender, Foucault and Therapy* (London and New York: Routledge, 2005).

O'Reilly, Patricia, 'New Religious Movements: Individualized Belief Systems and the Goddess'. Paper presented to The British Sociological Association Study of Religion Group, 11–13 April 2005, University of Lancaster.

Ong, Walter, *Orality and Literacy: The Technologizing of the Word* (London and New York: Methuen, 1982).

Orbach, Susie, *Fat is a Feminist Issue: A Self Help Guide for Compulsive Eaters* (Berkeley: Berkeley Publishing Group, 1990).

Osborne, June, 'What Price Would You Put on Dignity? How Much Do You Value Your Sense of Honour or Self-respect?' Sermon preached in Salisbury Cathedral, Sunday 30 July 2006http://www.salisburycathedral.org.uk/services. sermons.php?id=122, contacted 9 November 2006.

Otto, Rudolf, *The Idea of the Holy: An Inquiry into the Non-rational; Factor in the Idea of the Divine and its Relation to the Rational* (Oxford: Oxford University Press 1923).

Perry, Michael (ed.), *Deliverance: Psychic Disturbances and Occult Involvement* (London: SPCK, 1987).

Pieper, Josef, *Prudence* (trans. R. Winston and C. Winston; London: Faber and Faber 1959).

Pinkola Estes, Clarissa, *Women Who Run with the Wolves* (London: Rider, 1992).

Pollock, Sheldon I. 'The Divine King in the Indian Epic', *Journal of the American Oriental Society* 104 (1984), pp. 505–28.

Poole, Myra, *Prayer, Praise and Protest* (Norwich: Canterbury Press, 2001).

Porter J., *The Recovery of Virtue: The Relevance of Aquinas for Christian Ethics* (London: SPCK 1994).

Rahn, John, 'What is Valuable in Art, and Can Music Still Achieve It?' in John Rahn (ed.), *Perspectives in Musical Aesthetics* (New York: Norton, 1994).

Rankin, Marianne, *An Introduction to Religious Experience* (Lampeter, Wales: Religious Experience Research Centre, 2005).

Raphael, Melissa, *Female Sacrality* (Sheffield: Sheffield Academic Press, 1996).

_____*Introducing Thealogy: Discourse on the Goddess* (Sheffield: Sheffield Academic Press, 1999).

Redfearn, Joseph, *The Exploding Self: The Creative and Destructive Nucleus of the Personality* (Wilmette, Illinois: Chiron Publications, 1992).

RERC (Religious Experience Research Centre) accounts of Religious Experience, held at Lampeter University, Wales, UK.

Richter, Philip and Leslie J. Francis, *Gone But Not Forgotten: Church Leaving and Returning* (London: Darton, Longman & Todd, 1998).

_____'Gender Differences in Religious Disaffiliation: Viewing Matters From the Masculine Perspective'. Paper presented to The British Sociological Association Study of Religion Group, 11–13 April 2005, University of Lancaster.

Rizza, Margaret, *Awakening in Love* (Stowmarket: Kevin Mayhew, 2004).

Roach, M.E. and J.B. Eicher, *Dress, Adornment and Social Order* (New York: John Wiley & Sons Inc., 1965).

Robinson E., *The Original Vision: A Study of the Religious Experience of Childhood* (Oxford: RERC, 1977).

Robinson, Ken, *Out of Our Minds: Learning to Be Creative* (Oxford: Capstone, 2001).

Roose-Evans, James, *Passages of the Soul* (Shaftesbury: Element Books, 1994).

Rose, Stuart, 'Is the Word Spirituality a Word that Everyone Uses but Nobody Knows What Anybody Means by It?', *Journal of Contemporary Religion*, 16.2 (2001), pp. 193–207.

Ross, Malcolm, *The Creative Arts* (London: Heinemann, 1978).

Rouget, Gilbert, *Music and Trance: A Theory of the Relations Between Music and Possession*, (trans. Brunhilde Biebuyck; Chicago and London: University of Chicago Press, 1987).

Ruether, Rosemary Radford, *Sexism and God-Talk* (Boston: Beacon Press, 1983).

_____*Women-Church: Theology and Practice of Feminist Liturgical Communities* (London: Harper and Row, 1985).

_____*Women and Redemption: A Theological History* (Minneapolis: Fortress Press, 1988).

The Runnymede Trust, *Islamophobia: A Challenge for Us All* (Sussex: The Runnymede Trust Commission on British Muslims and Islamophobia, 1997), pp. 1–69.

Rye, Gill, 'Motherhood without Sacrifice: The Sacred without Sacrifice: Julia Kristeva's New Model of Mothering – An Exploration'. Paper presented at AHRB Seminar, *Gender, Myth and Spirituality*, 6 April 2003.

Sandoval, Chela, *Methodology of the Oppressed* (Minnesota: University of Minnesota Press, 2000).

Schafer, Murray, 'Where Does It All Lead?, *Australian Journal of Music Education* 12 (1973), pp. 3–5.

Schipperges, Heinrich, *The World of Hildegard of Bingen: Her life, Times and Visions* (trans. John Cumming; Tunbridge Wells: Burns and Oates and Collegeville, Minnesota: Novalis, 1997).

Schüssler Fiorenza, Elisabeth, *Bread not Stone: The Challenges of Feminist Biblical Interpretation* (Edinburgh: T.&T. Clark, 1984).

_____*Women Invisible in Society and Church* (Edinburgh: T. & T. Clark, 1985).

_____*Jesus and the Politics of Interpretation* (New York and London: Continuum, 2000).

_____*Wisdom Ways: Introducing Feminist Biblical Interpretation* (Maryknoll, New York: Orbis Books, 2001).

Schüssler Fiorenza, Elisabeth (ed.), *Searching the Scriptures: Volume Two: A Feminist Commentary* (London: SCM Press, 1994).

Selby, Peter, *Grace and Mortgage; The Language of Faith and the Debt of the World* (London: Darton, Longman & Todd, 1997).

Seller, Mary J., 'Genes, Genetics and the human Genome', in Celia Deane-Drummond, *Brave New World? Theology, Ethics and the Human Genome* (London and New York: T. & T. Clark, 2003), pp. 27–44).

Sheldrake, Philip, *Living Between Worlds: Place and Journey in Celtic Spirituality* (London: Darton, Longman & Todd, 1995).

_____*Spirituality and Theology* (London: Darton, Longman & Todd, 1988).

Shepherd, John and Peter Wicke, *Music and Cultural Theory* (Cambridge: Polity Press, 1997).

Shinoda Bolen, Jean, *Goddesses in Older Women: Archetypes in Women over Fifty* (New York: Quill, HarperCollins, 2001).

Soelle, Dorothee, *Christ the Representative: An Essay in Theology after 'The Death of God'* (Philadelphia: Fortress Press, 1967).

_____*Beyond Mere Obedience: Reflections on a Christian Ethic for the Future* (trans. Lawrence W. Denef; Minneapolis: Augsburg 1970).

_____*The Silent Cry: Mysticism and Resistance* (Minneapolis: Fortress Press, 2001).

Spelman, Elizabeth, *Inessential Woman: Problems of Exclusion in Feminist Thought* (Boston: Beacon Press, 1988).

Stark, R., 'Physiology and Faith: Addressing the "Universal" Gender Difference in Religious Commitment', *Journal for the Scientific Study of Religion*, 41 (2002), 495–507.

Steinwert, Tiffany, Paper given in Carter Heyward's class on Queer Theology, 28 April 2003 at the Episcopal Divinity School, Cambridge, Massachusetts.

Stewart, R. J., *Music and the Elemental Psyche: A Practical Guide to Music and Changing Consciousness* (Wellingborough: The Aquarian Press, 1987).

Struthers Malbon, Elizabeth, *Hearing Mark: A Listener's Guide* (Harrisburg, Pennsylvania: Trinity Press International, 2002).

Strong, Peggy, 'The Peabody Sisters of Salem' in Scribner (ed.), *Hawthorne Revisited* (Lenox Mass: Lenox Library Association, 2004), pp. 39–47.

Stuart, Elizabeth (ed.), *Daring to Speak Love's Name: A Gay and Lesbian Prayer Book* (London: Hamish Hamilton, 1992).

Sullivan, Lawrence E., *Enchanting Powers: Music in the World's Religions* (Harvard: Harvard University Press, 1997).

Sutherland, Jessie, *Worldview Skills: Transforming Conflict From the Inside Out* (Vancouver: Worldview Strategies, 2005).

Swinburne, Richard, *The Coherence of Theism* (Oxford: Oxford University Press, 1977).

Szerszynski, Bronislaw, 'That Deep Surface: The Human Genome Project and the Death of the Human' in Celia Deane-Drummond, *Brave New World? Theology, Ethics and the Human Genome* (London and New York: T. & T. Clark, 2003), pp. 145–63.

Tatman, Lucy, 'Wisdom' in *An A-Z of Feminist Theology* (eds. Lisa Isherwood and Dorothea McEwan; Sheffield: Sheffield Academic Press, 1996), p. 238.

Taylor, John V., *The Christlike God* (London: SCM Press, 1992).

Teish, Luisah, *Jambalaya: The Natural Woman's Book of Personal Charms and Practical Rituals* (San Francisco: Harper and Row, 1985).

Thalbourne M.A., L. Bartemucci, P.S. Delin, B. Fox and O. Nofi, 'Transliminality, Its Nature and Correlates', *The Journal of the American Society for Psychical Research*, 91 (1997), pp. 305–31.

Thorne, Brian, *Behold the Man: A Therapists' Meditations on The Passion of Christ* (London: Darton, Longman & Todd, 1991[revised 2006]).

Thornton, John, *Africa and the Africans in the Making of the Atlantic World 1400–1800,* (Cambridge and New York: Cambridge University Press, 2nd edn 1998).

Tillich, P. *Biblical Religion and the Search for Ultimate Reality* (Chicago: University of Chicago Press, 1964).

Tillman June B., 'Towards a Model of the Development of Musical Creativity: A Study of the Compositions of Children Aged 3–11.' Unpublished PhD Thesis, University of London Institute of Education, 1987).

———*Unfinished Journey* (London: Hildegard Press, 1988).

Todd Peters, Rebecca, *In Search of the Good Life: The Ethics of Globalization* (New York and London: Continuum, 2004).

Torjesen, Karen Jo, *When Women Were Priests: Women's Leadership in the Early Church and the Scandal of Their Subordination in the Rise of Christianity* (San Francisco: HarperSanFrancisco, 1990).

Tronto, J., 'Beyond Gender Difference to a Theory of Care', *Signs: Journal of Women in Culture and Society*, 12.4 (1987) pp. 644–63, [658].

Trible, Phyllis, *Texts of Terror: Literary-Feminist Readings of Biblical Narratives* (Philadelphia: Fortress Press, 1984).

Trzebiatowska, Marta, 'Habit Does Not a Nun Make? Religious Dress in the Everyday Lives of Polish Catholic Nuns'. Paper presented to The British Sociological Association Study of Religion Group, 11–13 April 2005, University of Lancaster.

Tseelson, E., *The Masque of Femininity* (London: Sage Publications, 1997).

Tubbs, Nigel, What is Love's Work? *Women: A Cultural Review, 9.1* (1998), pp. 34–46.

Turner, Bryan S., *The Body and Society* (Oxford: Basil Blackwell 1984).

Turner, Victor, *The Ritual Process: Structure and Anti-structure* (Baltimore: Penguin Books, [1969] 1974).

_____*Dramas, Fields and Metaphors: Symbolic Action in Human Society* (Ithaca NY: Cornell University Press, 1974).

Van Gennep, A. The Rites of Passage (Chicago: The University of Chicago, 1908).

Vernon, P.E. (ed.), *Creativity* (Harmondsworth: Penguin, 1970).

Virilio, P. & S. Lotringer, *Crepuscular Dawn* (New York: Semiotext(e), 2002).

Vygotsky, L. S., *Mind in Society* (Cambridge, MA: Harvard University Press, 1978).

Wallas, Carl, 'The Art of Thought', in P.E.Vernon (ed.), *Creativity* 1970: 91–97.

Ward, Elizabeth Stuart Phelps, *Chapters from a Life* (New York: Arno Press, 1896).

Ward, Hannah and Jennifer Wild (eds.), *Human Rites* (London: Mowbrays, 1995a).

Ward, Hannah and Jennifer Wild, *Guard the Chaos: Finding Meaning in Change* (London: Darton, Longman & Todd, 1995b).

Ward, Keith, '"The Awesome Scale of the Cosmos Should Change Our Priorities,"' *Church Times*, July 2005 p. 10.

Warner, Marina, *Alone of All Her Sex: The Myth and Cult of the Virgin Mary* (London: Picador 1985).

Warnock, Mary, *An Intelligent Person's Guide to Ethics* (London: Duckbacks, 2001).

Watson, J., *A Passion for DNA: Genes, Genomes and Society* (Oxford: Oxford University Press, 2001).

White, Michael, *Re-authoring Lives: Interviews and Essays* (South Australia: Dulwich Centre Publications, 1995).

Wijngaards, John, *The Ordination of Women in the Catholic Church: Unmasking A Cuckoo's Egg Tradition*, (London: Continuum, 2001).

Wilensky, H.L. Work, 'Careers and Social Integration', *International Science Journal 4* (1960), pp. 32–56.

Wilkinson, J., *The Bible and Healing: A Medical and Theological Commentary* (Edinburgh: Hansel Press, Grand Rapids: Eerdmans, 1998).

Williams, Rowan, *On Christian Theology* (Oxford: Blackwell, 2000).

Windeatt, B.A. (trans.) *The Book of Margery Kempe* (London: Penguin, 1985).

Winnicott, D., *Playing and Reality* (London: Tavistock, 1971).

Woolfson, Andrew, Radio 4, Start the Week, 5 December 2004, 9am.

Last page of *An Intelligent Person's Guide To Genetics* to be published by Duckworth Overlook, March 2005.

Wollstonecraft, Mary (ed. Miriam Brody,) *A Vindication of the Rights of Women* (Harmondsworth: Penguin (1975).

Wootton, Janet H., *Introducing a Practical Feminist Theology of Worship* (Sheffield: Sheffield Academic Press, 2000).

Wright, A., *Spiritual Pedagogy* (Oxford: Culham College Institute, 1998).

Yamani, Mai (ed.), *Feminism and Islam: Legal and Literary Perspectives* (Reading, Berkshire: Garnet Publishing, 1996).

Zappone, Katherine, *The Hope for Wholeness: A Spirituality for Feminists* (Connecticut: Twenty-Third Publications, 1991).

Printed in the United Kingdom
by Lightning Source UK Ltd.
130931UK00001B/15/A